Bond Like a Boss!
The Dad Playbook

72 Shared Adventures to Level Up Fun, Skills, and Lifelong Connections

Z.J. RAMSEY

Intergalactic Ink

ISBN: 979-8-9963265-0-1
Published by Intergalactic Ink
First Edition

DEDICATION

To little Elizabeth – You are more incredible than I ever could have imagined. May your life be filled with every bit of joy sparked by the moments in these pages.

CONTENTS

Quick Tip: Look for activities marked with an asterisk (*)—these are "Short & Sweet" options, perfect for when you want something fun and meaningful in less time. Great for those busy days!

PREFACE

The journey of creating *Bond Like a Boss!* started with a simple, yet profound realization: the invaluable impact of a father's active presence in a child's life. Growing up without a father, I often wondered what it would be like to have those special moments of shared laughter, learning, and love. This personal experience fueled my passion to provide fathers with a resource that could help them build the kind of meaningful connections I yearned for.

This book is born out of a deep desire to help dads savor every precious moment with their children. In a world where time seems to slip through our fingers, it's easy to miss the fleeting beauty of childhood. My goal is to ensure that fathers don't look back with regret, but instead, cherish a wealth of shared experiences and deep, loving relationships with their kids.

In developing this book, I focused on creating activities that are not only enjoyable but also accessible and enriching. Each activity had to meet a few key criteria: it needed to be simple enough to do with materials most people have on hand or can easily find, fun for both dads and kids, and beneficial in fostering different aspects of a child's development. The activities in this book cover a wide range of interests and personality types, ensuring every child feels included and engaged, whether they prefer hands-on crafting, thoughtful challenges, or lively outdoor fun.

What sets this book apart is its emphasis on the quality of the father-child relationship. It's not just about keeping kids entertained; it's about creating opportunities for dads to connect on a deeper level with their children. By fostering open communication and mutual understanding through these activities, my hope is that fathers and children will build a foundation of trust and love that will support them through life's many challenges.

Bond Like a Boss! is an invitation for fathers to be present, to engage fully, and to create lasting memories with their children. It's about cherishing the here and now, and building a legacy of love and connection that will endure for generations.

In shaping and refining this book, I also used AI to help polish my words, ensuring my ideas came through as clearly as possible. While AI provided support in clarity and flow, every activity, tip, and insight within these pages is a deeply personal expression of my own journey and vision.

Thank you for joining me on this journey. I hope this book inspires you to embark on each activity with enthusiasm and heart. May it help you create unforgettable moments, deepen your bond with your children, and experience the profound joy of being an active, involved father.

Z.J. Ramsey

INTRODUCTION

Welcome to *Bond Like a Boss!*, a guide designed to help you create unforgettable memories and build lasting bonds with your children. This book goes beyond simply offering activities; it opens the door to a world of adventures that can be tailored to fit your child's unique interests, personality, and age.

While this book is written with fathers in mind, the activities are designed for any parent or caregiver eager to create lasting memories and connections with their children. So, whether you're a mom, a grandparent, or another family member stepping into this role, you'll find these pages full of fun ways to strengthen your relationship with the kids in your life.

Each activity in this book comes with multiple variations and adaptations, turning one idea into several different experiences. Imagine finding a favorite activity that your child loves, and then discovering new ways to enjoy it together time and time again. Whether it's tweaking the rules, adding creative twists, or exploring new themes, you'll find that these activities never get old, effectively multiplying the fun.

The activities are thoughtfully organized by age group—ranging from preschoolers to high schoolers—with both indoor and outdoor options for each stage. However, these age guidelines are just that: guidelines. Most activities are appropriate for or can be easily adapted to suit a wide range of ages, skill levels, or interests. With a little creativity, you can modify a simple activity into something that challenges your child, ensuring it meets their current interests and developmental stage. You might even find that these experiences spark a new interest or hobby that becomes a lifelong passion.

Balancing life's demands can be challenging, and not every day allows for hours of engagement. That's why many activities in this book can be as involved or hands-off as you need them to be. For example, in activities like the Literary Adventure Lab, you can choose to be deeply involved in a collaborative project, or you can offer guidance and step back, letting your child's imagination take the lead. The choice is yours, and the flexibility ensures that these activities fit seamlessly into your life.

As you engage in these activities, it's important to remember that your role is to support and encourage, not to control or direct every move. Children learn and grow through exploration, experimentation, and even making mistakes. Offering guidance is wonderful, but it's crucial to let your child have the space to do things their way. This approach not only fosters independence but also builds confidence, as your child feels trusted to explore and create freely.

One of the most powerful ways to deepen your connection with your child during these activities is through active listening. When you listen attentively to their thoughts, ideas, and questions, you're showing them that their voice matters. This simple act can make your child feel valued and understood, laying the groundwork for a strong, trusting relationship.

At the end of each activity, I encourage you to take a moment to reflect together. Ask your child what they enjoyed the most, what they learned, or how they felt during the activity. You might also highlight specific moments that stood out—whether it was something funny that made you both laugh, a surprising part of the activity that caught you off guard, or even a challenge that you worked through together. This reflection not only reinforces the bonding experience but also helps your child develop critical reflective thinking skills that will serve them well in life.

To help guide these moments, I've included a section at the end of this introduction with general conversation starters and tips for connecting emotionally during the activities. Sharing personal stories or reflecting on similar experiences from your own childhood can be a wonderful way to build emotional connections. However, it's important to remember that these conversations should feel natural and unforced. Don't worry if you don't ask every question or if you don't have a perfect story to share. The goal is to enjoy the time together, not to follow a script.

While these moments of reflection and conversation can enhance your time together, it's also important to remember that not every activity needs to involve deep discussion. It's perfectly okay to enjoy quiet moments or simply revel in the shared experience. Sometimes, the joy of the activity and the company of each other is enough. Authentic connections often come from being fully present and enjoying the time together, whether that means having a deep conversation or just having fun in silence.

Bond Like a Boss! is designed to help you and your child connect in ways that feel genuine, meaningful, and fun. Let the activities guide you, but allow your relationship to unfold naturally. Here's to many adventures ahead, filled with laughter, learning, and love.

Maximizing Your Bonding Experience: Conversation Starters, Emotional Connection Tips, and Reflection Prompts

By asking thoughtful questions and being present, you can turn any activity into an opportunity to understand your child better, share feelings, and enrich your shared experiences. To help you connect on a deeper level with your child through the activities in this book, here are some general conversation starters, emotional connection tips, and reflection prompts that you can apply to any activity.

Conversation Starters

Use these prompts to spark interesting and meaningful conversations during your activities:

- **Exploring Feelings**: "You seemed really proud of yourself when you did that! How does it feel to accomplish something like this?"
- **Sharing Memories**: "This reminds me of something I used to do when I was your age. Do you want to hear about it?"
- **Funny Twist**: "What's the silliest thing that could happen while we do this? Let's think of the craziest possibilities!"
- **Perspective Shift**: "What do you think this would look like if we were tiny like ants? How would we do this differently if we were giants?"
- **Imagination Boost**: "If you could make this activity into a story or movie, what would happen next?"
- **Creative Thinking**: "Let's pretend this [object you're using] is magical. What kind of magic does it have, and what adventure will we go on?"
- **Inventiveness**: "If you could change one thing about this activity to make it even more fun, what would it be?"
- **Curiosity Questions**: "What do you think will happen if we try this differently? How do you think it would turn out if we [change a rule, add a new step, etc.]?"
- **Exploring Interests**: "What other things are you curious about that we could explore together? What would you love to learn more about?"

Emotional Connection Tips

Strengthening your bond requires more than just talking—it's about connecting emotionally too. Here are some tips:

- **Active Listening**: Give your full attention when your child is speaking. Nod, smile, and make eye contact to show that you value their thoughts and feelings.
- **Empathy and Understanding**: Acknowledge your child's emotions. If they express frustration or excitement, mirror that back to them by saying,

"I can see you're really enjoying this!" or "I understand this part is a bit tricky."

- **Personal Stories**: Share your own emotions and experiences related to the activity. This could be a childhood memory or how the activity reminds you of something important. This creates a deeper emotional connection.
- **Physical Affection**: Don't underestimate the power of a gentle touch, hug, or high-five during or after an activity. Physical gestures reinforce emotional bonds.
- **Encouragement and Praise**: Celebrate small successes and efforts. Simple phrases like, "I'm really proud of how you did that!" or "You have such great ideas!" can boost your child's confidence and deepen your connection.

Reflection Prompts

After the activity, take a moment to reflect together. This helps reinforce the experience and gives you both a chance to bond over what you've just shared:

- **Favorite Part**: "What was your favorite part of what we just did? Why did you like that the most?"
- **Learning Moments**: "What did you learn from this activity? Did anything surprise you?"
- **Feelings Check-In**: "How do you feel now that we've finished? Is there anything you want to talk about?"
- **Next Time Ideas**: "What would you like to do differently next time? Is there something you'd like to add or change?"
- **Personal Growth**: "Did you notice something new about yourself during this activity? How do you think this activity helped us work together?"

Putting It All Together

These conversation starters, emotional connection tips, and reflection prompts are designed to help you make the most of your time with your child. By being present, actively engaging, and taking the time to connect on a deeper level, you'll not only create lasting memories but also build a strong, trusting relationship that will support your child's growth and well-being.

Remember, it's not about getting every conversation perfect—it's about showing your child that you're there, you care, and you're interested in their thoughts, feelings, and ideas. Every moment you spend together is an opportunity to strengthen your bond and create a legacy of love and connection.

PRESCHOOLERS

ON THE

MOVE

INDOOR ADVENTURES

Get ready for some imaginative, indoor fun tailored for preschoolers! These activities focus on hands-on creativity and sensory play, from bubble art to indoor fishing. Preschoolers will enjoy colorful experiments, creative storytelling, and exciting obstacle adventures, keeping their little hands and minds busy while encouraging curiosity and learning right at home.

1

BUBBLE ART BLAST

Prepare to embark on a colorful and bubbly adventure with Bubble Art Blast! This delightful activity merges the playful act of blowing bubbles with the creative process of making vibrant and unique artwork. Imagine your preschooler's excitement as they blow colorful bubbles that burst into beautiful splatters on paper, creating a one-of-a-kind masterpiece. The experience not only fosters creativity and artistic expression but also provides a wonderful opportunity for quality bonding time.

Together, you can experiment with different colors and techniques, watch how the bubbles burst into fascinating patterns, and marvel at the whimsical results. This engaging activity is a fantastic way to introduce your child to the joys of art in a fun and interactive manner. Get ready for an artistic adventure where messiness is part of the fun and creativity knows no bounds.

Materials Needed:

- ☐ Bubble solution (store-bought or homemade with dish soap and distilled water)
- ☐ Food coloring
- ☐ Small bowls or cups
- ☐ Bubble wands (or pipe cleaners for DIY wands)
- ☐ White paper or cardstock
- ☐ Old newspapers or plastic sheet (for easy cleanup)
- ☐ Aprons or old clothes (to protect from potential stains)

Step-by-Step Instructions:

1. **Prepare Your Workspace:**
   - Cover your table or floor with old newspapers or a plastic sheet to catch any spills.
   - Ensure your preschooler is wearing an apron or old clothes to avoid staining their regular clothes.
   - Lay out the white paper or cardstock for your child to use as their canvas.
2. **Make the Colored Bubble Solution:**
   - Mix 3 cups of distilled water with ½ cup of dish soap if making your own solution from scratch.
     - **Note:** Tap water may have minerals that can hinder bubble formation, so distilled water is best.
   - Pour a small amount of bubble solution into several cups or bowls, one for each color you plan to use.
   - Add a few good squirts of food coloring to each bowl and mix well. Ensure the solution's color is intense and opaque.
   - As you're preparing the bubble solution, encourage your child to predict how the colors might blend and interact.
3. **Create Your Bubble Wands:**
   - If you don't have bubble wands, twist pipe cleaners into fun shapes for DIY bubble wands.
4. **Blow Colorful Bubbles:**
   - Dip the bubble wands into the colored solution and blow bubbles towards the paper.
   - Watch as the bubbles burst, leaving behind beautiful, colorful patterns.
   - Take breaks to admire the evolving artwork, discussing with your child what they see and how the colors and patterns are changing.
   - Experiment with layering different colors. Allow your child to observe how the colors mix or overlap, creating new shades and patterns.
   - Encourage your child to try different bubble-blowing techniques to create varied effects, like blowing harder for smaller bubbles or softer for larger ones.
5. **Let the Artwork Dry:**
   - Once your preschooler is satisfied with their creation, carefully set the paper aside to dry flat on a clean, dry surface. This can take anywhere

from 30 minutes to a few hours, depending on how much liquid is on the paper. Avoid stacking wet papers to prevent smudging or sticking.

Safety Considerations:

- Supervise your child while they are blowing bubbles to ensure they don't accidentally ingest or inhale the solution or get it in their eyes.
- Be cautious of slippery surfaces caused by spilled bubble solution, especially on floors, and clean up any spills promptly to prevent accidents.

Troubleshooting Tips:

- **Bubbles Not Forming:** Ensure the bubble solution has the right soap-to-water ratio. Add a bit more soap if needed or use distilled water instead of tap water.
- **Colors Too Light:** Add another squirt of food coloring to the bubble solution to intensify the color.
- **Bubbles Popping Too Quickly**: If the bubbles pop before reaching the paper, try holding the wand closer to the paper or blowing more gently to create larger, slower bubbles.
- **Paper Too Wet**: If the paper becomes too wet and starts to tear, use thicker paper or cardstock, and allow the artwork to dry slightly between bubble sessions.

Cleanup Tips:

- Check for any splatter on nearby surfaces and use damp cloths or paper towels to immediately wipe up any spills to prevent staining.
- If staining occurs, make a paste of banking soda or powdered cleanser and apply to the stain. Cover with plastic wrap and let it sit for a few hours before wiping or gently scrubbing the color off.

Variations and Adaptations:

- **Alternate Bubble Art Method:** Instead of blowing bubbles onto the paper, have your child blow into a straw placed in a bowl of colored bubble solution, creating a layer of bubbles that rise above the rim. Gently press a piece of paper onto the bubbles, then lift it off to reveal a colorful bubble print. Repeat with different colors for a layered effect.
- **Scented Bubbles**: Add a few drops of child-safe essential oils to the bubble solution to create scented bubble art, making the experience even more sensory-rich.
- **Glow-in-the-Dark Bubbles:** For a magical nighttime activity, mix equal parts glow-in-the-dark paint into your bubble solution. Adjust the mixture as needed—add more dish soap if bubbles aren't forming well, or increase the paint for a brighter glow.

- **Bubble Resist Art**: Draw or write on the paper with a white crayon before starting. The wax will resist the bubble solution, creating hidden designs that reveal themselves as the bubbles burst around them.
- **Outdoor Bubble Mural:** Tape large sheets of paper to a fence and create a giant bubble mural in the backyard. Use various sizes of bubble wands to change things up and create something truly spectacular!
- **Stencils and Templates**: Place stencils or templates on the paper before blowing bubbles. The bubbles will create colorful patterns around the stencils, leaving interesting shapes and designs.

Benefits:

- **Introduces Science Concepts**: Painting with bubbles sparks curiosity and interest in science by introducing basic principles such as color mixing, the behavior of liquids, and the properties of bubbles.
- **Boosts Creativity:** Blowing bubbles with different colors and watching them burst into unique patterns fosters creativity and artistic expression, encouraging children to explore art in a playful, hands-on way.
- **Develops Fine Motor Skills:** Enhances hand-eye coordination and fine motor control as children blow bubbles and manipulate bubble wands.
- **Strengthens Bonds:** Mixing colors, blowing bubbles, and watching the artwork come to life together creates moments of laughter and excitement, fostering a deeper connection. Celebrating the unique patterns made in the process further strengthens the bond through shared accomplishments.
- **Encourages Problem-Solving**: Children learn to adapt their technique to get the best results, such as adjusting the distance they blow the bubbles from or trying different colors, fostering problem-solving skills in a fun setting.

2

INDOOR FISHING FRENZY

Dive into an ocean of fun with a DIY indoor fishing game! This delightful activity transforms a simple tub or small pool into a lively fishing pond, complete with colorful, magnetic fish and a fishing rod. Your child will be hooked for hours as they cast their line and reel in a "big one." Not only is this game a blast, but it also helps develop their hand-eye coordination and patience. The beauty of this activity lies in its simplicity and the joy it brings to both the fisher and the proud parent.

As the game progresses, you'll see your little angler's skills improve with each catch. Whether it's cheering them on or playfully competing to see who catches the most fish, this engaging activity strengthens your bond and fills your home with laughter. The thrill of the chase, the satisfaction of a successful catch, and the inevitable giggles when a fish slips away all contribute to an afternoon of pure delight. It's a perfect way to spend quality time together, creating memories that will last a lifetime.

Materials Needed:

- ☐ Small pool or tub
- ☐ Cardstock or cardboard
- ☐ Paper clips
- ☐ Small magnets (Found at hardware or craft stores)
- ☐ Stick or dowel
- ☐ String
- ☐ Glue, scissors, markers
- ☐ Utility knife or drill
- ☐ Googly eyes (optional for fish, found at craft stores)
- ☐ Blue cloth or paper for water effect (optional)

Step-by-Step Instructions:

1. **Prepare the Fish:**
   - **Materials:** Cardstock or cardboard, scissors, paper clips, magnets, glue, markers, optional googly eyes
   - **Instructions:**
     - Draw fish shapes on cardstock and cut them out.
     - Encourage your child to decorate the fish with markers to make them colorful and fun.
     - Glue a small magnet to the fish's mouth.
     - Attach a paper clip to the fish's tail for added weight.
2. **Make the Fishing Rod:**
   - **Materials:** Stick or dowel, magnet, string, utility knife or drill
   - **Instructions:**
     - Use a stick or dowel as the rod
     - Drill a small hole or cut notches on one end of the rod to give the string something to grip onto, ensuring it doesn't fly off when cast.
     - Tie a piece of string to the end with the hole or notch.
     - Attach a small magnet to the end of the string. Ensure it's strong enough to pick up the magnetic fish.
3. **Set Up the "Pond":**
   - Place the small pool or tub in an open area.
   - Optionally, line the bottom with blue cloth or paper for a watery effect.
   - Scatter the magnetic fish in the pool or tub.
4. **Go Fishing:**
   - Show your child how to hold the fishing rod and cast the line into the "water".
   - Hand the fishing rod to your child and let them try to catch the fish by attracting the magnet to the fish's mouth.
   - Cheer for your child and offer tips to help them catch more fish.
   - If a fish slips away, turn it into a moment of humor and encourage your child to try again.
5. **Enhance the Experience:**
   - As your child catches each fish, you can introduce simple counting by tallying up the total number of fish caught.

- You can join in the fun by fishing alongside them, making it a playful competition to see who can catch the most fish.
- For added excitement, consider giving a small prize or treat for each fish caught. This could be a sticker, a piece of fruit, or just a high-five and some praise.

Safety Considerations:

- Ensure magnets are securely attached to prevent swallowing.
- Supervise the activity to avoid accidents with scissors or small parts.

Troubleshooting Tips:

- **Magnetic Fish Not Sticking**: Ensure that the magnets are clean and free from any debris. If needed, replace weak magnets with stronger ones.
- **Difficulty Catching Fish**: If your child is having trouble catching the fish, adjust the length of the fishing rod string to make it easier to control. You can also make the magnets on the fish and rod larger for a better connection.
- **Boredom:** If the game feels repetitive, add a variety of fish shapes, colors, or even other sea creatures to keep your child engaged and interested in the activity.

Cleanup Tips:

- Store the fishing game materials in a designated container or box so they're ready for the next use.
- Pretend the fish need to go back to their "school" (the container). Have your child guide them back as part of the cleanup process.

Variations and Adaptations:

- **Color Matching:** Create fish in different colors and ask your child to catch fish of a specific color.
- **Numbered Fish:** Number the fish and have your child catch them in numerical order to add an educational twist.
- **Alphabet Fishing**: Label each fish with a letter of the alphabet. Have your child fish for letters to spell out words, reinforcing their alphabet and spelling skills.
- **Timed Challenges**: Set a timer and see how many fish your child can catch within a certain time limit.
- **Story Time:** Create a story about each fish your child catches to enhance their imagination.
- **Glow-in-the-Dark Fishing**: Use glow-in-the-dark paint to decorate the fish and play the game in a dimly lit room for added excitement.

- **Fish Facts**: Write a simple fun fact on the back of each fish. When your child catches a fish, read the fact aloud, sharing interesting marine life knowledge and adding an educational twist to the game.

Benefits:

- **Enhances Hand-Eye Coordination**: Casting a line, aiming for the fish, and reeling it in strengthens hand-eye coordination and improves fine motor skills in a fun and engaging way.
- **Builds Confidence**: Each successful catch gives children a sense of accomplishment, boosting their self-esteem and encouraging them to take on new challenges with confidence.
- **Boosts Cognitive Skills**: Figuring out how to successfully catch a fish, especially when it slips away, helps children think critically and adjust their approach, building problem-solving abilities.
- **Strengthens Bonds:** Playing the game together fosters a sense of connection, as both participants share moments of laughter, teamwork, and playful competition, while celebrating each catch along the way.
- **Teaches Emotional Regulation**: Handling the ups and downs of missing a fish or successfully reeling one in teaches children how to manage emotions, helping them practice patience and perseverance in a safe, playful environment.

3

ADVENTURES IN STICKERLAND

Ignite your child's imagination with sticker storyboards! This creative activity involves using colorful stickers and large sheets of paper to craft unique scenes and narratives. Your child will have a blast as they bring their stories to life, placing stickers of characters, animals, and objects onto their storyboard. It's an engaging way to encourage storytelling and artistic expression, perfect for those rainy days or quiet afternoons.

As your child builds their storyboard, you'll see their creativity flourish. The collaborative process of choosing stickers, placing them just right, and weaving them into a story is a fantastic bonding experience. Laughter and excitement fill the room as you both dive into exciting worlds of your own making. This simple yet profound activity nurtures a sense of connection and joy that's hard to beat.

Materials Needed:

- ☐ Large sheets of paper or poster board
- ☐ Assorted stickers (characters, animals, objects, etc.)
- ☐ Markers and crayons

Step-by-Step Instructions:

1. **Set Up the Space:**
   - Lay out large sheets of paper on a flat surface.
   - Arrange the stickers within easy reach for your child.
   - Have markers and crayons ready for extra decorations.
2. **Create the Storyboard:**
   - Discuss with your child what kind of scene or story they want to create. It could be a day at the zoo, a space adventure, or a magical forest.
   - Help your child choose and place stickers on the paper to form the scene but let your child take the lead in deciding where to place each sticker.
   - As you place each sticker, ask your child questions to help develop the story: "What is this character doing here?" or "Where do you think this animal is going?"
   - Encourage your child to tell a story as they go, explaining who the characters are and what's happening.
   - Take turns adding stickers and contributing to the story. Add to the story by suggesting plot twists such as:
     - **Introducing New Characters**: Suddenly introduce a new character by placing a sticker or drawing one on the storyboard. Say something like, "And then, a mysterious knight appeared! What do you think he's here for?"
     - **Creating Challenges or Obstacles**: Add excitement by placing a sticker of a barrier, like a river or a mountain. Ask, "How are they going to cross this river? What will they do?"
     - **Adding Dialogue**: Give the characters voices, either by adding speech bubbles or voicing the characters yourself. Say, "Let's have this bear ask the frog, 'Why are you in such a hurry?' What do you think the frog will say?"
     - **Changing the Setting**: Suggest a sudden change in the scene, like "What if it suddenly started raining? Let's add some raindrops. What do the characters do now?"
     - **Introducing a Surprise**: Surprise your child with an unexpected event, like "Oh no! A dragon appears in the sky! What will our heroes do?"
     - **Encouraging Backstory Creation**: Ask your child to think about the characters' backgrounds: "Why do you think this

princess is in the forest? What happened before she got here?"

- **Creating Choices**: Offer choices to guide the story's direction: "Should the spaceship land on the moon or fly to another planet? You decide!"

3. **Add Details:**
   - Encourage your child to use markers and crayons to add background details, like trees, paths, stars, buildings, or speech bubbles.
4. **Tell the Story:**
   - Once the storyboard is complete, sit down with your child and admire your creation together. Encourage them to narrate the finished story and give it a title.

Safety Considerations:

- Ensure that small stickers are not a choking hazard for younger children.

Troubleshooting Tips:

- **Stickers Not Sticking:** Use glue to secure stickers that don't adhere well.
- **Running Out of Ideas:** Introduce new themes or combine stickers to create unique stories.

Cleanup Tips:

- Clean the table or workspace with a damp, soapy cloth to remove any sticky residue or marker stains.

Variations and Adaptations:

- **Sticker Theater**: Bring your storyboard to life by turning it into a charming miniature theater. Cut out the characters and props, mount them on popsicle sticks, and use them to perform an animated show on a makeshift stage.
- **Interactive Storyboards:** Create storyboards with movable parts, such as flaps or sliding elements, to hide and reveal different aspects of the story.
- **Sticker Collage Art**: Instead of a traditional storyboard, create abstract art pieces using stickers to form patterns, shapes, and designs. Encourage your child to experiment with color and composition.
- **Favorite Characters**: Focus on your child's favorite characters from books, movies, or TV shows. Create new adventures for these characters using stickers and their imagination.
- **Family Tale Time**: Create a storyboard starring your family members as the main characters, weaving them into delightful adventures and heartwarming stories.

- **Educational Themes:** Use stickers to create stories about the alphabet, numbers, or basic history like dinosaurs or the invention of telephones.

Benefits:

- **Develops Fine Motor Skills**: Handling stickers and placing them precisely on the storyboard helps develop fine motor control and hand-eye coordination.
- **Enhances Communication Skills**: Telling stories and explaining their sticker scenes enhances language development and communication skills.
- **Boosts Cognitive Development**: Deciding where to place stickers and how to build their story helps develop problem-solving and decision-making abilities.
- **Encourages Patience and Focus**: Engaging in a creative task that involves multiple steps, such as selecting stickers and arranging them, encourages sustained attention and patience, especially as children refine their work.
- **Strengthens Bonds**: Collaborating on creating stories together builds a deeper connection through shared imagination and laughter, strengthening the relationship through joint creative expression.
- **Promotes Emotional Expression**: Crafting storyboards using stickers allows children to explore and express their emotions through the characters and scenes they create, helping them articulate feelings in a playful way.

4

CARDBOARD BOX TOWN EXTRAVAGANZA

Get ready to transform your living room into a bustling mini-metropolis! With a few cardboard boxes, some markers, and a sprinkle of imagination, you and your preschooler will build a vibrant cardboard box town. Picture your living space filled with colorful buildings, winding roads, and bustling parks, all crafted from simple materials. Each box becomes a unique structure - a towering skyscraper, a quaint little house, or even a whimsical shop. Together, you'll design and decorate each building, creating a rich tapestry of a town where toy cars zoom through streets, action figures embark on adventures, and imaginative stories unfold.

The creativity flows freely as you both dive into this hands-on activity, crafting a custom-built cityscape that evolves with every addition. Your child will be brimming with excitement as they navigate their miniature world, making up tales of the town's residents and their daily lives. It's a day of construction, exploration, and endless storytelling, right in the heart of your home.

Materials Needed:

- ☐ Various sizes of repurposed cardboard boxes (delivery boxes, cereal boxes, etc.)
- ☐ Markers, crayons, or colored pencils
- ☐ Tape or glue
- ☐ Scissors (child-safe)
- ☐ Construction paper, stickers, and other decorative items (optional)
- ☐ Toy cars, dolls, and action figures for added fun (optional)

Step-by-Step Instructions:

1. **Gather Your Materials:**
   - Collect a variety of cardboard boxes. These could range from small shoeboxes to larger shipping boxes.
   - Lay out all your decorating supplies, including markers, crayons, and any other craft items you have on hand.
   - Bring in toy cars and action figures to populate the town (optional).
2. **Design and Decorate:**
   - Before starting, spend a few minutes brainstorming with your child about what kind of buildings you want to include in your town. Will there be a school, a grocery store, or a fire station?
   - Begin by flipping each box upside down so that the open side becomes the bottom of the building.
   - Use markers, crayons, or colored pencils to draw windows, doors, and other details on each box. Encourage your child to decorate their buildings however they like—maybe with flowers in the windows or a sign for the shop.
   - **Optional:** For added detail, you can cut out doors or windows and tape or glue construction paper to create roofs, awnings, or other features.
3. **Build Your Town:**
   - Arrange the decorated boxes on the floor to create streets and blocks. You can use the whole room or designate a specific area as your town's location.
   - Use construction paper, or simply draw directly on the floor with chalk or tape, to create roads connecting the buildings. Add a few intersections or roundabouts to make it interesting!
   - Set up parks or green spaces by cutting out pieces of green construction paper or using a green towel as a park where your child can place cardboard trees or benches.
   - As you work together, suggest ideas like adding a crosswalk or a fountain in the park, and discuss the importance of these features in a real town.
4. **Playtime:**
   - Let your child drive toy cars through the streets and have the dolls or action figures visit different buildings (optional).
   - Encourage your child to create imaginative scenarios about the residents and what's happening in their new mini-metropolis.

Safety Considerations:

- Supervise the use of scissors to ensure safe handling.
- Ensure the play area is free of small objects that could pose a choking hazard.

Troubleshooting Tips:

- **Limited Space:** If space is tight, build the town on a large piece of cardboard or a table to keep it contained.
- **Running Out of Supplies:** Use household items like paper cups, plastic containers, and paper towel rolls to extend the town's features.
- **Short Attention Span:** Break the activity into smaller sessions to maintain your child's interest.

Cleanup Tips:

- Designate a storage area for the cardboard town pieces to easily rebuild it later. If space is limited, carefully collapse the boxes before storing.
- Challenge your child to see who can put away the most supplies or stack the most boxes in a set amount of time. Use a timer to add excitement, and celebrate when the cleanup is completed quickly and neatly.

Variations and Adaptations:

- **Themed Town:** Create themed towns like a beach town, space colony, or dinosaur park.
- **Light Up the City:** Add small LED lights or glow sticks inside some buildings for a magical nighttime effect.
- **Interactive Features:** Add ramps and tunnels using toilet paper rolls and cardboard scraps.
- **Weather Elements:** Create elements like a cardboard sun, rainclouds, or snowflakes to change the town's weather.
- **Neighborhood Project:** Build different sections of the town over multiple days, expanding the city gradually.
- **Storybook Town:** Base the town on your child's favorite book or movie, recreating familiar scenes and characters.

Benefits:

- **Enhances Creativity:** Designing and decorating buildings from cardboard encourages imaginative thinking and artistic expression, allowing children to explore their creative potential.
- **Develops Fine Motor Skills:** Cutting, gluing, and drawing help improve hand-eye coordination and dexterity as children work with their hands to

bring their ideas to life.

- **Encourages Problem-Solving:** Figuring out how to construct buildings or create specific features, like windows or doors, fosters problem-solving abilities and resourceful thinking.
- **Builds Confidence**: Seeing their ideas take shape boosts a child's sense of accomplishment and confidence, encouraging them to take pride in their creative work.
- **Strengthens Bonds:** Working together to build and design the town fosters teamwork and communication, creating a shared sense of accomplishment that deepens bond between you and your child.
- **Promotes Storytelling:** Playing in the cardboard town stimulates storytelling as children invent characters, scenarios, and adventures that unfold within the town, enhancing narrative skills and imagination.

5

KITCHEN BAND BONANZA

Turn your kitchen into a vibrant music studio and unleash your child's inner rock star with Kitchen Band Bonanza! This dynamic activity transforms everyday items into part of an exciting orchestra. Watch as your preschooler discovers the joy of creating their own music using pots, pans, wooden spoons, and more.

Packed with creative twists, this fun-filled session takes kitchen music-making to a whole new level. It's not just about burning off energy but also nurturing a love for music and rhythm. Picture the delight on your child's face as they experiment with different sounds, from banging on pots to shaking spice jars and tapping plastic containers. The Kitchen Band Bonanza is all about exploration, creativity, and joyful noise-making, transforming an ordinary day into an unforgettable musical adventure. It's a fantastic way to bond and create lasting memories filled with laughter and spontaneous jam sessions.

Materials Needed:

- ☐ Pots, pans, bowls
- ☐ Wooden spoons, ladles, spatulas
- ☐ Plastic containers
- ☐ Spice jars

Step-by-Step Instructions:

1. **Gather Instruments:**
   - Collect various kitchen items like pots, pans, bowls, and wooden spoons. Choose items that are durable and safe for your child to handle.
   - Use plastic containers and spice jars for added variety and softer sounds.
2. **Setup:**
   - Arrange these items within easy reach for your preschooler, either on the floor or on a low, stable surface.
   - Ensure the area is clear of breakables and sharp objects.
3. **Demonstrate:**
   - Show your child how to create different sounds by tapping on the pots and pans with wooden spoons, shaking spice jars, and tapping on plastic containers.
   - Encourage your child to explore and experiment with the different sounds each item makes. Let them see how using different utensils or hitting different parts of the items changes the sound.
4. **Jam Session:**
   - Once your child is familiar with the "instruments," it's time to let loose! Encourage them to play freely, making as much cheerful noise as they like.
   - Join in with clapping or playing along with another kitchen instrument.
   - Engage your child by playing simple games like repeating each other's rhythms or creating a "call and response" pattern where one person starts a rhythm and the other completes it.
5. **Wind Down the Session:**
   - After the initial excitement, gently guide your child toward quieter activities. Suggest exploring softer sounds or using plastic containers for a quieter jam session.
   - Transition to a calming activity, such as singing a lullaby together while lightly tapping on a pan or container to maintain a musical theme while winding down.

Safety Considerations:

- Avoid using glass or sharp objects to prevent accidents.
- Ensure that heavier pots and pans are placed in a way that they won't tip

over easily.

Troubleshooting Tips:

- **Too Loud:** Move the activity to a space where the noise won't be disruptive or use softer items like plastic containers.
- **Child Loses Interest:** Introduce new items or make up fun songs to keep them engaged.

Cleanup Tips:

- Check for any scattered items on the floor to prevent tripping hazards.

Variations and Adaptations:

- **Sound Experiments:** Explore sound by changing water levels in pots and other kitchen items, discovering the different tones and pitches they create when tapped.
- **Musical Parade:** Turn your home into a parade route, marching with your instruments and creating a lively, musical procession that winds through the rooms.
- **Musical Scavenger Hunt:** Turn the instrument gathering phase into a scavenger hunt where your child has to find specific items that make particular sounds.
- **Sing-Along:** Combine your musical play with a sing-along, belting out favorite nursery rhymes or songs while playing your kitchen instruments.
- **Obstacle Course:** Set up an obstacle course where your child has to play an instrument at each station.
- **Create a Music Video:** Record your jam session and then watch it together, turning your musical adventure into a fun, homemade music video.

Benefits:

- **Encourages Creativity:** Creating spontaneous rhythms and sounds encourages free-form creative expression, allowing children to explore music without boundaries or instructions.
- **Encourages Musical Exploration**: Using everyday kitchen items to create sounds introduces children to the basics of music, helping them discover different rhythms, beats, and tones in a playful environment.
- **Boosts Motor Skills**: Banging, tapping, and shaking different kitchen instruments improve fine and gross motor coordination, helping preschoolers refine their hand-eye coordination and muscle control.
- **Strengthens Bonds:** Collaborating on fun, musical "jam sessions" fosters stronger connections through shared creativity and playfulness, creating

opportunities for laughter, teamwork, and spontaneous moments of joy.

- **Promotes Sensory Development**: Experimenting with various textures, sounds, and movements engages multiple senses, enhancing sensory development and awareness in a hands-on way.

6

SENSORY EXPLORATION STATION

Immerse your preschooler in a world of tactile exploration with an enhanced Sensory Exploration Station! This engaging activity invites your child to dive into a bin filled with various textured materials such as rice, beans, or pasta. The sensory experience is enriched with sorting, measuring, and discovering hidden treasures. Your little one will delight in the different sensations and sounds, all while developing fine motor skills, sensory awareness, and early math concepts.

As you join in the fun, demonstrating different ways to interact with the materials, you'll both enjoy moments of discovery and creativity. This activity not only entertains but also provides a calming and therapeutic experience, perfect for curious minds eager to explore and learn through touch. Dive into this sensory adventure and watch as your child's imagination and skills flourish.

Materials Needed:

- ☐ Shallow plastic bin
- ☐ Sensory materials (dried rice, beans, pasta, etc.)
- ☐ Spoons, cups, small toys
- ☐ Measuring cups and spoons
- ☐ Small containers for sorting
- ☐ Magnifying glass (optional)

Step-by-Step Instructions:

1. **Prepare the Bin:**
   - Get a shallow plastic bin and fill it with a sensory material like dried rice, beans, or pasta.
   - Ensure the bin is placed on a stable surface.
2. **Add Tools:**
   - Provide tools like spoons, cups, small toys, measuring cups, and containers for added fun.
   - Arrange the tools around the bin for easy access.
3. **Interactive Play:**
   - Let your child explore the bin, feeling the textures and using the tools to scoop, pour, and measure.
   - Encourage your child to sort the materials into different containers, use the measuring cups to understand volume, and find hidden toys.
4. **Guided Learning:**
   - Demonstrate different ways to play with the materials, such as creating patterns, counting the number of items, or using the magnifying glass to examine textures closely.
   - Engage your child with questions and challenges, like "Can you find all the blue objects?" or "How many spoonfuls fit into this cup?"

Safety Considerations:

- Supervise your child to prevent choking hazards and ensure safe play.
- Be mindful of allergies, and choose sensory materials that are safe for your child's health.

Troubleshooting Tips:

- **Child Loses Interest:** Periodically update the sensory bin with new materials and create themes that align with your child's interests (e.g., ocean, farm, construction) to keep the activity engaging and exciting.

Cleanup Tips:

- Place a large mat or old sheet under the sensory bin to catch any spilled materials. This makes it easier to gather and clean up everything in one go.
- Have designated containers or bins for storing sensory materials to keep everything organized and ready for the next play session.

Variations and Adaptations:

- **Sorting Sensory Bin**: Include various objects that your child can sort by color, size, or type, using cups or containers to organize them.
- **Hidden Treasures:** Bury small toys or objects in the sensory material for a fun treasure hunt.
- **Seasonal Bins:** Use seasonal items like artificial autumn leaves or snowflakes to change up the sensory experience. You can find these at dollar stores.
- **Alphabet Sensory Bin**: Bury plastic letters in the bin and encourage your child to find and identify the letters, or spell out simple words.
- **Nature Sensory Bin**: Use materials from nature such as sand, pebbles, leaves, and sticks. Add small animal figurines to create a mini forest or beach scene.
- **Magnetic Sensory Bin**: Fill the bin with sand or rice and bury magnetic objects. Provide a magnetic wand or magnets for your child to discover and explore the magnetic properties of different items hidden in the bin.
- **Puzzle Sensory Bin:** Hide pieces of a simple puzzle in the sensory materials and have your child find and assemble the puzzle pieces.
- **Mystery Sensory Bin**: Cover the bin with a cloth and have your child reach in to identify objects by touch alone, adding an element of surprise and guessing.

Benefits:

- **Promotes Sensory Exploration:** Interacting with different materials engages multiple senses, including touch, sight, and sound, helping to strengthen your child's ability to process and respond to sensory stimuli.
- **Develops Fine Motor Skills:** Manipulating small items, scooping, pouring, and sorting materials help to develop precise hand movements and strengthen fine motor control.
- **Encourages Creativity and Imagination:** With endless possibilities for interaction, the sensory bin encourages imaginative play, allowing your child to invent stories and scenarios as they explore the materials.
- **Strengthens Focus and Attention**: The immersive nature of the activity helps develop the ability to focus for longer periods, as children become engrossed in the tactile experience and the hidden treasures they discover.
- **Strengthens Bonds:** Engaging in the activity together fosters a sense of connection and cooperation, creating moments of shared discovery and communication during play.
- **Supports Emotional Regulation**: The calming nature of tactile play

offers a soothing experience, helping children regulate their emotions and reduce stress through gentle, repetitive actions.

7
INDOOR OBSTACLE ADVENTURE ZONE

Transform your home into a thrilling playground with Indoor Obstacle Adventure Zone! This dynamic activity turns everyday household items into a challenging and fun obstacle course. Using cushions, blankets, and furniture, you can create tunnels to crawl through, hurdles to jump over, and balance beams to navigate. Your preschooler will love the physical challenge and excitement of completing the course, while also enhancing their motor skills and problem-solving abilities.

As you cheer them on and maybe even join in the action, you'll create an atmosphere of encouragement and fun. A DIY indoor obstacle course offers endless variations and can be tailored to suit your child's abilities and imagination, ensuring an energetic and laughter-filled playtime. Embrace the opportunity to turn your living space into a hub of adventure, sparking joy and active engagement for both you and your child.

Materials Needed:

- ☐ Cushions and pillows
- ☐ Blankets and sheets
- ☐ Furniture (chairs, tables)
- ☐ Tape (for marking boundaries; masking or painter's tape work great)

Step-by-Step Instructions:

1. **Set the Stage:**
    - Begin by clearing a large space in your living room or any room with enough space to move around.
2. **Create the Course:**
    - **Tunnels and Crawling Spaces:** Drape blankets or sheets over chairs or small tables to create tunnels. Encourage your child to crawl through them on their hands and knees.
    - **Hurdles to Jump Over:** Stack pillows or cushions at different heights for your child to jump over. Start with smaller hurdles and gradually increase the difficulty based on your child's ability.
    - **Balance Beam:** Lay down a long cushion, a strip of tape, or a rolled-up blanket to serve as a balance beam. Challenge your child to walk along it, trying to keep their balance.
    - **Obstacle Paths:** Use tape or string to mark paths on the floor. These could be zigzag paths to follow, spots to hop between, or a line to walk along.
    - Mark starting and ending points with tape.
3. **Explain the Course:**
    - Show your child how to navigate each part of the course.
    - **Optional:** Demonstrate crawling under tables, jumping over cushions, and walking along the balance beam.
4. **Go!:**
    - Let your child to complete the course, helping them as needed. Cheer them on and offer encouragement as they conquer each part of the adventure.

Safety Considerations:

- Ensure the play area is free of sharp objects, fragile items, and tripping hazards to prevent injuries.
- Use plenty of cushions, pillows, and blankets to create soft landing areas and reduce the risk of bumps and bruises.
- Make sure that chairs, tables, and other furniture used in the obstacle course are stable and won't tip over easily.
- Always supervise your child during the activity to provide assistance and ensure they navigate the course safely.

Troubleshooting Tips:

- **Running Out of Space**: If space is limited, create a smaller, more compact course with quick transitions between obstacles. Focus on creative use of vertical space with activities like crawling under tables or climbing onto couches.
- **Course Too Difficult**: Simplify challenging obstacles by lowering heights, shortening distances, or reducing the complexity. Offer additional guidance and encouragement to help your child navigate the course confidently.
- **Child Gets Tired**: Shorten the course or include designated rest stations where your child can take a quick break and catch their breath before continuing.

Cleanup Tips:

- Turn cleanup into a role-playing activity. Pretend to be superheroes, robots, or construction workers tasked with cleaning up the site. Use playful dialogue and actions to keep your child engaged.

Variations and Adaptations:

- **Puzzle Obstacle Course**: Integrate simple puzzles or problem-solving tasks at each station. For example, your child has to match colors, complete a small puzzle, or find a hidden object before moving to the next obstacle.
- **Themed Obstacle Course**: Create a themed obstacle course based on your child's favorite interests, such as a pirate adventure, superhero training camp, or space exploration. Incorporate props and decorations that match the theme to make it even more immersive.
- **Animal Obstacle Course**: Encourage your child to move like different animals through the course. They can crawl like a bear, hop like a frog, or slither like a snake, adding a playful twist to the activity.
- **Timed Challenge**: Introduce a timed element where your child tries to complete the course as quickly as possible. Track their best times and encourage them to beat their own records.
- **Fitness Obstacle Course**: Between obstacles, add small challenges like doing five jumping jacks, a little spin, or hopping on one foot to promote physical fitness and coordination.
- **Story-Based Course:** Create a narrative for the obstacle course where your child is on a mission, like rescuing a stuffed animal friend or finding hidden treasure. Narrate the story as they progress through the course.
- **Toy Rescue Mission:** Place small toys at different points along the course. Your child's mission could be to collect them all as they navigate

through the obstacles.

- **Musical Obstacles:** Play music and pause it periodically; when the music stops, your child must freeze in place until it starts again.

Benefits:

- **Promotes Physical Activity:** The dynamic nature of the obstacle course promotes physical exercise, helping your child burn energy in a fun and engaging way, even in an indoor setting.
- **Teaches Resilience**: Overcoming obstacles and persisting through challenges in the course helps foster resilience, teaching your child the value of perseverance and encouraging them to keep trying even after setbacks.
- **Develops Gross Motor Skills**: Navigating through tunnels, jumping over hurdles, and balancing on beams help improve your child's gross motor skills, including coordination, strength, and balance.
- **Boosts Problem-Solving Skills:** Figuring out how to move through each obstacle encourages critical thinking and problem-solving, as your child experiments with different ways to complete the course.
- **Strengthens Bonds**: Working together to build and complete the course strengthens relationships by fostering communication, cooperation, and encouragement during active play.
- **Builds Confidence**: Completing challenges successfully boosts your child's self-esteem and confidence, reinforcing their belief in their ability to overcome obstacles.

OUTDOOR FUN

Step outside for some engaging, outdoor exploration perfect for preschoolers! These activities embrace the natural energy and excitement of the outdoors, offering a mix of nature-themed crafts, playful games, and discovery challenges. From crafting nature bracelets to shadow play in the sun, each activity turns any outdoor space into a fun-filled adventure, building memories and making the most of the great outdoors.

8

NATURE BRACELET PURSUIT

Turn a simple walk into a creative craft session with nature bracelets. Picture a leisurely walk through a park or garden, where every step brings a new discovery. As you wander, your child's eyes light up with excitement, spotting vibrant leaves, delicate flowers, and intriguing twigs to collect. These small natural treasures become the jewels of their unique bracelet. Wrapping a strip of tape around their wrist, sticky side out, transforms it into a canvas for nature's art. Each found item is carefully placed, creating a wearable masterpiece that tells the story of your walk.

The bracelet grows more beautiful with every addition, a testament to your child's keen eye and creativity. Once complete, the nature bracelet becomes a cherished accessory, a reminder of the day's adventure and the beauty of the natural world. It's a simple yet enchanting way to blend exploration with creativity, turning an ordinary stroll into a magical crafting experience.

Materials Needed:

- ☐ Wide tape (masking tape works well)
- ☐ Scissors

Step-by-Step Instructions:

1. **Prepare the Tape:**
   - Cut a piece of wide tape long enough to wrap around your child's wrist.
   - Wrap it around their wrist sticky side out, forming the bracelet.
   - **Optional:** Join in on the fun by wrapping a piece of tape around your own wrist for your child to decorate for you.
2. **Go on a Nature Walk:**
   - Head out to your yard, local park, or any natural area where you can find a variety of leaves, flowers, and small natural items.
   - Encourage your child to explore and collect small treasures like vibrant leaves, delicate flowers, and interesting twigs to add to their bracelet.
3. **Create the Bracelet:**
   - As your child finds each item, help them gently press it onto the sticky side of the tape. Encourage them to be creative with the placement, mixing different shapes, textures and colors.
   - Once the bracelet is full or your walk comes to an end, admire the finished piece together. Talk about each item they've chosen and what made it special.
4. **Share the Story:**
   - Encourage your child to share the story of their bracelet with other family members or friends. They can explain where they found each item and why they chose it, which adds to the bonding experience and makes the activity more meaningful.

Safety Considerations:

- Ensure your child avoids touching or picking any plants that could be harmful, such as poison ivy, poison oak, or plants with thorns.

Troubleshooting Tips:

- **Running Out of Tape:** Bring extra tape in case the first bracelet gets full or damaged.
- **Losing Interest:** Make it a game by setting challenges like finding specific colors or shapes.

Cleanup Tips:

- Wash hands thoroughly after handling outdoor materials.
- If your child wants to keep the bracelet for longer, consider placing a clear

adhesive tape over the top to secure the items or taking a photo of it to preserve the memory.

Variations and Adaptations:

- **Themed Collections**: Create themed bracelets based on specific criteria, such as only using items that are a certain color, shape, or type (e.g., only flowers, only leaves).
- **Interactive Story Bracelet**: As you collect items, create a story together. Each item added to the bracelet represents a part of the story, enhancing creativity and narrative skills.
- **Seasonal Bracelets:** Create bracelets in different seasons to showcase the changing colors and textures of nature throughout the year, like fresh blossoms in spring or colorful leaves in fall.
- **Scented Bracelet**: Focus on collecting fragrant items like herbs, flowers, or pine needles, creating a bracelet that not only looks beautiful but also smells wonderful.
- **Memory Bracelet:** Collect items from special places and memorable events to create a cherished keepsake that tells the story of your adventures together.

Benefits:

- **Boosts Observational Skills**: Searching for and identifying different plants, flowers, and leaves enhances your child's observational abilities and attention to detail.
- **Encourages Outdoor Exploration**: Exploring parks or gardens in search of natural treasures promotes curiosity about the surroundings, transforming a simple walk into an exciting adventure filled with discovery.
- **Enhances Fine Motor Skills**: Picking up small items and sticking them onto the tape helps develop your child's fine motor skills and hand-eye coordination.
- **Strengthens Bonds:** Creating the bracelet together fosters a deeper connection through joint exploration and creativity. This shared experience enhances communication and builds meaningful moments as you engage with nature side by side.
- **Provides Educational Opportunities:** Discussing the different items collected teaches children about various plants, flowers, and elements of nature, while also introducing basic concepts of botany and ecology, enriching their understanding of the natural world.

9

SHADOW PLAY SOIREE

Embrace the power of the sun and spark your child's imagination with Shadow Play Soiree. This outdoor activity turns a sunny day into a canvas for creativity, using shadows to make fun shapes and stories. By experimenting with different poses and simple props, your child can create fascinating shadow scenes, and you'll enjoy the imaginative playtime together. Whether it's making shadow animals or crafting shadow art, this activity is a wonderful way to enjoy the outdoors and stimulate your child's creativity.

As the sun casts long shadows, watch as your child discovers the magic of light and dark, creating large and small silhouettes that dance on the ground. Props like toys or household items add another layer of fun, transforming everyday objects into whimsical shadow puppets. Each new shadow form sparks a story or a playful scenario, filling your outdoor space with the laughter and wonder of discovery. This sunlit activity becomes a treasured memory of imaginative play and exploration.

Materials Needed:

- ☐ Sunny day
- ☐ Flat, open area
- ☐ Props like toys or household items (optional)

Step-by-Step Instructions:

1. **Find a Sunny Spot:**
   - Head outside on a sunny day and find a flat, open area where the sun casts clear, long shadows. Early morning or late afternoon often works best as the sun is lower in the sky, creating more pronounced shadows.
2. **Create Shadow Shapes:**
   - Encourage your child to use their body to make different shadow shapes. Ask them to stretch their arms, jump, or make animal shapes like a roaring lion or a flapping bird.
   - Show them how moving closer or farther from the ground changes the size of their shadow.
   - Try creating shapes together. For example, hold hands and form a circle or create an arch by reaching for each other's hands overhead.
3. **Invent Shadow Stories:**
   - Use the shadows to create stories or scenes. For example, pretend to be superheroes flying through the sky, with your shadows showing off your best superhero poses.
   - Introduce props like toys or household items to add to the shadow play. For example, a toy dinosaur can stomp through an imaginary forest, or a stick can become a magic wand in a shadow play adventure.
   - Take turns narrating parts of the story while the other person acts it out with shadows. Encourage creativity and fun twists in the plot.

Safety Considerations:

- Ensure the play area is free of hazards that could cause tripping or injury.
- Time flies when you're having fun so consider using sunscreen.

Troubleshooting Tips:

- **Cloudy Weather:** If the sun goes behind the clouds, switch to indoor shadow play with a flashlight.
- **Short Attention Span:** Change up the activity by introducing new props or challenges.

Cleanup Tips:

- Turn cleanup into a fun game by having your child become a cleanup superhero, gaining special powers with each prop they collect and put away.

Variations and Adaptations:

- **Shadow Art:** Trace shadows on the ground or a large piece of paper with crayons or chalk. Fill in the shapes with colorful drawings to create a lasting piece of shadow art.

- **Night Shadows:** Use a flashlight or lantern to create shadows at night.
- **Themed Stories:** Create shadow stories based on favorite books or movies.
- **Shadow Charades**: Play a game of charades using only shadows to act out different animals, objects, or actions, and have others guess what the shadow is portraying.
- **Shadow Sculptures**: Arrange objects into interesting shapes or towers, then position them to cast cool, abstract shadows that look like sculptures.
- **Shadow Dance Party**: Play some music and have a shadow dance party where everyone creates fun and funky shadow shapes as they dance.

Benefits:

- **Encourages Imagination:** Experimenting with different shapes, poses, and props stimulates your child's imagination as they create unique shadow scenes and stories.
- **Channels Energy Constructively:** Engaging in shadow play helps channel your child's natural energy into focused, creative play, offering a productive way to engage their enthusiasm and curiosity.
- **Teaches Science Concepts:** Playing with shadows helps children learn basic principles of light, geometry, and how objects interact with sunlight, fostering a natural curiosity about science.
- **Strengthens Bonds:** Collaborating on shadow scenes and stories strengthens the bond as you and your child share ideas, laugh, and connect through creative play.
- **Enhances Communication Skills:** Narrating stories and describing shadow creations helps children develop language and communication skills, building confidence in self-expression.

10

SPRINKLER SPLASH BASH

Transform a hot day into a watery wonderland with Sprinkler Splash Bash! This activity turns your yard into a mini water park, where your preschooler can revel in the joys of running, jumping, and splashing through the refreshing spray of a garden sprinkler. The sheer delight of cooling off while playing outside creates lasting memories of fun and laughter.

As you join in the splashing or simply watch with joy, you'll be sharing in a delightful bonding experience. Sprinkler Splash Bash not only provides a fun way to beat the heat but also encourages physical activity and outdoor play, making it a perfect summer adventure. Prepare for an afternoon of sunny, splashy fun that your child will remember fondly.

Materials Needed:

- ☐ Garden sprinkler
- ☐ Garden hose
- ☐ Swimsuits
- ☐ Towels
- ☐ Sunscreen (waterproof)
- ☐ Water toys (balls, buckets, or inflatable toys; optional)

Step-by-Step Instructions:

1. **Setup:**
   - Place a garden sprinkler in an open area of your yard.
   - Attach the garden hose to the sprinkler.
   - **Optional:** Position the sprinkler so it catches the sunlight just right, creating rainbows for your child to chase and play in. To maximize the chances of creating a rainbow, position the sprinkler so that you and your child have the sun at your back while looking at the water spray.
   - Apply sunscreen to protect your child's skin from sunburn.
2. **Turn on Water:**
   - Adjust the water pressure to a gentle spray that's not too intense for your preschooler.
3. **Play:**
   - Encourage your child to run through the sprinkler, jump over the spray, and splash in the water.
   - Introduce water toys like balls, buckets, or inflatable toys to add variety to the play (optional).
   - **Optional:** If you're joining in, grab some water toys or jump right into the fun with your child. You can play catch with a ball through the sprinkler's spray, lead a game of 'Follow the Leader,' or see who can make the biggest splash.
4. **Wrap Up:**
   - Once the fun winds down, take a moment to talk about the fun they had, sharing your favorite parts of the splash bash together.

Safety Considerations:

- Ensure the play area is free of hazards like rocks or sharp objects.
- Apply sunscreen to your child's skin and reapply as needed, especially if they'll be playing in the sun for an extended period.

Troubleshooting Tips:

- **Water Pressure Issues:** If the spray is too strong, adjust the water pressure or move the sprinkler to a different spot.
- **Water Too Cold**: If the water is too cold for your child's comfort, run the hose in the sun for a few minutes before starting to warm up the water slightly.
- **Child Hesitant:** Start by running through the sprinkler yourself to show how fun it is.

Cleanup Tips:

- Dry off your child with towels and change them into dry clothes.
- Drain any excess water from the hose and store it and the sprinkler properly to prevent damage.

Variations and Adaptations:

- **Sprinkler Limbo:** Play a game of limbo under the sprinkler spray.
- **Sprinkler Simon Says**: Play a game of Simon Says with water-themed commands like "Simon says jump over the sprinkler" or "Simon says run through the water." Add extra fun by spraying the sprinkler at key moments.
- **DIY Slip 'n Slide:** Use a plastic tarp and some tear-free baby soap to create a slip 'n slide for extra excitement. (Ensure you promptly remove the tarp after play to prevent lawn damage.)
- **Obstacle Course:** Set up an obstacle course around the sprinkler, with stations for jumping over hoses, crawling under pool noodles, and racing through sprinklers for an added challenge.
- **Sprinkler Freeze Dance**: Play music while your child runs through the sprinkler, and pause the music at random intervals. When the music stops, they have to freeze in place under the spray until it starts again.
- **Water Balloon Blast:** Add biodegradable water balloons into the mix, where you and your child can toss balloons at targets or each other while running through the sprinkler. (Always keep a close watch on your child around balloons, as they can be a choking hazard.)
- **Sprinkler Hide-and-Seek**: Add a watery twist to a classic game of hide-and-seek. Your child hides while you control the sprinkler, trying to find them by spraying the water in different directions.

Benefits:

- **Reduces Screen Time**: Engaging in outdoor fun provides a healthy alternative to screens, promoting active play and reducing reliance on electronic devices.
- **Introduces Safe Water Play**: Helping young children become comfortable with water in a controlled and safe environment lays the foundation for future swimming skills.
- **Provides Sensory Stimulation:** The varying pressure and temperature of the water offer sensory stimulation, enhancing a child's tactile awareness and sensory processing.
- **Strengthens Bonds:** Engaging in playful water games together creates opportunities for shared laughter and joy, strengthening bonds through

positive, memorable experiences.

- **Enhances Gross Motor Skills**: Jumping, running, and navigating through the water spray strengthens large muscle groups while improving balance and coordination, refining overall physical skills.

11

SIDEWALK CHALK-A-PALOOZA

Grab your sidewalk chalk and watch as your driveway or sidewalk transforms into a burst of creativity! From vibrant patterns to whimsical characters, your preschooler can fill the pavement with their imaginative masterpieces. As you join in the artistic fun, you'll foster a love for creativity and provide an opportunity for quality time together.

Watching your child's imagination come to life with each stroke of chalk is a magical experience that brings joy to both of you. Sidewalk Chalk-a-Palooza is not just about drawing; it's about exploring creativity, expressing ideas, and enjoying the simple pleasures of outdoor art. Grab some chalk and let your child's artistic talents shine in this fun and engaging activity.

Materials Needed:

- ☐ A large, flat outdoor surface (driveway, sidewalk, or patio)
- ☐ Variety of brightly colored sidewalk chalk
- ☐ A spray bottle filled with water (fun effects; optional)
- ☐ Hose or water bucket and sponge (for easy cleanup)
- ☐ Old clothes (optional)

Step-by-Step Instructions:

1. **Gather Chalk:**
   - Get a variety of brightly colored sidewalk chalk.
   - Ensure the chalk is non-toxic and safe for children.
2. **Choose Your Canvas:**
   - Find a safe, flat area like a driveway or sidewalk where you and your child can comfortably draw.
   - Clear the area of any debris or obstacles.
3. **Draw Together:**
   - You might want to start by showing your child how to hold the chalk for different effects—using the side for shading or the tip for fine lines.
   - Begin by drawing simple shapes or lines to get your child started. Encourage them to experiment with different colors and patterns. You can draw alongside them or collaborate on a big picture together.
   - Encourage your child to draw whatever comes to mind, from shapes and patterns to imaginative scenes.
   - As your child draws, ask them to tell you a story about their picture. This helps spark their imagination and language skills. You can join in by adding your own ideas or expanding on their story.
   - **Optional:** Use the spray bottle to lightly mist the chalk drawings for a fun, blended watercolor effect. Let your child discover how the water changes the chalk colors.
4. **Celebrate the Artwork:**
   - Once your child is finished, take a step back and admire the masterpiece together. Praise their creativity and ask them to explain their drawings.
   - Consider taking photos of your child interacting with their drawings. They can pretend to ride a chalk-drawn bike, stand under a drawn rainbow, or jump over drawn puddles—creating a fun and memorable photo series.

Safety Considerations:

- Make sure the drawing area is away from traffic and other hazards. Supervise your child closely, especially near driveways or streets.
- Ensure your child stays hydrated and wears sunscreen if you're spending a lot of time outside.

Troubleshooting Tips:

- **Chalk Breaks:** Keep extra pieces of chalk handy or show your child how they can still use the smaller pieces to create different effects.
- **Child Gets Frustrated:** Suggest simpler designs or help them with their drawing to keep the fun going.
- **Lost Interest:** If your child loses interest, suggest drawing something they love, like their favorite animal or a rainbow. Incorporate movement by drawing a path or road for toy cars to follow.

Cleanup Tips:

- Keep the art around for a while or use a hose or bucket of water and a sponge to wash it away together, turning cleanup into another playful activity.
- Turn broken chalk pieces into a "Chalk Treasure Hunt." Challenge your child to find and collect all the "hidden treasures" (broken pieces) within a set time. Celebrate their success by counting the pieces together and giving a high-five or small reward for completing the hunt.

Variations and Adaptations:

- **Chalk Spray Paint**: Crush small leftover pieces of sidewalk chalk (Crayola works best for vibrant colors) into a fine powder using a mortar and pestle or by placing the chalk in a baggie and hammering it. Mix with water, pour into a spray or squeeze bottle, and let your child spray or squeeze the paint to create large, colorful designs.
- **Themed Drawings:** Choose themes like animals, outer space, or underwater scenes to guide your art session.
- **Learning with Chalk:** Use the chalk to practice letters, numbers, or shapes. Turn the drawing session into an educational activity by drawing and discussing different animals, plants, or objects.
- **Weather-Themed Art**: Have your child draw scenes that depict different types of weather, like sunny days, rainy afternoons, or snowy landscapes. This can be a fun way to explore and discuss weather while being creative.
- **Life-Sized Self-Portraits**: Have your child lie down on the sidewalk, trace their outline, and then let them fill it in to create a life-sized self-portrait. They can add their favorite clothes, accessories, and even imaginary features.
- **Chalk Mosaic Art**: Use tape to create sections on the pavement and fill each section with different colors and patterns to create a stunning chalk mosaic. Peel away the tape to reveal a beautiful, intricate design.
- **Chalk Races:** Draw a race track on the ground and have fun racing toy

cars or running along the track with your child.

- **DIY Chalk Rubbings**: Place leaves, coins, or textured objects under a piece of paper on the sidewalk, and rub chalk over the paper to create imprints. This combines art with a bit of scientific exploration of textures.
- **Chalk Shadow Tracing**: Place objects on the sidewalk in the sun and trace their shadows with chalk. Your child can then color in the shapes or turn them into different drawings.
- **Interactive Games:** Draw classic games like hopscotch, tic-tac-toe, or a giant board game grid on the sidewalk. Play these games together, combining art with interactive fun.
- **3D Art:** Experiment with simple 3D chalk techniques, like drawing a long shadow next to an object or using perspective to create the illusion of depth, bringing the artwork to life.
- **Chalk Obstacle Course**: Create a fun obstacle course on the sidewalk using chalk. Draw paths to follow, shapes to jump on, and lines to balance along, turning the activity into a physical and creative challenge.
- **Chalk Puzzles**: Draw simple puzzles or mazes with chalk for your child to solve. These could be as easy as connecting dots to form a picture or finding their way through a chalk-drawn labyrinth.
- **Message in Chalk**: Encourage your child to help create positive or inspirational messages on the sidewalk for neighbors and passersby to enjoy. You can write the words while they add drawings, patterns, or colorful decorations around the message. It's a great way to spread kindness and brighten someone's day.
- **Chalk Countdown**: Create a countdown to an exciting event, like a birthday or holiday, by drawing a new picture each day on the sidewalk leading up to the event. It builds anticipation and adds a fun, daily ritual.
- **Chalk Art Museum**: Create a gallery of sidewalk art by drawing several different "pieces" along a walkway or driveway. Take a tour of your own sidewalk art museum, discussing each piece like you're in a real gallery.
- **Community Chalk Walk**: Organize a neighborhood chalk event where kids and parents come together to create a long, continuous mural on the sidewalk. It's a great way to foster community spirit and teamwork.

Benefits:

- **Develops Spatial Awareness**: Working on a large surface helps children understand spatial relationships, proportions, and the use of space in art.
- **Boosts Confidence and Self-Esteem**: Successfully creating and showcasing their artwork gives children a strong sense of accomplishment, boosting their confidence and self-esteem.

- **Fosters Creativity and Imagination**: Playing with sidewalk chalk on a wide-open canvas allows children to express their creativity and imagination, allowing them to bring their ideas to life in a fun, tangible way.
- **Strengthens Bonds:** Working together on a large-scale art project allows you and your child to share creative ideas, collaborate on designs, and celebrate each other's contributions, fostering a deep sense of connection and mutual appreciation.
- **Supports Emotional Expression**: Art provides a safe and constructive outlet for children to express their emotions, helping them process and communicate their feelings.

12

TINY TOT TREASURE TROT

Embark on an exciting adventure with Tiny Tot Treasure Trot! This activity transforms your backyard into a treasure island, where your little pirate can hunt for hidden treasures. By hiding small toys or objects around the yard and providing simple clues or a map, you'll create an exciting and engaging game. The thrill of the hunt and the joy of discovering each hidden item make this a perfect activity for sparking curiosity and imagination.

As you guide your child through the treasure hunt, you'll enjoy the shared excitement and bonding moments. Tiny Tot Treasure Trot is not just a game; it's an adventure that fosters exploration, problem-solving, and the joy of discovery. Prepare for a day of fun and treasure-finding excitement that will delight and engage your preschooler.

Materials Needed:

- ☐ Small toys or objects to hide
- ☐ Simple map or verbal clues
- ☐ Bag or bucket for collecting treasures

Step-by-Step Instructions:

1. **Prepare Treasures:**
   - Collect small toys or objects to hide around the yard. Choose items that your child enjoys and can easily recognize.
   - Ensure the items are safe and appropriate for your child's age.
2. **Hide Treasures:**
   - Place the items around the backyard in easy-to-find spots, such as under bushes, behind rocks, or in the sandbox.
   - Consider hiding the items at different heights for added fun.
3. **Create the Clues:**
   - Depending on your child's age and ability, you can choose to guide them using one of the following methods:
     - **Draw a Simple Map:** Sketch a basic map of the backyard, marking the treasure locations with pictures or symbols that your child can easily recognize.
     - **Use Picture Clues:** Alternatively, create visual clues by drawing simple pictures or taking close-up photos of the hiding spots. These picture clues can be shown to your child one at a time as they search for each treasure.
     - **Provide Verbal Clues:** For a more interactive experience, give verbal hints, such as "The treasure is near something tall," or "Look by the place where we plant flowers," to guide your child to the hidden items.
4. **Start the Hunt:**
   - Provide your child with a small bucket or bag to collect the treasures as they find them. This adds to the sense of accomplishment and makes the treasures feel special.
   - Give your child the treasure map or the first clue, and explain how to use it to find the hidden treasures.
   - As your child searches, offer encouragement and gentle guidance if needed, helping them stay engaged and excited about the hunt.
   - Celebrate each discovery with high-fives, cheers, or a little pirate dance, making the experience joyful and rewarding.
   - Once all the treasures have been found, gather together to admire the collection and talk about the adventure.

Safety Considerations:

- Ensure the play area is free of hazards like sharp objects or unsafe surfaces.

- Make sure that the toys or objects used are age-appropriate and not small enough to pose a choking hazard.
- Supervise the entire activity to prevent wandering off or injury.

Troubleshooting Tips:

- **Difficulty with Clues:** Simplify the clues or help them find the first few treasures to keep the experience enjoyable and frustration-free.
- **Lost Treasures:** As you hide each treasure, be sure to mark it on your map or make a quick note to avoid forgetting any locations.
- **Uncooperative Weather:** If the weather isn't cooperating, bring the treasure hunt indoors, hiding treasures in different rooms and turning your home into a treasure island.

Cleanup Tips:

- If the hunt involved digging or playing in the dirt, wash your child's hands and sanitize any toys or objects that were used in the hunt.

Variations and Adaptations:

- **Themed Hunts**: Customize the hunt with different themes, such as a dinosaur dig or a fairy garden adventure, using themed clues, toys, and decorations.
- **Color or Shape Hunt**: For a more educational twist, hide objects of a certain color or shape and ask your child to find all the items that match the criteria.
- **Puzzle Piece Hunt**: Hide pieces of a simple puzzle around the yard, and have your child collect and assemble them as they find each piece, adding an extra layer of challenge and fun.
- **Timed Treasure Hunt**: Add a bit of excitement by timing the treasure hunt, encouraging your child to find all the treasures before the time runs out, with a small reward at the end.
- **Glow-in-the-Dark Hunt**: Create a nighttime or indoor hunt using glow-in-the-dark treasures or flashlights, turning the hunt into a magical, luminous adventure.
- **Role Reversal Hunt**: Let your child take the lead by hiding the treasures for you to find. This reversal fosters their sense of independence, boosts creativity, and allows them to experience the joy of guiding the game.

Benefits:

- **Encourages Exploration**: Searching for hidden treasures encourages preschoolers to explore their surroundings and engage with the world in a hands-on way, fostering a natural sense of curiosity and adventure.

- **Develops Problem-Solving Skills**: Interpreting clues and finding hidden treasures enhances your child's critical thinking and problem-solving abilities in a fun and engaging way.
- **Promotes Physical Activity:** Running, jumping, and moving around the yard during the treasure hunt promotes physical exercise, helping to improve coordination, balance, and overall motor skills.
- **Improves Focus and Attention**: Concentrating on clues and staying engaged in the search helps children improve their focus and ability to maintain attention, even in an exciting and active setting.
- **Strengthens Bonds:** The excitement of searching for and finding hidden treasures creates meaningful moments of connection, as the shared adventure fosters teamwork and brings joy through collective success.
- **Teaches Patience and Persistence**: The process of searching for hidden items teaches your child patience and the value of persistence when facing challenges.

KINDERGARTENERS

UNLEASHED

INDOOR ADVENTURES

Let your kindergartener's imagination run wild indoors! This set of activities includes everything from "roughing it" in the living room to creating recycled art. Each activity combines creativity and hands-on fun, such as rolling marbles to create colorful artwork or transforming household items into imaginative crafts. You'll also find DIY Playdough Adventures and Storytime Theater, all designed to keep them engaged, build skills, and share joyful moments together.

13

MARBLE PAINTING MARVELS

Dive into a world of colorful creativity with marble painting! This fun and messy activity involves placing a piece of paper in a shallow box, adding a few drops of paint, and rolling marbles through the paint to create unique artwork. Picture the excitement on your child's face as they watch the marbles zigzag across the paper, leaving vibrant trails of color behind. This activity is not just about creating art; it's about experiencing the joy of unexpected results and embracing the beauty of randomness.

As you guide your child through this artistic adventure, you'll see their eyes light up with each new pattern that emerges. The unpredictable movement of the marbles makes every painting unique, sparking their curiosity and delight. The tactile experience of handling the marbles and the visual feast of swirling colors provide a rich sensory experience. Sharing in their joy and wonder, you'll find this activity strengthens your bond and creates lasting memories of creative play.

Materials Needed:

- ☐ Marbles
- ☐ Thick paper or cardstock
- ☐ Shallow box or tray (large enough to hold the piece of paper)
- ☐ Washable paint
- ☐ Tongs or spoons (for handling marbles; optional)

Step-by-Step Instructions:

1. **Prepare the Box:**
   - Place a sheet of paper or cardstock in the bottom of the shallow box or tray. Make sure it fits snugly so it doesn't move around when the marbles roll.
2. **Add the Paint:**
   - Squeeze a few drops of different colored paint onto the paper.
3. **Create Your Masterpiece:**
   - Drop the marbles into the box and tilt it to roll them through the paint, watching as the marble rolls through the paint and creates colorful patterns on the paper.
   - Encourage your child to experiment with different movements: tilting the box gently for slow, winding trails or more vigorously for fast, zigzag patterns.
   - Continue adding paint and rolling marbles until you're satisfied with the artwork.
   - Consider making it a team effort by holding one side of the box while your child holds the other. Together, you can tilt the box in unison, guiding the marbles across the paper to create a shared work of art. This cooperative approach adds an extra layer of bonding to the creative experience.
4. **Admire the Artwork:**
   - Once your child is satisfied with their painting, carefully lift the paper out of the box and set it aside to dry.
   - Use this time to talk about the different patterns and colors, asking your child what they see and how they feel about their creation.

Safety Considerations:

- Keep a close eye on your child to prevent marbles from becoming a choking hazard.
- Ensure the paints used are non-toxic and washable, suitable for young children.

Troubleshooting Tips:

- **Colors Mixing Too Much**: To prevent colors from mixing too much and becoming muddy, use fewer colors at a time or allow each layer of paint to dry slightly before adding more.
- **Marbles Sticking:** Clean marbles periodically to prevent paint buildup.

Cleanup Tips:

- Cover the workspace with newspaper or a disposable tablecloth.
- Have a small bucket of soapy water and paper towels nearby to clean hands and marbles quickly.

Variations and Adaptations:

- **Glow-in-the-Dark Creations:** Use glow-in-the-dark paint and create artwork in a dimly lit room. Turn off the lights afterward to see the marbles' paths glow on the paper!
- **Texture Fun:** Add small amounts of sand or glitter to the paint for a textured effect.
- **Rolling with Variety**: Instead of just marbles, use different round objects like small balls, beads, little pinecones, or even toy cars to create various patterns and textures.
- **Seasonal Themes:** Tailor the colors and patterns to match different seasons or holidays—use pastels for spring, vibrant colors for summer, earthy tones for fall, and cool blues and whites for winter.
- **Storytelling Art:** Create a story or scene with the marble painting and add details with markers.
- **Salty Effects**: Sprinkle a little salt on the wet paint. As the paint dries, the salt will create interesting textures and effects, adding an extra dimension to the artwork.

Benefits:

- **Boosts Creativity:** Painting with marbles encourages children to explore colors, patterns, and textures, fostering their creativity and imagination.
- **Enhances Fine Motor Skills:** Rolling marbles and controlling their movements helps improve hand-eye coordination and fine motor skills.
- **Boosts Focus and Concentration**: Creating marble paintings requires children to focus on their movements and decisions, helping them develop better concentration and attention to detail.
- **Encourages Experimentation:** The unpredictable nature of marble painting teaches kids to enjoy the process and embrace unexpected outcomes.
- **Strengthens Bonds**: Working together on marble paintings provides opportunities to collaborate, share ideas, and celebrate your creations, fostering meaningful interactions and deeper emotional connections.
- **Introduces Basic Science Concepts**: Watching how marbles move and how colors mix introduces children to basic principles of motion and color theory in a fun, hands-on way.

14

RECYCLED ART CRAFTING SPREE

Turn trash into treasure with this eco-friendly crafting activity. Using materials that would typically be tossed out, such as cardboard boxes, plastic bottles, and old magazines, you and your kindergartener can craft imaginative masterpieces. Whether you decide to create whimsical sculptures, colorful masks, or intricate collages, the possibilities are endless. This activity is not just about crafting; it's about teaching your child the value of recycling and sustainability.

Your little one will delight in the creative challenge, and you'll find joy in the hands-on bonding experience. So, gather your supplies, clear a space, and let the artistic adventure begin! The crafting area becomes a hub of creativity, filled with the vibrant colors of paint and the textures of various materials. As you both work on your projects, the room buzzes with excitement and the satisfaction of turning everyday items into extraordinary works of art.

Materials Needed:

- ☐ Various recycled materials (cardboard, plastic bottles, old magazines, etc.)
- ☐ Scissors (child safe)
- ☐ Glue
- ☐ Markers, paint, and other decorative items
- ☐ Tape

Step-by-Step Instructions:

1. **Gather Materials:**
   - Collect various recycled materials from around your home. Items such as cardboard boxes, plastic bottles, old magazines, bottle caps, and egg cartons work well. Consider materials with unique textures, like using sandpaper for a rough texture or bubble wrap for interesting patterns.
   - While gathering materials, consider talking about why recycling is important and how reusing materials can help the environment. This can be done in a simple, age-appropriate way.
   - Set up a crafting area with all the necessary supplies.
2. **Choose a Project:**
   - Sit down with your child to brainstorm project ideas such as a sculpture, mask, or collage. Encourage your child to think creatively by asking questions like, "What do you think we can make with this bottle?" or "How can we use these old magazines in our artwork?"
   - Plan the project together, sketching out ideas and deciding how to use the available materials.
3. **Create and Decorate:**
   - Use scissors and glue to cut and assemble the recycled materials. Help your child with any difficult cuts or assembly steps.
   - Encourage your child to decorate their creation with markers, paint, and other decorative items. They can add finishing touches like glitter, stickers, or pieces of fabric for added texture and color.
   - While crafting, consider sharing fun facts or tell stories about recycling, like how a plastic bottle can be recycled into a fleece jacket or how paper is made from trees.
   - **Optional:** Take turns adding to the creation instead of letting your child have all the fun. You can start by making part of the project, and then your child can add the next piece. This makes the process interactive and encourages teamwork and shared creativity.
4. **Showcase the Art:**
   - Praise your child's creativity and effort, regardless of the outcome. Say things like, "I love how you used the bottle caps for eyes!" or "Your collage is so colorful!"
   - Display the finished artwork in a special place in your home, such as on a shelf, table, or wall.

Safety Considerations:

- Supervise the use of scissors, glue, and any other tools to ensure safety.

- Ensure all recycled materials are clean and free of any harmful substances before use.

Troubleshooting Tips:

- **Running Out of Materials:** Keep a stash of extra recycled materials for future projects, so you always have supplies on hand.
- **Paint Not Sticking to Surfaces**: If paint isn't adhering well to certain materials, lightly sand the surface or apply a base coat of primer to help the paint stick better.
- **Materials Not Sticking**: If your glue isn't holding the materials together, try using stronger adhesive options like double-sided tape or hot glue (handled by Dad).

Cleanup Tips:

- Use an old tablecloth or newspapers to cover the crafting area to make cleanup easier.
- Keep a small trash bag or bin nearby to collect scraps and trash as you go, preventing clutter from piling up.

Variations and Adaptations:

- **Material Scavenger Hunt**: Turn gathering recycled materials into an adventure. Go around the house together, looking for items that can be used. Make it a fun game by giving it a theme, like a "Treasure Hunt for Crafting Gold."
- **Functional Art**: Create items that have a practical use, like pencil holders from tin cans, bird feeders from plastic bottles, or bookmarks from cereal boxes. This adds an element of functionality to the fun.
- **Seasonal Themes:** Create crafts based on different seasons or holidays, such as making ornaments for Christmas or pumpkins for Halloween.
- **Mixed Media:** Combine recycled materials with other art supplies like clay, fabric, or natural elements like pebbles and twigs.
- **Storytelling:** Create characters or props for a story and put on a puppet show, integrating creativity with narrative skills.
- **Fashion Show**: Create wearable art from recycled materials, such as hats, jewelry, or costumes, and have a mini fashion show to display your creations.
- **Art from Around the World**: Explore different cultures by using recycled materials to create art inspired by traditional crafts from around the world, like African masks, Native American dreamcatchers, or Mexican paper flowers.

Benefits:

- **Encourages Creativity:** Using recycled materials to create art allows children to think outside the box, transforming everyday items into imaginative and original creations.
- **Teaches Sustainability:** Crafting with recycled items introduces the concept of sustainability, helping children understand the value of reusing materials and reducing waste, fostering an early sense of environmental responsibility.
- **Develops Fine Motor Skills:** Cutting, gluing, and arranging small materials improves fine motor skills, hand-eye coordination, and dexterity.
- **Strengthens Bonds:** Crafting together creates meaningful moments of connection, allowing for open conversations, laughter, and mutual enjoyment of the creative process.
- **Promotes Problem-Solving**: Deciding how to use different shapes, textures, and materials in art projects encourages problem-solving and resourcefulness, as children figure out creative ways to combine elements into a cohesive piece.

15

DIY PLAYDOUGH ADVENTURES

Homemade playdough is easy to make and provides endless fun for kindergarteners. Kids will love squishing, rolling, and shaping their own creations. Plus, making the playdough together adds an extra layer of enjoyment. This method is quick, simple, and safe for kids to help with. With just a few common kitchen ingredients, you can whip up a batch of colorful, non-toxic playdough that will keep your kiddo entertained for hours.

The tactile experience of playing with dough enhances fine motor skills and creativity, making it a fantastic hands-on activity for children. Playdough also offers educational opportunities, such as learning about colors and shapes, as well as developing problem-solving skills through imaginative play. Enjoy the simplicity and joy of making and playing with homemade dough.

Materials Needed:

- ☐ 2 cups all-purpose flour
- ☐ 1 cup salt
- ☐ 2 tablespoons vegetable oil (any cooking oil will do)
- ☐ 3/4 to 1 cup water
- ☐ Food coloring (optional)
- ☐ Mixing bowls
- ☐ Spoon
- ☐ Disposable gloves (to prevent stains from food coloring; optional)

Step-by-Step Instructions:

1. **Set Up Your Workspace:**
   - Clear a table or countertop and gather all the ingredients and tools. This is a great chance to involve your child by letting them help set up.
2. **Mix Dry Ingredients:**
   - In a large bowl, combine the flour and salt. This is a perfect time to talk to your child about the basics of measuring.
   - Stir together until thoroughly mixed.
3. **Add Oil:**
   - Add the vegetable oil to the dry ingredients and mix well.
4. **Add Water Gradually:**
   - Slowly add the water to the mixture, starting with 3/4 cup. Mix until the dough starts to come together. If the dough is too dry or crumbly, add a little more water, a tablespoon at a time, until the desired consistency is reached.
5. **Add Color (Optional):**
   - If you want to color your playdough, either add the food coloring to the water or divide the dough into portions and add a few drops of food coloring to each portion. Knead the dough until the color is evenly distributed.
6. **Knead the Dough:**
   - Knead the dough for a few minutes until the texture is soft and consistent. Encourage your child to use their hands and feel the texture. This part is all about sensory play and having fun!
7. **Playtime:**
   - Give your child tools like cookie cutters, utensils, or a rolling pin to shape and play with the dough. Join in by making your own shapes or characters!
   - Use this time to explore creativity. Encourage your child to create different shapes, animals, or even pretend food. Ask them questions about what they're making and let their imagination lead the way.

Safety Considerations:

- Supervise to prevent ingestion of too much salt, especially for younger children who may confuse it with food.

Troubleshooting Tips:

- **Too Sticky:** If the dough is too sticky, add more flour gradually until the desired consistency is reached.

- **Too Dry:** If the dough is too crumbly, add a bit more water a tablespoon at a time.
- **Too Soft**: If the playdough is too soft and loses shape easily, add a little more salt to the mixture to firm it up.

Cleanup Tips:

- Use a damp cloth to wipe down surfaces where playdough has been used to avoid any dried residue.
- Store playdough in airtight containers or resealable plastic bags to keep it fresh for future use. It can last 1-3 months this way before drying out.

Variations and Adaptations:

- **Glitter Playdough:** Mix in a sprinkle of fine glitter to the playdough to give it a sparkly, magical appearance.
- **Nature Impressions:** Use leaves, flowers, or shells to make impressions in the playdough.
- **Color-Changing Playdough**: Use thermochromic pigments (which change color with temperature) to make playdough that changes color when warmed by your hands or cooled in the fridge. These pigments are affordable and readily available online.
- **Themed Creations:** Create playdough figures based on favorite characters or themes like animals, fairies, or space.
- **Learning Shapes:** Use the playdough to teach shapes, letters, and numbers by forming them together or using alphabet and number cookie cutters.
- **Textured Playdough**: Mix in materials like rice, sand, or beads to add texture, giving your child a new sensory experience and challenging them to create different designs.
- **Playdough Monsters**: Provide googly eyes, pipe cleaners, and small plastic accessories to create fun and quirky playdough monsters or creatures.
- **Scented Playdough:** Add a few drops of essential oils (like sage, lemon, or peppermint) or mix in kitchen spices (such as cinnamon or vanilla extract) to create scented playdough for a multi-sensory experience. Remind your child that the playdough is for playing, not eating, even though it smells delicious.
- **Calming Playdough**: Add a few drops of calming essential oils like chamomile or lavender and introduce soft colors, creating a calming playdough perfect for winding down before bed.

- **Seasonal Playdough**: Create playdough that reflects the seasons, such as orange and black with pumpkin spice for fall, red and green with peppermint for winter, or pastel colors with floral scents for spring.

Benefits:

- **Fosters Early Learning:** DIY playdough introduces basic concepts such as mixing, measuring, and color blending, laying the foundation for early math and science skills.
- **Stimulates Creativity and Imagination**: The open-ended nature of playdough allows children to create whatever they can imagine, fostering creativity and encouraging imaginative play.
- **Enhances Fine Motor Skills**: Squishing, rolling, and shaping the dough helps develop fine motor skills, strengthening hand muscles and improving dexterity essential for writing, drawing, and other tasks.
- **Strengthens Bonds:** Creating and playing with playdough together provides valuable one-on-one time, fostering communication and collaboration through shared creativity and fun.
- **Promotes Emotional Regulation**: The sensory nature of playdough can have a calming effect, helping children release stress and regulate their emotions through hands-on, tactile engagement.

16

LIVING ROOM CAMPOUT

Bring the adventure of camping indoors by transforming your living room into a cozy campsite for a night of unforgettable fun with your little one. Picture this: a tent pitched between the couch and coffee table, sleeping bags sprawled out, and the soft glow of flashlights illuminating your impromptu adventure. This activity captures the magic of camping without needing to brave the elements, offering a delightful blend of comfort and excitement. Break out the microwave for some gooey s'mores and let the evening's adventure begin!

As you share stories by your imaginary campfire and snack on treats, the atmosphere becomes charged with laughter and bonding. Your kindergartener's eyes will light up with each tale and flashlight shadow, making it a night of cherished memories. The indoor camping setup turns your home into a world of adventure and connection, where the joy of togetherness takes center stage. It's an easy, memorable way to break the routine and bring a touch of wilderness indoors.

Materials Needed:

☐ Small tent or blankets and furniture for fort-building

☐ Sleeping bags or blankets and pillows

☐ Flashlights, glow sticks, or battery-powered lanterns

☐ A variety of snacks (e.g., s'mores ingredients, trail mix, granola bars)

☐ Books or story ideas

Step-by-Step Instructions:

1. **Set Up the Tent:**
    - Find a suitable spot in the living room, like between the couch and coffee table.
    - Pitch a small tent or create a makeshift one using blankets draped over furniture.
2. **Prepare the Sleeping Area:**
    - Lay out sleeping bags or blankets inside the tent.
    - Arrange pillows for added comfort.
3. **Gather Lighting:**
    - Provide flashlights, glow sticks, or battery-powered lanterns for a cozy, campfire-like glow.
    - Consider using fairy lights to add a magical touch to the campsite.
4. **Prepare Snacks:**
    - Arrange a selection of easy-to-eat snacks like popcorn, fruit, or Rice Krispie Treats.
    - **Make Indoor S'mores**:
        - Gather ingredients: graham crackers, marshmallows, and chocolate bars.
        - Use the microwave to melt the marshmallows and chocolate between the graham crackers.
        - Enjoy the gooey, delicious s'mores together.
5. **Share Stories:**
    - Sit together in the tent or around the "campfire" area.
    - Take turns telling stories, using flashlights to create shadows and enhance the atmosphere.
6. **Reflect and Discuss:**
    - After the activities, take some time to reflect on the fun you had. Talk about what you enjoyed most and plan for your next indoor camping adventure.

Safety Considerations:

- Ensure there are no fire hazards when setting up blankets and furniture.
- If using a lantern, ensure it's battery powered or rechargeable to reduce fire hazards.

Troubleshooting Tips:

- **Not Enough Space**: If the living room feels too cramped, consider rearranging furniture temporarily or using a smaller tent. Alternatively, create a "half-tent" by draping a blanket over just one side of the couch.
- **Tent Stability:** Secure blanket forts with additional pillows, cushions, or furniture to provide more stability. You can also use heavy books or clips to anchor blankets.
- **S'mores issues:** Microwave marshmallows in short intervals to prevent overheating.
- **Child Getting Overexcited**: Include calming activities like reading a story or playing soft music to help settle down before bedtime.

Cleanup Tips:

- Make cleanup part of the fun by singing a camping song or turning it into a game, like a race to see who can pick up the most items.

Variations and Adaptations:

- **Picnic:** Incorporate an indoor picnic with sandwiches and juice boxes.
- **Theme Nights:** Choose a specific theme, such as "Enchanted Forest" or "Marooned on Mars" and decorate the tent and living room accordingly. Use stuffed animals, themed stickers, and appropriate sound effects to enhance the atmosphere.
- **Nature Sounds:** Play nature sounds or soft music in the background to enhance the camping atmosphere. You can even make it a game by challenging your child to identify different sounds like bird calls, rain, or wind.
- **Campfire Games:** Include board games, card games, or games like "20 Questions," "I Spy," or "Simon Says" with a camping twist to play inside the tent.
- **Campfire Sing-Along**: Create a playlist of campfire songs or use instruments to have a sing-along session. Use homemade shakers or drums to add rhythm, and encourage your child to make up their own verses or songs.
- **Crafts:** Include a craft session where you create simple nature-themed crafts, like leaf rubbings or paper campfires with red and orange construction paper. Use the crafts to decorate your campsite.
- **Surprise Camp Challenges**: Write down fun challenges on slips of paper, such as "Tell a ghost story," "Act like your favorite animal," or "Do 10 jumping jacks." Draw challenges randomly during the campout to keep the excitement going.

- **Lights Out Adventure**: Plan a "lights out" adventure where you turn off all the lights and navigate the house using only flashlights. Create challenges like finding specific items or following a glow-stick trail to make it more exciting.
- **Weather Simulation**: Simulate different weather conditions by playing soundtracks of rain, wind, or thunderstorms while cozying up in the tent. Use a spray bottle to create a light "rain" effect or a fan for a "breezy" experience, making the campout feel like a true outdoor adventure.
- **Flashlight Tag**: Play a game of flashlight tag by turning off the lights and using flashlights to tag each other. This adds a fun, active element to the campout and helps burn off some energy before bedtime.
- **Mini Hikes**: Plan "mini hikes" around the house where you explore different "terrains" and "landscapes." Use pillows as stepping stones, a rolled-up rug as a "river," and create a map of the house with these terrains labeled to guide your adventure.

Benefits:

- **Provides a Safe Adventure:** Offers the excitement of camping in a safe, familiar environment, making it perfect for young adventurers who aren't ready for the great outdoors.
- **Promotes Communication**: Sharing stories around the "campfire" encourages children to express themselves, enhancing their verbal skills and confidence in storytelling.
- **Teaches Problem-Solving**: Setting up the campsite, arranging sleeping areas, and improvising with household items provide opportunities for kids to learn basic problem-solving and organizational skills.
- **Strengthens Bonds:** Engaging in collaborative activities like setting up tents, sharing campsite tasks, and storytelling around the "campfire" fosters a deep sense of connection and builds stronger bonds.
- **Stimulates Curiosity**: The campout setup invites children to ask questions and learn about camping, nature, and the outdoors, nurturing their natural curiosity.

17

STORYTIME THEATER

Turn your child's favorite tales into an unforgettable theatrical adventure by bringing storytime to life with costumes, props, and a dash of imagination. Your kindergartener will love transforming into beloved characters and watching you perform alongside them. This engaging activity not only entertains but also nurtures their narrative skills and boosts confidence as they take on various roles. Prepare to dive into the world of make-believe and craft a storytime experience that will be cherished forever.

The interactive and creative nature of Storytime Theater fosters a deep love for reading and storytelling, making it a fantastic way to spend quality time together. As you both perform, you'll enhance your child's comprehension and expressive abilities in a fun and dynamic way.

Materials Needed:

- ☐ Favorite storybook
- ☐ Simple props (e.g., hats, scarves, household items)
- ☐ Costumes (optional)
- ☐ Interactive elements (e.g., flashlight for dramatic lighting, media player for sound effects; optional)
- ☐ A small space to perform

Step-by-Step Instructions:

1. **Choose a Story:**
   - Sit down with your child and pick out a favorite storybook or story they love. Choose a story that has plenty of characters and action to make the performance exciting.
2. **Gather Costumes and Props:**
   - Look around the house for items that can serve as costumes and props, like scarves for capes or hats for crowns. Everyday items can be transformed into magical accessories with a bit of imagination.
   - Let your child decorate props using craft supplies if they'd like.
   - Use props like flashlights for dramatic lighting or sheets as capes.
   - Include sound effects and other interactive elements to enhance the performance.
3. **Assign Roles:**
   - Decide who will play which characters.
   - Consider switching roles during the performance to keep it dynamic and fun.
4. **Read and Act:**
   - Start by reading the story out loud, pausing to act out the scenes.
   - Use different voices and gestures for each character to bring them to life.
   - Encourage your child to be animated and imaginative. Let them use their creativity to add new elements to the story or change how a character behaves.
5. **Applaud and Discuss:**
   - After the performance, give applause and praise your child's efforts.
   - Discuss the story and talk about what they liked best and if they would change anything about the tale.

Safety Considerations:

- Ensure props and costumes are safe and non-restrictive to prevent tripping or other accidents during performances.

Troubleshooting Tips:

- **Reluctant Performer:** Encourage a shy child by starting with simple roles and gradually building confidence.

Cleanup Tips:

- Turn cleanup into part of the story by narrating a "cleanup adventure" where the characters tidy up their castle or stage. This keeps the fun going while getting the job done.

Variations and Adaptations:

- **Story Remix:** Encourage your child to create alternative endings or new scenes.
- **Mystery Bag Theater**: Fill a bag with random household items. Let your child pull out items one by one and use them as props to create spontaneous, imaginative stories.
- **Silent Storytelling**: Try acting out a story without words, using only gestures and expressions. This variation emphasizes non-verbal communication and creativity.
- **Interactive Stories:** Create a "choose your own adventure" format where the audience can make choices that affect the plot.
- **Freeze Frame**: During the performance, anyone can call out "freeze!" and everyone must stop moving. Then, the caller changes one thing about the scene (like a character's mood or the setting), and the story continues from there. This keeps the performance dynamic and exciting.

Benefits:

- **Develops Problem-Solving Skills**: Acting out different scenarios helps children think on their feet and come up with solutions, enhancing their problem-solving and critical thinking skills.
- **Improves Language Skills**: Engaging in storytelling boosts vocabulary and helps kids practice speaking clearly and expressively.
- **Enhances Emotional Awareness:** Promotes empathy and emotional understanding through shared storytelling and character exploration.
- **Strengthens Bonds:** Working together on a story helps you bond through shared laughter and teamwork, deepening your connection by supporting and enjoying each other's creativity.
- **Builds Confidence:** Performing in front of you builds your child's self-esteem and confidence by encouraging them to take on various roles, express themselves, and feel proud of their performance.

OUTDOOR FUN

Unleash the adventurous spirit of your kindergartener with these outdoor activities! From custom kite-making to riding and conquering a bike obstacle course, these activities are all about embracing the outdoors. Watch as your child explores the wonders of nature during a scavenger hunt or enjoys the thrill of a backyard bug hunt. Whether they're planting their very own mini garden or creating a collage out of nature's wonders, each activity encourages exploration, physical play, and joyful learning in the great outdoors.

18

CUSTOM KITE CREATION STATION

Dive into an afternoon of creative fun and outdoor adventure by making a custom kite with your little one. Together, you'll design and construct a unique kite from simple materials, turning a few basic supplies into a flying work of art. Your kindergartener will be amazed as their handmade kite takes shape and even more thrilled when it finally takes to the skies.

Watching the kite soar high above is a magical experience, filled with excitement and pride. The process of crafting and flying a kite is not only an excellent bonding activity but also a wonderful way to spend a sunny day outdoors. Get ready to chase your kite as it dances in the wind, creating joyful memories that will last a lifetime.

Materials Needed:

- ☐ Simple kite-making kit or DIY materials:
    - o Sticks (for the frame)
    - o Paper or plastic bag (for the sail)
    - o String (for the bridle)
    - o Roll of ribbon (½ - 1 inch wide; for the tail)
    - o Ruler (optional)
- ☐ Markers, stickers, or paint for decoration
- ☐ Scissors
- ☐ Tape or glue

Step-by-Step Instructions:

1. **Build the Kite:**
   - **Gather Materials**:
     - Collect the kite kit or gather sticks, paper or a plastic bag, string, and tape/glue.
   - **Assemble the Frame**:
     - Tie two sticks together in a cross shape, ensuring they are securely fastened.
     - Secure the string to the point where the sticks intersect, creating the kite's bridle.
   - **Cut and Attach the Sail:**
     - Lay the kite frame on your piece of paper or plastic. Use a marker or pencil to draw a dot at each end of both sticks, then use a ruler to connect the dots to outline the kite shape.
     - Carefully cut out the kite shape along the drawn lines.
     - Place the cut kite shape over the frame and use tape or glue to secure the edges of the kite shape to the frame. Smooth out any wrinkles or bubbles to make sure it's snug and flat.
   - **Attach the Tail**:
     - Attach a long ribbon to the bottom of the kite with tape. 2-3 times the length of the kite is a good place to start.
     - Ensure the tail is long enough to help stabilize the kite during flight.
     - Use this time to discuss with your child how the tail will help the kite fly and why it's important. For example: "The kite ribbon helps the kite fly straight and not get wobbly or spin around. Think of it like the kite's balance helper. Just like when you spread your arms out to keep your balance while walking on a log, the ribbon helps the kite stay steady in the sky."
2. **Decorate:**
   - Let your child decorate the kite with colorful markers, stickers, and other craft supplies, adding unique designs and personal touches to make it truly their own.
3. **Fly the Kite:**
   - **Find the Right Spot**:
     - Choose an open space free from trees and power lines, such as a park or beach.

- **Launch the Kite**:
  - Let your child hold the kite up and run to catch the wind.
  - Gradually release the string as your child runs, allowing the kite to lift off the ground.
  - Celebrate the successful flight with cheers and high-fives.
- **Teach Control**:
  - Show your child how to control the kite by gently pulling on the string and adjusting the angle to keep it flying high.
  - Encourage them to experiment with different movements to see how the kite responds.

Safety Considerations:

- Fly kites in open areas away from power lines and trees.
- Supervise your child closely to prevent the kite string from getting tangled or causing harm.
- If your kite gets stuck in power lines, **do not** attempt to retrieve it yourself. Power lines carry high-voltage electricity, and touching them or the kite string can cause serious injury or even death. Stay at least 10 feet away and contact your local utility company immediately for assistance. Always prioritize safety over retrieving the kite.

Troubleshooting Tips:

- **Flight Issues:** Adjust the tail length or balance of the kite if it doesn't fly well. Generally speaking, the stronger the wind, the longer the tail you need.
- **Wind Conditions:** Wait for a day with moderate wind; too little or too much wind can make kite flying difficult.
- **Stuck in a Tree:** Tie a small weight (like a tennis ball) to a rope and throw it over the branch holding the kite. Gently pull on the rope to shake the branch and dislodge the kite. Avoid pulling too hard, as this could break the branch and cause it to fall, potentially injuring you or your child.
- **Stuck in Power Lines:** Never attempt to retrieve a kite from power lines. Stay clear and contact your local utility company immediately for safe removal.

Cleanup Tips:

- Coil the kite string neatly to avoid tangles and store it in a dry place.

Variations and Adaptations:

- **Shape Experiments:** Create kites in different shapes, like diamonds or deltas. Test each shape to see which flies best, encouraging your child to guess why some shapes fly higher or longer, sparking curiosity and discovery.

- **Themed Kites:** Create kites based on your child's favorite characters, animals, or themes, like mermaids, dinosaurs, or outer space.
- **Night Flying:** Add glow-in-the-dark paint or tape to the kite for a magical nighttime flying experience. For an even more dazzling display, attach small LED lights to create vibrant, glowing patterns as your kite soars through the night sky.
- **Kite-Themed Educational Stations**: Set up educational stations around the kite-flying area with fun facts about wind, flight dynamics, and kite history. Integrate learning with the activity for an educational twist.
- **Kite and Drone Combo**: Integrate drones with kites for a combined flying experience. The drone can be used to capture aerial footage of the kite and the surrounding scenery.
- **Kite Flight Challenges**: Introduce different flight challenges, such as keeping the kite in the air for a certain amount of time, performing tricks, or navigating through obstacles.
- **Historical Kite Designs**: For a more advanced project, explore historical kite designs from different cultures and recreate them as part of a historical exploration activity. This can be a great way for older kids to learn about the significance and flight characteristics of traditional kites.

Benefits:

- **Boosts Confidence**: Successfully creating and flying their own kite gives children a sense of accomplishment and boosts their self-esteem.
- **Promotes Active Play:** Flying a kite is a fun outdoor activity that encourages physical movement and exploration, promoting a healthy lifestyle.
- **Encourages STEM Learning**: Building and flying a kite helps children understand how the kite's shape and structure affect its ability to stay in the air, introducing them to basic STEM concepts in a hands-on way.
- **Strengthens Bonds:** Working together on the kite allows you and your kindergartener to share the excitement of seeing your creation fly, reinforcing your bond through the shared joy of your collective achievement.
- **Enhances Visual-Spatial Awareness**: Designing and flying a kite helps children develop visual-spatial skills as they learn to gauge distances, angles, and the effects of wind on their kite's flight.

19

RIDE AND CONQUER OBSTACLE COURSE

Turn a simple bike ride into an exhilarating adventure with a custom obstacle course. Set up a variety of obstacles in your driveway or a safe, open area, and challenge your child to navigate through them. This activity is not just about riding a bike; it's about incorporating fun and challenging elements that will test and improve your child's coordination, balance, and problem-solving skills. Whether it's weaving through cones, navigating a zigzag path, or circling around makeshift obstacles, your child will be thrilled with the exciting new way to ride their bike.

You'll enjoy watching them conquer each challenge with a smile. As they gain confidence and skill, each lap through the course becomes a testament to their growing abilities. The air fills with the sound of laughter and the whirring of bike wheels, creating a lively and joyful atmosphere. This outdoor adventure transforms a regular bike ride into a memorable experience of fun and achievement.

Materials Needed:

- ☐ Cones or large plastic cups
- ☐ Chalk or tape (for marking paths)
- ☐ Household items (buckets, boxes, hula hoops, pool noodles, etc.)
- ☐ A safe, open area (driveway, backyard, or park)
- ☐ Bike and helmet for your child
- ☐ Wooden planks or plywood (for ramps; optional)
- ☐ A stopwatch (for timing; optional)

Step-by-Step Instructions:

1. **Set Up the Course:**
   - Choose a safe area for the obstacle course. A flat driveway, backyard, or park with minimal traffic is ideal.
   - Use cones, large plastic cups, wooden planks, or household items to create variety of obstacles. Start simple with a few straight-line challenges, and then add more complexity with zigzags, weaving challenges, circles, and tight turns.
2. **Mark the Path:**
   - Use chalk to draw paths between the obstacles. This will help guide your child through the course.
   - Create a starting point and a finish line to give a sense of progression.
3. **Explain the Course:**
   - Walk through the course with your child, explaining how to navigate each obstacle. Optionally, take a moment to set the scene like a storybook:
     - You could say something like, "Today, you're a brave explorer venturing into the wild jungle. Ahead of you are challenges that only the bravest can overcome. Are you ready to embark on this daring adventure?"
     - Use a dramatic voice to make it sound like a grand adventure. Describe the obstacles as they relate to the story theme. For example, "First, you'll face the River of Doom, where you must weave through the rocks to avoid falling into the rushing water!"
   - **Optional:** Demonstrate how to ride through the course, showing techniques for weaving and turning.
4. **Conquer the Course:**
   - Start the course together by cheering your child on as they tackle the first obstacle. You can walk alongside or watch from the sidelines, giving them encouragement and tips as they go.
   - Optionally, enhance the experience by narrating your child's ride through the course as a daring adventure or a thrilling sports event. Use imaginative storytelling or lively sports commentary to bring the course to life, making each obstacle an exciting challenge to overcome. Try phrases like:
     - “Watch as our fearless explorer approaches the giant snake pit—will they be able to zigzag through the twisting turns and escape unharmed?”
     - “And they’re off! Look at that speed as they navigate the first turn,

heading straight for the zigzag section. Can they make it without slowing down? Yes, they can! What a fantastic display of agility!"

- Offer supportive comments if they struggle: "Even the greatest adventurers stumble, but our hero doesn't give up. Look at that determination as they try again!"

- Encourage your child to gradually increase the speed as they become more confident.
- If they're ready, time their laps with a stopwatch to add a fun, competitive element. See if they can beat their own time on each lap.

5. **Celebrate and Innovate:**
   - After your child completes the course, take a break to enjoy a special snack or drink together. Use this time to talk about what was the most fun, what was challenging, and think about new ideas for the next time you tackle the course.
   - As you share your thoughts, get excited about what's next—transforming the course into a new adventure. Add fresh challenges or change the layout to keep the activity exciting. You could introduce new obstacles like a low-hanging rope to duck under or a tight squeeze between two cones.
   - Encourage your child to come up with their own ideas for the course. This not only keeps them engaged but also helps develop their problem-solving and creative thinking skills.

Safety Considerations:

- Ensure your child wears a helmet and appropriate safety gear including knee pads, elbow pads, and gloves, to protect them from falls.
- Supervise the activity to prevent accidents and provide assistance if needed.
- Have a basic first aid kit readily available for minor scrapes or injuries that might occur during the activity.

Troubleshooting Tips:

- **Difficulty Navigating Obstacles:** Adjust the difficulty of the obstacles based on your child's age, skill level, and comfort with biking. Start with simpler challenges and gradually increase complexity.
- **Lack of Confidence:** Provide encouragement and let your child practice riding skills in a simpler setting before tackling the obstacle course.

Cleanup Tips:

- Make cleanup a playful race to see who can collect the most cones, cups, and household items used for the course.

Variations and Adaptations:

- **Traffic Cop Adventure:** Take on the role of a traffic cop, complete with a toy whistle and makeshift stop signs. Direct your child through the course, giving funny or challenging instructions, like "Stop! Traffic jam ahead!" or "Green light, go fast!" This adds a playful, imaginative element to the course and helps your child follow directions.
- **Theme Course:** Design the course around a theme, such as "Magical Pony Ride," "Dinosaur Jungle," or "Cowboy Rodeo." Tailor the obstacles and decorations to match the theme, and use related props and costumes to enhance the experience.
- **Night Rider:** Set up the course with glow sticks or LED lights for a fun evening challenge. This adds an exciting twist to the activity and helps develop your child's spatial awareness.
- **Skill Challenges**: Add specific challenges such as "keep a beanbag on your head while riding through the cones" or "navigate the course while carrying a small stuffed animal on your handlebars."
- **Sensory Stations**: Integrate sensory stations into the course where your child can experience different textures, sounds, or materials. For example, have a station with sand to ride through or a tunnel with crinkly fabric.
- **Scavenger Hunt**: Combine the obstacle course with a scavenger hunt by hiding small items or clues around the course. Your child must find these items while navigating through the obstacles.

Benefits:

- **Improves Physical Fitness**: Navigating an obstacle course requires strength, endurance, and agility, helping your child improve their overall physical fitness and health.
- **Enhances Coordination and Balance**: By steering and maneuvering through various obstacles, your child practices maintaining control and balance, which enhances their coordination and fine motor skills.
- **Develops Problem-Solving Skills:** Figuring out how to navigate through the course encourages your child to think critically and solve problems on the spot.
- **Strengthens Bonds:** Cheering your child on as they navigate the course and celebrating their successes together creates positive, shared experiences that strengthen your emotional connection.
- **Boosts Confidence:** Successfully completing each obstacle gives your child a sense of achievement and boosts their self-confidence.

Obstacle Course Starter Pack

Get the fun started with these easy obstacle ideas! Use them to turn any space into an exciting bike course that keeps your child laughing, learning, and pedaling. Whether you're looking to challenge their riding skills or just add some variety to playtime, these flexible options can be mixed and matched to fit your child's abilities and your available space.

---

1. **Pool Noodle Tunnel:** Set up pool noodles by bending them into arches and securing the ends into the ground by attaching them to stakes. Arrange these arches in a series to create a tunnel that your child can ride through, adding a fun and colorful element to the course.
2. **Water Spritz:** Set up a light sprinkler or spray bottles in a section where your child gets a gentle mist of water as they ride through, adding a refreshing element to the course.
3. **Spiral and Figure Eight Loop:** Use rope, chalk, or tape to create different looping patterns like spirals and figure eights. Have your child ride through these varied loops, focusing on making smooth turns and maintaining a steady pace.
4. **Tight Corners:** Create a section of the course with sharp turns, marked out with cones, requiring precise handling and slower speeds to navigate.
5. **Speed Bumps:** Lay down a few rolled-up towels as soft speed bumps that your child has to ride over, adding a fun little bump in their path.
6. **Low Bridge:** Stretch a piece of rope or a pool noodle across two stakes at a low height, creating a low "bridge" they have to duck under while riding.
7. **Slalom Course:** Set up a series of cones or markers in a straight line for your child to weave through, focusing on their steering and maneuvering skills.
8. **Elevated Ride:** Set up a small, low ramp leading to a raised platform (like a sturdy board on bricks). Encourage your child to ride up, pause on the platform, and then carefully ride down. This introduces a new dimension and tests their balance.
9. **Ball Toss Challenge:** Set up a station where your child has to toss a small ball into a bucket while riding by. This obstacle combines hand-eye coordination with bike control.
10. **Balloon Pop:** Attach balloons to a low-hanging string or on poles. Your child has to ride by and bump into the balloons or pop them with a small stick.

11. **Obstacle Retrieval:** Place small objects along the course that your child has to pick up and carry to a designated spot without stopping their bike.
12. **Color Zone Paths:** Use colored chalk to draw different paths or lanes. Assign each color a different action (e.g., red path = slow ride, blue path = stand while pedaling, green path = pedal fast). This helps introduce variety and new riding techniques.
13. **Water Bottle Knockdown:** Place half-filled plastic water bottles along a section of the course. Challenge your child to gently knock them over with their front wheel while maintaining balance.
14. **Bridge Over 'Rivers':** Lay down a couple of planks over "rivers" marked by chalk lines or garden hoses. Guide your child to balance and ride over these "bridges" without falling into the "water."
15. **Swinging Pendulum:** Hang a lightweight, soft item (like a pool noodle or a foam ball) from a tree branch or a makeshift stand. Have your child ride through without touching the swinging object, adding a fun moving element to the course.

20

MINI GARDEN PLANTING PARTY

Get your hands dirty in a magical gardening adventure with your kindergartener by creating a mini garden bursting with color and life! Choose easy-to-grow herbs or flowers, and dive in together to make planting an exciting, hands-on experience. Witness the wonder in your child's eyes as they dig into the soil, discover wiggly earthworms, and see tiny sprouts bursting from the ground. Whether you have a backyard or just a few pots on a sunny windowsill, this mini garden can bring boundless joy and a sense of accomplishment.

As you nurture your garden, you'll find endless opportunities for meaningful conversations about nature. Watch your child develop a sense of responsibility as they learn how sunlight, water, and care help plants grow. Guide them in watering and caring for each tender sprout, creating a space where they can explore, learn, and bond with you. This shared journey of nurturing life will grow not only your garden but also your connection, bringing laughter, learning, and memories that will last far longer than the blooms.

Materials Needed:

- ☐ Small pots (with drainage holes) or a garden bed
- ☐ Potting soil
- ☐ Seeds or seedlings (e.g., herbs, flowers)
- ☐ Watering can or spray bottle
- ☐ Gardening tools (child friendly)
- ☐ Labels or popsicle sticks (for marking plants; optional)
- ☐ Journal (to track growth and changes; optional)

Step-by-Step Instructions:

1. **Choose Plants:**
    - Select easy-to-grow plants, such as herbs or flowers, that are suitable for your climate and let your child pick the ones that spark their interest.
2. **Prepare the Garden Space:**
    - Choose a designated area for your gardening activity. This could be a corner of your backyard, balcony, or even a sunny windowsill inside.
    - Gather and arrange all the supplies you'll need, like pots, soil, seeds, and tools, so they're easily accessible and ready for use.
    - **Optional:** Let your child paint and decorate the pots before planting. This adds an art component to the activity, making the garden truly their own creation.
    - Clear any weeds or debris if planting in a garden bed.
3. **Planting:**
    - **In Pots:**
        - Help your child fill the pots about three-quarters full with potting soil.
        - Make small holes in the soil with your fingers or a small tool, about half an inch deep.
        - Place a seed in each hole and cover lightly with soil, or dig small holes for seedlings and gently pack soil around them.
    - **In a Garden Bed:**
        - Show your child how to loosen the soil with a small trowel to create an aerated space for planting.
        - Add a fresh layer of potting soil.
        - Mark out where each plant will go, spacing them out according to the instructions on the seed packet or care tag for optimal growth.
        - Help your child create small holes (about half an inch deep) for seeds or slightly larger ones for seedlings.
        - Place a seed or seedling in each hole and cover lightly with soil.
    - Write the name of each plant on popsicle sticks or labels and place them in the pots or in the garden bed next to the plants for easy identification (optional).
4. **Watering and Care:**
    - Show your child how to properly water their plants using a watering can or spray bottle, ensuring the soil is moist but not waterlogged.

- Explain the importance of regular watering and provide guidance on sunlight and general plant care.
- **Note:** Specific care instructions can typically be found on the backs of seed packets or plant tags.
- Set up a simple daily routine with your child to check on the plants. Make sure they understand when to water the plants and how to feel the soil to see if it needs moisture.
- Celebrate small milestones like the first sprout or bloom, and encourage your child to share their excitement about the growing plants.

Safety Considerations:

- Supervise closely and use age-appropriate tools specifically designed for young children. These tools are usually smaller, lighter, and have rounded edges to minimize the risk of injury.
- While most herbs are safe for humans, some can be harmful to pets like dogs, cats, and other animals. It's crucial to select plants that are non-toxic if you have any pets at home. Consult your vet for a comprehensive list, but some common herbs to avoid include chives, mint, oregano, and lavender.

Troubleshooting Tips:

- **Seeds Not Sprouting**: Make sure the soil is loose and not packed too tightly, as compacted soil can hinder seed growth. Ensure you're using fresh seeds as older or improperly stored ones may fail to sprout. A seed-starting mix designed for germination can also improve results.
- **Poor Growth**: Ensure seeds are planted at the right depth, getting enough sunlight, and watered correctly.
- **Watering Issues**: Teach your child about the right amount of water by checking soil moisture. Set a simple watering schedule to prevent over or under-watering.
- **Pests:** Teach your child about different types of insects and how some can be pests. Use child-safe, natural pest control options to protect the plants.
- **Impatience with Growth**: Keep interest high by choosing fast-growing plants or measuring and observing growth together regularly. This helps show progress even if it's slow.
- **Accidentally Damaged Plants**: Teach gentle handling and involve your child in caring for damaged plants. Use it as a lesson on how plants can recover with proper care.

Cleanup Tips:

- If using pots, lay down some newspaper or a plastic sheet to catch any spilled soil, making cleanup easier.

Variations and Adaptations:

- **Garden Journal:** Start a garden journal with your child to track the growth of your mini garden. Your child can draw pictures of the plants, while you jot down dates of planting, watering schedules, and observations about weather or new growth. This reinforces learning about plant care and creates a memorable keepsake of your gardening journey together.
- **Decorative and Themed Gardens:** Personalize your mini garden with fun elements like animal figurines, action figures, or butterfly stakes. To make it even more magical, choose a theme like a Fairy Garden with tiny houses and flowers, a Dinosaur Garden with toy dinosaurs and ferns, or a Space Garden with "moon rocks" and star-shaped decorations.
- **Planting for Pollinators:** Plant a variety of flowers that attract butterflies, bees, and hummingbirds, such as zinnias, borage, calendula, and alyssum. This variation teaches your child about the importance of pollinators and creates a vibrant, living space full of activity and life.
- **Pizza Garden**: Grow ingredients commonly used in pizza-making, such as basil, thyme, tomatoes, and bell peppers. Once harvested, use your homegrown ingredients to make pizzas together, enjoying the fresh flavors and the reward of your gardening efforts.
- **Sensory Garden**: Focus on plants that engage the senses, such as lemon balm for smell, lamb's ear for touch, and brightly colored flowers for sight.
- **Recycled Container Garden**: Use recycled items like old boots, tin cans, or plastic bottles as plant containers. Decorate them with paint or stickers. This variation teaches the importance of recycling and adds a creative twist to traditional gardening.
- **Grow Your Name**: If planting in a garden bed, arrange seeds in the shape of your child's name. As the seeds sprout, they will see their name growing in green!
- **Nighttime Gardening**: Plant moonflowers or other night-blooming plants. Take your child out in the evening to see how these special plants behave differently from those that bloom in the daytime.
- **Vertical Garden**: Use a trellis or vertical planter to grow climbing plants like beans or ivy. This is perfect for small spaces and teaches children about different ways plants can grow.
- **Science Experiment Garden**: Incorporate simple experiments, such as comparing the growth of plants in different types of soil, the effect of

different amounts of sunlight or water, or the impact of different types of music on plant growth.

- **Plant Swap Party**: Host a plant swap where your child can exchange plants or seeds with friends or neighbors. This adds a social element and introduces them to new plants and gardening ideas.
- **Community Garden Plot**: If possible, participate in a community garden. This allows your child to interact with other gardeners, learn from different people, and experience a larger-scale gardening effort.

Benefits:

- **Fosters a Connection to Nature**: Gardening allows children to directly interact with soil, plants, and insects, deepening their appreciation for the natural world while teaching the importance of nurturing living things and instilling values of environmental stewardship.
- **Provides Educational Experience:** Planting a mini garden introduces children to fundamental science concepts like the life cycle of plants, the importance of sunlight, water, and soil, and how nature supports growth.
- **Promotes Healthy Eating Habits**: Growing herbs, vegetables, or fruits encourages children to taste and enjoy fresh produce, fostering a lifelong interest in healthy, nutritious food.
- **Encourages Problem-Solving Skills**: Encountering and addressing gardening challenges, such as pests or weather conditions, helps children develop critical thinking and practical problem-solving abilities.
- **Strengthens Bonds**: Sharing the process of planting, nurturing, and harvesting fosters communication and builds closer relationships through shared achievements.
- **Boosts Confidence**: Watching their plants grow and thrive gives children a sense of pride and accomplishment, boosting their confidence and self-esteem.

21

NATURE SCAVENGER HUNT

Take your child on a journey of discovery, seeking out nature's hidden gems with a thrilling scavenger hunt! Create a list of treasures to find, like vibrant leaves, smooth pebbles, or colorful flowers, and set off on an adventure to uncover them. See your child's eyes light up with excitement at each new discovery, and share in the triumph of ticking off items together. Whether you're exploring a local park or just the neighborhood, this scavenger hunt turns every outing into an unforgettable adventure.

Each find is a spark for curiosity—discuss the shapes, colors, and textures, and watch as your child's fascination with nature grows. Celebrate the thrill of each discovery, and bond over the shared sense of accomplishment. This hands-on adventure not only builds keen observation skills but also fosters a lifelong love for exploring the wonders of the natural world together.

Materials Needed:

- ☐ Scavenger hunt list
- ☐ Pencil or crayon
- ☐ Small bag or bucket for collecting items
- ☐ Magnifying glass (optional)

Step-by-Step Instructions:

1. **Create a List:**
    - Write a list of items to find in nature (e.g., a red leaf, a sparkly rock). Keep the list manageable with around 5-10 items.
    - Include a variety of items like different types of leaves, flowers, rocks, or even specific insects.
2. **Go on a Hunt:**
    - Head outside to your backyard, a local park, or a nature trail. Make sure it's an area where the items on your list can be found.
    - Give your child the bag or bucket for collecting items and help your child find the items on the list.
    - Encourage your child to look closely and use their observation skills to find each item.
    - As you walk, take time to observe your surroundings.
3. **Celebrate Finds:**
    - When your child finds an item from the list, stop and examine it together. Use this as an opportunity to talk about the item—its color, texture, shape, and even its importance in nature.
    - Optional: Use a magnifying glass for a closer look at the textures.
4. **Reflect and Share:**
    - Once all items are found or you've spent enough time exploring, spend a few minutes talking about the highlights of the hunt.
    - Take a moment to thank nature for the adventure. This simple act can instill a sense of respect and gratitude for the environment, teaching children to appreciate and care for the world around them.
    - Ask your child what their favorite part was, what surprised them the most, and what they would like to find next time.

Safety Considerations:

- Keep a close watch on your child during the scavenger hunt to ensure they stay within safe areas and don't wander off.
- Educate your child on recognizing and avoiding harmful plants like poison ivy, poison oak, or thorny bushes.

Troubleshooting Tips:

- Hard-to-Find Items: Offer clues or hints to guide your child, or adjust the list to include more commonly found items. You can also substitute with similar items or simply move on to the next, keeping the momentum and fun alive.

Cleanup Tips:

- Return collected items to nature or use them in a craft project.
- Before leaving, do a quick sweep of the area to ensure no personal items (hats, water bottles, etc.) are left behind.
- Pick up any litter you find along the way to teach environmental responsibility.

Variations and Adaptations:

- **Photo Hunt:** Instead of collecting items, give your child a camera or smartphone to take photos of each find.
- **Alphabet Hunt**: Create a list that includes items for each letter of the alphabet. For example, "A" could be for acorn, "B" for bark, and so on. This variation is both fun and educational, helping with letter recognition and vocabulary building.
- **Themed Hunts**: Choose a specific theme, like "Insects and Bugs," "Colors of Nature," or "Shapes in the Wild," and create a list of related items.
- **Mystery Bag**: Use a bag with clues written on cards. Each clue leads to a specific item or area. As your child pulls out a card, they follow the clue to the next find, adding a fun mystery element to the hunt.
- **Magic Potion Hunt**: Pretend you're wizards or fairies collecting ingredients for a magic potion. Each item on the list is a "magical ingredient" needed to make a potion, adding an imaginative twist.
- **Learning Nature Names**: Turn the hunt into a learning experience by helping your child identify and name the plants, trees, or flowers they find. Use a simple field guide or app (e.g., Seek) to make it educational.

Benefits:

- **Enhances Observation Skills**: Searching for specific items sharpens children's ability to notice details like color, texture, and shape, training them to notice small differences and unique characteristics in their environment.
- **Fosters a Love for Nature**: Direct interaction with nature helps children build an early connection to the environment, sparking a lifelong interest in environmental conservation and respect for living things.
- **Encourages Curiosity and Discovery**: The thrill of finding hidden objects triggers curiosity, encouraging children to explore, ask questions, and develop a mindset of continuous learning.
- **Improves Focus and Concentration**: Staying engaged in the search for items helps children practice focusing on tasks for longer periods,

strengthening their ability to concentrate.

- **Strengthens Bonds:** Working together on the scavenger hunt, celebrating each found item, and overcoming challenges as a team help deepen emotional connections through a shared sense of adventure and discovery.
- **Develops Problem-Solving Skills:** Children must think critically about where to look for items, adapt their strategies, and overcome challenges, developing flexible thinking and the ability to tackle challenges creatively.

Scavenger Hunt Jumpstart

Can't hold back the excitement? Kick off your hunt instantly with this starter list!

☐ **A Smooth Rock** - Find a rock that's smooth to the touch.

☐ **A Pinecone** - Look for a pinecone that has fallen from a tree.

☐ **A Twig Shaped Like a Letter** - Find a twig that looks like a letter from the alphabet.

☐ **A Small Bug** - Look for a small bug crawling on the ground or on a plant.

☐ **A Spider Web** - Look for a spider web glistening in the sunlight.

☐ **A Dandelion** - Find a dandelion puffball ready to be blown.

☐ **A Fallen Leaf Bigger Than Your Hand** - Look for a large fallen leaf.

☐ **A Flower with More Than Five Petals** - Find a flower that has more than five petals.

☐ **A Tree with Moss** - Find a tree that has green moss growing on its trunk.

☐ **A Bird Singing** - Listen for and locate a bird that is singing a cheerful tune.

22

BACKYARD BUG HUNT

Turn your backyard into an exciting safari with a Backyard Bug Hunt. Kids love the thrill of exploration, and you'll be surprised how a simple hunt for creepy crawlies can transform your backyard into a jungle of discovery. Imagine the look on your child's face when they find a ladybug or a colorful beetle—pure joy!

This activity is perfect for curious little explorers and provides a hands-on way to learn about insects and their habitats. It's an engaging way to teach your child about nature and the importance of even the smallest creatures in our ecosystem. Through careful observation and gentle handling, children gain an appreciation for biodiversity and the intricate world of insects. Enjoy the adventure of discovering the tiny wonders that inhabit your backyard and foster a sense of respect and curiosity in your young explorer.

Materials Needed:

- ☐ Small jars or plastic containers (with lids and air holes)
- ☐ Magnifying glass
- ☐ Notebook and pencil or crayons (for recording findings)
- ☐ Bug identification book or app (e.g., Seek, iNaturalist; optional)
- ☐ Small paintbrush (to gently handle bugs; optional)

Step-by-Step Instructions:

1. **Preparation:**
   - Gather all materials and explain the plan to your child.
   - If your jars or containers don't already have air holes, use a hammer and a small nail to carefully poke several small holes in the lids. Make sure the holes are evenly spaced and large enough for air to pass through, but small enough so the bugs can't escape.
   - Let your child decorate the notebook with crayons, markers, or stickers. This personal touch makes it feel like their own special field journal, and builds excitement for the upcoming hunt (optional).
2. **Start Hunting:**
   - Explore your backyard with your child, looking under rocks, peeking under leaves, and searching in the grass. These are prime spots to find bugs.
   - Show your child how to carefully lift objects, checking for creatures hiding underneath.
   - Explain to your child the importance of being gentle with the bugs. Remind them that you're only observing the bugs and will release them back where you found them once you're done.
3. **Capture and Observe:**
   - When you find a bug, gently place it in a container for closer observation.
   - Use the magnifying glass to examine its features.
   - As your child discovers bugs, encourage them to observe closely and ask questions. "How many legs does it have?" or "What color is the bug?" These questions engage their curiosity.
   - Discuss the characteristics of each bug, such as color, size, and behavior.
   - Consider using a bug identification book or app to learn more about each find, like the names of the different species and their role in the ecosystem.
4. **Document Findings:**
   - Encourage your child to document their discoveries by drawing the bugs in the notebook.
   - Discuss what makes each bug unique and help them jot down interesting facts like color, size, and where it was found. This simple journaling adds an educational element and reinforces observational skills.

5. **Release:**
   - Once your child has had a good look at the bugs, gently release them back where you found them. Use the small paintbrush to help guide the bugs back to safety if needed.
   - Teach the importance of returning bugs to their natural habitat.
6. **Reflect on the Adventure:**
   - After the bug hunt, chat with your child about their favorite finds and what they learned. Ask them to describe their favorite bug or share something new they discovered about insects.

Safety Considerations:

- Be cautious of any potentially harmful bugs, like bees, wasps, spiders, or insects with bright warning colors, and teach your child to recognize and avoid them.
- Be aware of any insect-related allergies your child may have. Keep an antihistamine or epinephrine auto-injector (if needed) on hand in case of an allergic reaction.
- Ensure your child handles insects gently to avoid harm.
- When using jars or containers to observe bugs, ensure they have air holes so insects can breathe. Limit the time bugs are kept in these containers before releasing them.

Troubleshooting Tips:

- **Lack of Bugs:** Try different times of day or areas of the yard to find more bugs. Mornings or evenings tend to be more active times for certain insects.
- **Fear of Bugs:** Reassure and educate your child about the benefits of bugs in the ecosystem. Start with harmless, slow-moving insects like ladybugs or pillbugs to ease their fears. Demonstrate handling or observing the bugs first to show there's nothing to worry about.

Cleanup Tips:

- Make sure all insects are gently released back into their original habitats after observation.
- Rinse out containers and clean any tools before storing them and the notebook for next time.
- Wash hands thoroughly with soap and water after handling bugs, dirt, or plants.

Variations and Adaptations:

- **Bug Hunt Races**: Turn the bug hunt into a race! Time your child to see how many bugs they can find in a certain amount of time. For added fun, race together to see who can spot the most bugs.

- **Night Hunt:** Turn the activity into an evening adventure by using flashlights to search for nocturnal insects like moths, fireflies, or crickets.
- **Bug Song and Dance**: Combine the hunt with music! After each bug discovery, make up a fun song or dance that represents the bug's movements or sounds.
- **Bug-Themed Scavenger Hunt**: Add an extra layer of fun by creating a scavenger hunt checklist. Include different types of bugs or specific insect features (e.g., wings, antennae, six legs) for your child to find and check off during the hunt.
- **Bug Fact Cards**: Create or print insect fact cards with fun facts about common backyard bugs. As your child finds each bug, you can read the card together, turning the hunt into an educational experience about each species.
- **Bug Storytelling Adventure**: Have your child create a story or adventure around the bugs they find. This encourages imaginative play, where each bug can become a character in a story of their own creation.
- **Insect Craft Creations:** After the hunt, set up an arts and crafts session where your child can use materials like markers, clay, and natural elements to bring their insect discoveries to life in imaginative ways.

Benefits:

- **Develops Observation Skills**: Searching for insects sharpens children's ability to focus on small details, helping them improve their attention to their environment and notice subtle differences in size, shape, and movement.
- **Provides Hands-On Learning**: Direct interaction with insects allows children to learn about biology, habitats, and ecosystems in a tangible and memorable way, enhancing their understanding of the natural world.
- **Builds Curiosity and Scientific Thinking**: The hands-on nature of bug hunting stimulates curiosity and inquiry-based learning. Children ask questions, make observations, document findings, and start thinking like young scientists.
- **Fosters Respect for Nature**: By observing insects in their natural habitats, children develop a sense of respect for even the smallest creatures, learning that every living thing plays a role in the ecosystem.
- **Teaches Responsibility and Care**: Through careful observation and gentle handling of bugs, children learn the importance of treating living things with care and responsibility, reinforcing empathy for other

creatures.

- **Strengthens Bonds:** Working together to find and observe insects creates moments of shared excitement and curiosity, fostering a deeper connection through the joy of exploring nature side by side.
- **Improves Problem-Solving Skills**: As children search for bugs in various environments, they learn to think critically about where insects might be hiding, adapting their strategies and enhancing their problem-solving skills.

23

NATURAL WONDERS COLLAGE

Turn your next afternoon stroll into an artistic adventure with a nature-inspired collage! This activity combines the excitement of exploring the outdoors with the joy of crafting a unique collage from natural materials. Collect leaves, flowers, twigs, and stones during your walk and use them to create a beautiful artwork. Your kindergartner will love the hunt for natural treasures and the chance to arrange them into a stunning masterpiece.

This activity not only fosters a connection with nature but also encourages creativity and fine motor skills. As you work together on the collage, you'll share moments of discovery and artistic expression, making this project a memorable and enriching experience. Embrace the beauty of nature and creativity in this delightful and bonding activity.

Materials Needed:

- ☐ Leaves, flowers, twigs, stones (collected from a nature walk)
- ☐ Small bag or basket (for collecting materials)
- ☐ Cardboard or construction paper
- ☐ Glue or tape
- ☐ Markers or crayons (optional)

Step-by-Step Instructions:

1. **Collect Materials:**
   - Head out on a short walk around your neighborhood, local park, or backyard.
   - As you explore, encourage your child to search for interesting natural items to collect such as leaves, flowers, and twigs.
   - Allow your kindergartener to lead the way and decide what to collect. This helps foster independence and curiosity as they gather their "treasures."
2. **Prepare a Base:**
   - Once you're back from your walk, clear a flat workspace and lay down the construction paper or cardboard for the collage base.
   - Lay out all the collected materials, letting your child sort through their finds and decide which pieces they want to include in the collage.
3. **Create the Collage:**
   - Help your child plan where they want to place the nature items on the collage. You can talk about grouping similar objects together (like a "leaf corner" or "stone section"), or let them arrange the materials randomly for a more abstract look.
   - Encourage them to think creatively! Maybe the leaves can be turned into the shape of a tree, or flowers can be arranged to look like a sun.
   - Once they're happy with the arrangement, start gluing the items down. If you're using liquid glue, apply small dots of glue and press the nature items gently in place. If using a glue stick, apply it directly to the items and press them onto the paper.
   - Make sure to help with the more delicate items to avoid tearing or crumbling.
   - If your child wants, they can use crayons or markers to add drawings around the natural materials, creating a scene or adding details to complete the artwork.
4. **Admire and Celebrate:**
   - Once the collage is complete, sit back with your child and just enjoy looking at it together. Let them proudly show off their favorite parts, whether it's a special leaf or a colorful arrangement they made.
   - Point out something you admire about their work. Maybe it's how they grouped things together or how a certain item stood out to you.
   - Talk about the fun you had collecting everything. Maybe bring up a funny moment from the walk or a discovery that surprised you both.

  - Wrap things up with something playful—a fist bump, silly handshake, or even plan what you'll do with the next collection of treasures!

Safety Considerations:

- Avoid sharp or toxic items, like thorny plants, poisonous berries, or mushrooms. If you're unsure, guide them toward common, safe plants like leaves or flowers.
- Keep an eye on the size of collected materials, especially with younger children, to prevent choking hazards from small stones or tiny objects.
- If your child has allergies, be mindful of collecting items that could trigger reactions (such as certain flowers or pollen). Bring any necessary medication, like antihistamines, just in case.

Troubleshooting Tips:

- **Materials Not Sticking:** Try using a stronger adhesive or pressing the objects more firmly. You can also try using double-sided tape for more challenging materials.
- **Items Wilt or Dry Out**: If flowers or leaves wilt quickly, encourage your child to use them as soon as they are collected. Alternatively, press them between books to flatten and preserve them for future projects.

Cleanup Tips:

- Lay down old newspapers or a plastic sheet to catch any glue or debris.
- Keep a small box handy to store any unused, sturdy nature items like pebbles, pressed flowers, or pinecones. This not only makes future craft activities easier but also reduces waste.
- Have a trash bag nearby for quick collection of unwanted materials. Any unused leaves, twigs, or flowers should be returned to nature or disposed of in a compost bin if possible.
- Involve your child by turning the cleanup into a game. Pretend you're going on one last "mini-hunt" to gather all the leftover materials or tools, making it fun while getting the job done.

Variations and Adaptations:

- **Seasonal Nature Collage Series**: Create a series of collages, each representing a different season. Over time, you and your child can collect materials during each season's nature walk, making a full "year of nature" collage collection.
- **Pressed Flower Art**: After collecting flowers and leaves, press them between books for a few days. Once they're flattened, create a delicate collage that looks more like a framed piece of botanical art.

- **Sensory Nature Collage**: Instead of just focusing on appearance, incorporate items that stimulate other senses. Collect fragrant flowers, rough bark, or soft moss to create a collage that's also a sensory experience your child can touch and smell.
- **Nature Collage Frames**: Instead of making the collage the artwork itself, use natural materials to decorate the frame of a picture or photo.
- **Memory Board**: Turn the collage into a memory board by gluing down materials that represent special places or moments. For example, leaves from a favorite park or flowers from a recent family trip.

Benefits:

- **Encourages Healthy Outdoor Habits**: The activity promotes spending time outdoors, encouraging children to enjoy fresh air and physical activity while engaging in a creative pursuit.
- **Enhances Creativity**: Gathering natural items and arranging them into a collage encourages children to think creatively, experimenting with colors, shapes, and textures to create unique artwork.
- **Develops Fine Motor Skills:** The process of collecting small items and manipulating them into place on the collage helps refine children's fine motor skills, improving their hand-eye coordination and dexterity.
- **Strengthens Bonds:** Working together to collect materials and create the collage provides a shared experience that strengthens the bond between parent and child, fostering open communication and cooperation.
- **Boosts Problem-Solving Skills**: Deciding how to arrange different materials in the collage helps children develop problem-solving abilities as they figure out how to best use each item for their design.

EARLY-ELEMENTARY

EXPLORERS

INDOOR ADVENTURES

Bring adventure indoors with activities perfect for early-elementary explorers! This set features everything from LEGO challenges that test creativity to DIY slime that sparks excitement. Activities like indoor bowling and the Mini Zen Garden Sanctuary encourage children to think creatively, solve problems, and relax—all while having a blast at home. Whether creating a thriving cardboard box town, or cooking up some memorable moments in the kitchen, each activity is designed to engage young minds while fostering curiosity and hands-on fun.

24

INDOOR BOWLING MANIA

Prepare to transform your living room into a lively bowling alley, where you and your child can enjoy hours of fun! With empty plastic bottles standing in for pins and a soft ball ready to roll, the excitement begins as you set up the makeshift lanes. The simplicity of the materials belies the endless joy this activity brings, as each turn offers a new opportunity for triumph or hilarious misadventure. The thrill of watching the ball glide down the lane and the anticipation of a strike create a delightful, shared experience.

As the game progresses, your living room fills with cheers and playful banter, making every attempt to knock down the pins an event to remember. The casual competition and the joy of achieving that perfect roll bring about a sense of camaraderie and accomplishment. The dynamic atmosphere, filled with laughter and encouragement, transforms an ordinary day into a memorable, joy-filled adventure.

Materials Needed:

- ☐ 10 empty plastic bottles (same size)
- ☐ A soft ball (like a foam or rubber ball)
- ☐ Masking tape or chalk (optional, for marking the lane)
- ☐ A scoreboard and marker (optional, for keeping score)

Step-by-Step Instructions:

1. **Set Up the Pins:**
   - Fill the plastic bottles with a small amount of water or rice to weigh them down slightly, but not too much—they should still be easy to knock over. Secure the caps tightly.
   - Arrange the bottles in a traditional bowling pin formation (a triangle) at the end of a hallway or open space.
   - Ensure the bottles are stable and evenly spaced.
2. **Mark the Lane:**
   - Use masking tape or chalk to create a bowling lane leading up to the pins. This helps guide your child and makes the game feel more official.
   - Make the lane as long or short as you like, depending on the space available and your child's skill level.
3. **Start Bowling:**
   - Take turns rolling the ball toward the pins to try and knock them down.
   - Encourage your child to aim and roll the ball gently to avoid causing any damage.
   - Cheer for each other and celebrate every roll, whether it's a strike, a spare, or even a gutter ball! Make the experience full of laughter, whether the pins topple or stay standing.
4. **Keep Score (Optional):**
   - Use a simple scoring system to keep track of points. Award a point for each pin knocked down.
   - If you want to make it more competitive, keep a running total and see who scores the highest after a set number of rounds.
5. **Reset and Repeat:**
   - After each round, reset the pins and continue bowling.
   - Encourage your child to try different techniques, such as rolling the ball faster or slower, to see what works best.

Safety Considerations:

- Move breakable or valuable items out of the room or far from the bowling area before starting the game to avoid accidental damage.
- Use a soft ball to prevent any damage or injury.

Troubleshooting Tips:

- Pins Falling Over Too Easily: Fill the bottles with a bit more water, rice, or sand to add weight and stability.
- **Space Constraints:** Adjust the size of the lane and number of pins to fit your available space.

Cleanup Tips:

- Create a specific area or box for storing the bottles and ball, making it easy to find and set up the game next time.
- For added fun, let your child decorate the official bowling box, turning it into a creative project that adds personal flair and makes cleanup more enjoyable.

Variations and Adaptations:

- **Glowing Alley:** Use glow-in-the-dark tape or paint to decorate the pins and ball, then dim the lights for an exciting nighttime bowling experience.
- **Obstacle Bowling:** Add soft obstacles like pillows or cushions along the "lane" that the ball must navigate around before reaching the pins.
- **Themed Bowling:** Decorate the pins and lane according to a theme, such as "Robot Factory" or "Flower Power."
- **Pin Knockdown Power-Ups**: Assign each pin a "power-up," like extra points, a free turn, or bonus time. Your child earns these rewards based on which pins they knock down, keeping the game exciting and varied.
- **Bowling with a Twist**: Create different rules for each round, such as rolling the ball while sitting down, bowling backward, or using a "slow-motion" roll.
- **Blindfold Bowling**: Challenge your child to roll the ball while blindfolded, relying on you to give verbal directions on where to aim. Then switch roles! This adds an element of trust and teamwork to the game.

Benefits:

- Enhances Hand-Eye Coordination: Rolling the ball to hit specific targets improves your child's hand-eye coordination and helps develop precise motor skills.
- **Promotes Problem-Solving**: Figuring out how to adjust their aim, strength, or ball placement to hit the pins requires problem-solving, encouraging your child to think critically and adapt.
- **Promotes Physical Activity:** Indoor bowling gets children up and moving, helping them stay active and burn energy, especially when it's too cold or rainy to play outside.

- **Boosts Math Skills:** Keeping track of scores introduces basic math skills, like counting pins and adding up scores, which helps reinforce number recognition and addition.
- **Strengthens Bonds:** The shared experience of playing, cheering each other on, and celebrating each attempt creates moments of connection and strengthens bonds through laughter and collaboration.
- **Encourages Sportsmanship:** Playing a friendly game of bowling teaches the importance of taking turns, following rules, and congratulating others.

25

LEGO INNOVATION LAB

Unleash a world of imagination with your child through exciting LEGO challenges. Picture a session where creativity knows no bounds as you and your child build fantastical structures and daring designs. The room fills with laughter and concentration as together you decide to construct the tallest tower or the most intricate bridge. Each colorful brick becomes a part of a grand story, transforming your living room into a bustling construction site where ideas come to life.

As you build, you might find yourselves inventing new challenges or adding unexpected twists to your creations. Perhaps your tower needs to withstand an imaginary earthquake, or your bridge must support the weight of your child's heaviest book. The process is filled with trial and error, success and learning. In these moments, you and your child not only create wonderful memories but also learn to think creatively and solve problems together, turning a simple pile of LEGO bricks into a source of endless adventure.

Materials Needed:

- ☐ A variety of LEGO bricks
- ☐ A flat surface to build on
- ☐ A timer (optional)

Step-by-Step Instructions:

1. **Set a Challenge:**
   - Pick a fun challenge like "build a tower taller than Dad's golf bag", "create a bridge that can hold your heaviest book," or "create a sculpture that must balance on a single LEGO brick." Make it interesting and a bit tricky to spark creativity.
   - For added fun, use a timer to set a specific challenge, such as building the tallest tower in 10 minutes. This adds an element of friendly competition and encourages faster problem-solving.
   - Explain the challenge clearly to your child and set any rules or guidelines.
2. **Build Together:**
   - Dive into the pile of LEGO bricks and start building. Offer help but let your child take the lead. It's all about teamwork and creativity.
   - Encourage your child to think outside the box and try different approaches.
3. **Evaluate and Improve:**
   - Once the masterpiece is complete, test it out. Does the tower stand tall? Does the bridge hold the book? Discuss what worked, what didn't, and how it could be improved.
   - Celebrate the successes and talk about what was fun, what was tricky, and what they might want to build next time.

Safety Considerations:

- Supervise younger children to ensure they don't put small pieces in their mouths.
- Keep the building area tidy to avoid stepping on LEGO bricks, which can be painful.

Troubleshooting Tips:

- **Challenge too hard:** Scale it back. Instead of a tower taller than a golf bag, aim for one taller than the coffee maker.
- **Running out of bricks:** Combine different sets or get creative with what you have. Limitations can lead to the most inventive solutions.

Cleanup Tips:

- Use a large tray or a blanket to build on. When you're done, just lift the corners and pour the bricks back into the box.
- Make it a game: set a timer and challenge your child to see how many bricks they can pick up before the timer runs out!

Variations and Adaptations:

- **Theme Build:** Choose a theme like "Starport Station" or "Poseidon's Paradise" to add an imaginative twist.
- **Blindfolded Build:** One person describes the building steps while the other builds blindfolded. Hilarity ensues.
- **Mystery Bag Build**: Put a random selection of LEGO bricks in a bag, and your child has to create something from whatever pieces they pull out. This forces creativity with limited resources and adds a surprise element.
- **Reverse Engineering:** Take apart an existing LEGO creation and challenge each other to rebuild it from memory.
- **Build and Trade**: Have a "build and trade" session where you each build something, then swap creations and add new features to the other person's design. It's a fun way to collaborate and see how different minds work.

Benefits:

- **Promotes Creativity:** Building with LEGO bricks encourages children to think outside the box, experimenting with different designs, colors, and shapes to bring their imaginative ideas to life.
- **Enhances Problem-Solving Skills**: LEGO challenges, like constructing stable towers or designing functional bridges, teach children to assess situations, try different strategies, and adapt to overcome obstacles.
- **Introduces Basic Engineering Concepts**: Children naturally engage with basic engineering principles like balance, stability, and weight distribution while building LEGO structures, laying the foundation for STEM learning.
- **Teaches Resilience Through Failure**: When a structure falls or a design doesn't work as expected, children learn the value of trying again, building resilience and a growth mindset that embraces failure as part of learning.
- **Strengthens Bonds:** Building LEGO creations together provides quality bonding time, fostering open communication, shared laughter, and a sense of accomplishment as you complete projects together.
- **Boosts Confidence:** Successfully completing a complex build or inventing a creative new design boosts children's confidence in their abilities, reinforcing their belief in their problem-solving and creative skills.

26

MINI ZEN GARDEN SANCTUARY

Create a little slice of tranquility with a miniature Zen garden, a type of Japanese rock garden known as Karesansui! Using a shallow tray, sand, and small rocks, you and your child can craft a peaceful oasis that's both fun to make and soothing to maintain. Imagine the serene atmosphere as you both use a fork or small rake to draw intricate patterns in the sand, rearranging rocks to create a harmonious design. This activity offers a perfect blend of creativity and relaxation.

As you work on your Zen garden together, you'll find it to be a calming and meditative experience. The process of creating and maintaining the garden encourages mindfulness and patience. Sharing this peaceful activity with your child can become a cherished ritual, providing a quiet moment of connection amidst the hustle and bustle of daily life.

Materials Needed:

- ☐ Shallow tray or dish
- ☐ Craft sand
- ☐ Small rocks
- ☐ Fork or small rake
- ☐ Decorations (e.g., miniature figurines, plants, crystals; optional)

Note: *Alternatively, consider a Zen garden kit that includes most materials, though it may feel less personalized.*

Step-by-Step Instructions:

1. **Prepare the Tray:**
   - Let your child pour the sand into the shallow tray until it's about 1–2 inches deep.
   - Make sure the sand is evenly distributed across the surface by shaking the tray gently or spreading it with your hand.
2. **Arrange Rocks:**
   - Together, choose a few rocks or pebbles to place in the sand.
   - Discuss where to place them, encouraging your child to think about how the arrangement feels balanced and peaceful.
   - Let your child rearrange the rocks as many times as they like until they feel satisfied with the layout.
3. **Create Patterns:**
   - Give your child a small rake or fork to start creating patterns in the sand. Show them how to gently drag the rake to form waves, lines, or circles around the rocks.
   - Encourage them to experiment with different designs, explaining that there's no right or wrong way to do it—just go with what feels calming and natural.
4. **Add Decorations (Optional):**
   - Enhance the garden by adding miniature figurines, crystals, or incorporating small plants like succulents or air plants for a touch of greenery and charm. These can add a personal touch and make the garden more visually interesting.
5. **Maintain the Garden:**
   - Regularly change patterns and rearrange rocks to keep the garden fresh and engaging. This ongoing interaction helps maintain its calming effect.
   - Explain to your child that they can rake the garden and change the arrangement whenever they feel like it. It can be a peaceful daily or weekly ritual to help them relax and refocus.

Safety Considerations:

- Ensure close supervision while working with small items like rocks and figurines, as they could be choking hazards for younger children.
- Opt for child-safe, non-toxic sand that's free from dust or harmful additives. If using colored sand, ensure the dye is non-toxic and safe for handling.

Troubleshooting Tips:

- **Messy Sand:** Use a tray with higher edges to contain the sand better and minimize spills.
- **Sand Clumping**: If the sand becomes clumpy or sticks together, it might be absorbing moisture from the air. Keep the garden in a dry place and gently stir or sift the sand to break up clumps.
- **Limited Decorations:** Get creative with natural elements from your surroundings, such as twigs, leaves, or shells.
- **Child Losing Interest**: If your child becomes disinterested, introduce a challenge by suggesting new designs or patterns to create, such as spirals, waves, or shapes.

Cleanup Tips:

- Keep the tray in a safe place away from heavy traffic to prevent spills and disturbances.

Variations and Adaptations:

- **Personalized Symbols:** Allow your child to include personal, meaningful objects like a favorite small figurine, a special rock, or a tiny sculpture. This can make the garden more personal while still maintaining the tranquil spirit.
- **Bedtime Zen Ritual**: Incorporate the Zen garden into a nightly routine where your child creates a new design before bed. This calming activity becomes a special moment to share together, helping them wind down peacefully.
- **Interactive Storytelling:** Use the Zen garden as a backdrop for storytelling. Create stories about the placement of rocks, the flow of sand patterns, and the elements within the garden, making the experience more engaging and imaginative.
- **Cultural Learning:** Integrate learning about the history and philosophy of Zen gardens. Share stories or read books about the origins and meanings behind these gardens, enhancing the educational aspect of the activity.
- **Themed Zen Gardens:** Create themed Zen gardens that incorporate elements reflecting different seasons or environments. For example, use autumn-colored sand and leaves for a fall theme, or incorporate tiny seashells and blue sand for a beach theme.
- **Meditative Patterns:** Encourage the creation of traditional Zen garden patterns such as circles, waves, and spirals. Research different designs together and experiment with replicating them in your miniature garden.

- **Artistic Expression:** Introduce elements of Japanese art by including miniature versions of traditional Japanese lanterns, pagodas, or bridges. These can be crafted from clay or purchased as small figurines.
- **Gratitude Stones:** Paint small stones with words of gratitude or positive affirmations and incorporate them into the Zen garden. This adds a reflective and mindful element to the activity.

Benefits:

- **Supports Emotional Well-Being**: Engaging in this quiet, soothing activity provides an outlet for relaxation, helping children calm down, regulate their emotions, and feel more balanced.
- **Enhances Creativity:** Designing patterns and arrangements stimulates artistic expression, allowing kids to explore their creative potential.
- **Promotes Mindfulness:** The calming act of raking sand and arranging rocks encourages children to focus on and enjoy the present moment, helping them develop mindfulness and stress-relief techniques.
- **Strengthens Bonds:** The collaborative effort of designing patterns and maintaining the garden fosters a sense of connection and shared tranquility, deepening the bond through peaceful, creative moments.
- **Encourages Emotional Expression**: The Zen garden can be used as a non-verbal tool for emotional expression, allowing children to reflect their feelings through the patterns and designs they create.

27

DIY SLIME FACTORY

Step into the world of gooey fun with your very own DIY Slime Factory right in your kitchen. The excitement starts as you gather simple ingredients and prepare to mix up some colorful, stretchy slime. Watching the transformation from liquid to slime is nothing short of magical, captivating your child's curiosity and enthusiasm. The process of adding glitter and food coloring allows for endless customization, making each batch of slime a unique creation.

As the slime comes together, the real joy is in the hands-on play. Stretching, squishing, and molding the slime provides a sensory delight, sparking imagination and creativity. The kitchen becomes a hub of activity, filled with laughter and exclamations of wonder at the slime's tactile properties. This messy, enjoyable activity not only entertains but also fosters a sense of discovery and experimentation, creating lasting memories of scientific fun. So, get ready to get slimy!

Materials Needed:

- ☐ White school glue (8 oz bottle or 1 cup)
- ☐ Baking soda (½ teaspoon)
- ☐ Contact lens solution (2 tablespoons, must contain boric acid)
- ☐ Food coloring (optional)
- ☐ Glitter or confetti (optional)
- ☐ Large mixing bowls
- ☐ Spoons or spatulas
- ☐ Measuring cups and spoons

Step-by-Step Instructions:

1. **Prepare the Ingredients:**
   - In a mixing bowl, pour in the contents of the 8 oz bottle (1 cup) of white school glue.
   - Add a few drops of food coloring and glitter (or confetti) if you want to make your slime colorful and sparkly.
   - Stir until the color is evenly mixed.
2. **Create the Slime:**
   - Add ½ teaspoon of baking soda to the glue mixture and stir thoroughly. The baking soda helps to firm up the slime, making it stretchy and fun to play with.
   - As you mix, ask your child how they think the baking soda is changing the slime. Get them thinking by saying, "What do you think will happen next?" or "Does it look more like slime yet?" This will keep them engaged and excited to see what happens.
   - Gradually add 2 tablespoons of contact lens solution to the mixture, a little at a time. This is the activator that will turn the glue into slime. The more you add, the thicker the slime becomes. Experiment to find the right consistency for you and your child.
   - Stir vigorously. The mixture will start to come together and start to pull away from the sides of the bowl. If it's not forming after stirring, add a bit more contact lens solution.
3. **Knead the Slime:**
   - Once the slime begins to form, take it out of the bowl and knead it with your hands. This helps improve its texture and make it more stretchy.
   - If the slime is still too sticky after kneading for a few minutes, add a tiny bit more contact lens solution (just a few drops at a time) and continue kneading.
   - Consider turning this step into a fun challenge by seeing who can stretch their slime the farthest. Let your child experiment with how far they can pull it before it breaks.
4. **Play and Experiment:**
   - Now that your slime is ready, it's time to have fun! Stretch, squish, and even blow bubbles with the slime.
   - Encourage silly play by seeing who can make the most creative shapes, like slime snakes or pancakes, or just enjoy the satisfying feeling of playing with it together.

  - When playtime is over, store the slime in an airtight container or a resealable plastic bag to keep it fresh for future play. Proper storage will help the slime last for several days.

Safety Considerations:

- Ensure your child doesn't ingest the slime or the ingredients.
- Supervise your child during the activity to prevent any mess-related mishaps.

Troubleshooting Tips:

- **Slime Too Sticky:** Add more contact lens solution a few drops at a time until the slime reaches the desired consistency.
- **Slime Too Runny:** Add a bit more baking soda to firm it up.
- **Slime too Firm:** Add more glue or a bit of baby oil to the mixture and knead until the mixture softens.

Cleanup Tips:

- Cover the table or workspace with a plastic tablecloth or newspaper to make cleanup easier.
- Set up a hand cleaning station with a bowl of soap and water or wet wipes for easy cleanup of sticky hands.
- Soak the mixing bowls and utensils in warm, soapy water immediately after use to make cleaning easier.
- Wipe down all surfaces with a damp cloth and a mild cleaner to remove any leftover slime or glitter. Make it a fun game by seeing who can clean their area the fastest.
- Check the floor for any slime spills or sticky spots. Use a damp mop or cloth to clean up, ensuring no slippery areas are left behind.

Variations and Adaptations:

- **Glow-in-the-Dark Slime:** Add glow-in-the-dark paint or powder to the slime mixture for an extra magical effect.
- **Fluffy Slime:** Add shaving cream to the glue mixture before adding the activator to make an incredibly light and fluffy version. The result is a soft, cloud-like slime that's super satisfying to squish.
- **Clear Slime:** Use clear school glue instead of white glue to create a shimmering, crystal-clear effect.
- **Crunchy Slime:** Add small plastic beads to the slime for a satisfying, crunchy texture. The mix of slime and solid elements provides a unique sensory experience.

- **Galaxy Slime**: Create mesmerizing galaxy-themed slime by combining dark colors (black, blue, purple) with glitter and star-shaped confetti. Swirl the colors together for a cosmic effect that's out of this world!
- **Jelly Cube Slime**: Add small, sponge-like cubes (you can cut up a soft kitchen sponge) to the slime for a squishy, jelly-like effect. The cubes absorb the slime, giving it an intriguing texture. For this version, use less activator in the slime as the cubes absorb moisture and will make the slime thicker.
- **Butter Slime**: Create a smooth, soft butter slime by adding soft clay to the slime mix. This version has a silky, pliable texture that makes it easy to mold and shape.
- **Ocean Slime**: Mix in blue food coloring, seashells, and tiny plastic sea creatures to create an underwater-themed slime. Your child can pretend to be exploring the ocean with their slimy creation.
- **Color-Changing Slime**: Use thermochromic pigments that react to temperature, so when the slime is warmed up in your child's hands or cooled in the fridge, it changes color. These pigments are affordable and readily available online.

Benefits:

- **Develops Fine Motor Skills**: Mixing ingredients and manipulating the slime—stretching, pulling, and shaping—helps children develop fine motor skills, strengthening hand muscles and improving dexterity.
- **Introduces Basic Science Concepts**: Making slime teaches children about the science of mixing materials, such as the transformation from liquid to solid, sparking curiosity about chemistry and scientific reactions.
- **Encourages Experimentation**: As children try different ingredients and textures, they learn to experiment and explore what works and what doesn't, fostering a mindset of discovery and hands-on learning.
- **Strengthens Bonds:** Creating slime together encourages teamwork and problem-solving, allowing for shared moments of success and fun that deepen the connection between you and your child.
- **Improves Problem-Solving Skills**: If the slime doesn't turn out as expected, children learn to adjust the ingredients, teaching them how to troubleshoot and solve problems through trial and error.

28

MINI CHEF ACADEMY

Turn your kitchen into a culinary playground, where the delicious scent of fresh ingredients fills the air as you teach your child the basics of cooking. Choose a simple and fun recipe, such as homemade pizza or colorful cookies, and watch their eyes light up as they get hands-on with measuring, mixing, and kneading. The kitchen buzzes with excitement and chatter, each step of the process becoming a moment of learning and joy. Your child will love the opportunity to get messy and creative, transforming ordinary ingredients into a tasty masterpiece.

As the dough rises or the cookies bake, you'll find yourselves chatting about the different ingredients, why certain steps are important, and maybe even sharing your own childhood memories of cooking. The anticipation builds as the timer counts down, culminating in the satisfaction of tasting your joint creation. These moments spent together in the kitchen do more than just fill your bellies; they create lasting memories and instill a sense of accomplishment and pride in your child. Cooking together becomes a cherished ritual, blending the joy of creation with the pleasure of sharing a meal.

Materials Needed:

- ☐ Ingredients for the chosen recipe (e.g., dough, cheese, toppings for pizza)
- ☐ Basic kitchen tools (bowls, measuring cups, spoons, etc.)
- ☐ Aprons (optional)

Step-by-Step Instructions:

1. **Choose a Recipe:**
   - Select a simple, child-friendly recipe that you both will enjoy making and eating.
   - Make sure you have all the ingredients and tools needed for the recipe.
2. **Prepare Your Workspace:**
   - Clear and clean your kitchen counter or table.
   - Lay out all the ingredients and tools for easy access. Let your child help gather everything from the pantry or fridge—this makes them feel involved right from the start.
   - If using the oven, preheat it, explaining to your child why it's important.
   - **Optional:** Encourage your child to wear an apron to add a fun "chef" feel to the activity.
3. **Read the Recipe Together:**
   - Sit with your child and read through the recipe aloud, explaining each step in simple terms. This helps them understand the process and builds anticipation.
4. **Measure Ingredients:**
   - Start by measuring out the ingredients so they're ready to be mixed in. Let your child pour flour, sugar, or other items into the measuring cups. Guide them in leveling off ingredients to get the correct amount. This is a great way to practice basic math skills like counting and fractions (half a cup, etc.).
   - Encourage your child to guess what each ingredient might add to the recipe (e.g., "What do you think sugar does in cookies?").
5. **Cook Together:**
   - Hand your child a spoon or whisk to mix the ingredients together and follow the recipe step-by-step.
   - You can help your child when needed, but allow them to take the lead in stirring, kneading, or cracking an egg. This is the part where things might get a little messy, but it's all part of the fun!
   - While the food cooks or bakes, chat about the ingredients you used or tell a story from your own childhood cooking experiences. The waiting period can be filled with fun conversations about how the food will taste once it's done.
6. **Taste and Enjoy:**
   - Once the food is ready, sit down together and enjoy the fruits of your

labor.

- Discuss what you like best about your creation and what you might change next time.
- If the dish doesn't turn out as expected, reassure your child that it's okay. Share stories of your own kitchen mishaps to show that everyone makes mistakes.

Safety Considerations:

- Always supervise your child when using sharp tools or hot appliances, and teach them to stand back when opening the oven.
- When using mixers, blenders, or other kitchen appliances, supervise closely. Teach your child to keep their hands and hair away from moving parts, and unplug appliances when not in use.
- If your child is using a real knife, guide them on how to hold and use it properly. Teach them to always cut away from their body and keep fingers out of the way.
- Ensure all ingredients are safe for your child's dietary needs.
- Make sure your child is wearing fitted clothes that won't dangle into food or flames.
- Be prepared for minor accidents like cuts or burns by keeping a basic first aid kit within reach.
- Make sure your child washes their hands thoroughly before cooking and after handling raw ingredients, especially raw meat or eggs, to prevent the spread of bacteria.
- When working with raw ingredients like meat or eggs, ensure separate cutting boards are used, and wash surfaces and surfaces immediately after handling them.
- If your child is old enough to help near the stove, teach them to always turn pan handles inward to avoid knocking them over.

Troubleshooting Tips:

- **Recipe too complex:** Choose a simpler one with fewer steps or ingredients. Opt for no-bake recipes or dishes that require minimal cooking to keep it manageable and fun.
- **Ingredient Unavailability**: If you're missing an ingredient, use it as an opportunity to teach about substitutions. For example, use yogurt instead of sour cream or honey instead of sugar, explaining how substitutions can alter the recipe.
- **Forgotten Steps**: If a step is missed, don't panic. Use it as a learning opportunity to discuss how recipes work and what might happen when

steps are skipped, emphasizing experimentation.

- **Overcooked or Undercooked Food**: Involve your child in setting timers and checking the oven or stovetop regularly. Teach them simple methods to test for doneness, like inserting a toothpick into baked goods.
- **Child loses interest:** Assign engaging tasks like stirring, sprinkling toppings, or decorating. Keep instructions brief and lively to maintain their enthusiasm throughout the activity.

Cleanup Tips:

- Have a damp cloth ready to wipe up spills immediately.
- Use a large tray to contain ingredients and minimize mess.
- Keep a large bowl on the counter for discarding food scraps, eggshells, and wrappers. This keeps the workspace tidy and reduces trips to the garbage can.
- After all food preparation is complete, wipe down countertops and tables with a food-safe sanitizer to maintain hygiene.
- Make cleanup part of the experience. Frame it as "tidying up our kitchen just like chefs do" to keep it fun and engaging. Alternatively, make a game out of tidying up by assigning a "cleanup challenge" where your child races to put items away before you finish wiping down the table.

Variations and Adaptations:

- **Culinary Dress-Up**: Dress up as chefs with hats and aprons. You can even create your own chef hats as a craft activity before you start cooking.
- **Alphabet Cooking**: Choose a letter and make foods that start with that letter, like 'B' for banana bread or 'T' for tacos, making it a fun educational activity.
- **DIY Salad Bar:** Set up a variety of toppings and let your child create their own salad.
- **Smoothie Creation:** Mix different fruits, yogurt, and juice to create delicious smoothies.
- **Pizza Party:** Make individual mini pizzas with various toppings, letting your child get creative with their combinations.
- **Healthy Snacks Creation**: Focus on making healthy snacks like energy balls, veggie sticks with dip, or fruit kebabs. Teach your child about nutrition and making healthy food choices.
- **Culinary Colors:** Make the activity a learning moment by adding food coloring to dough or icing and discussing color combinations with your child.

- **Cultural Storytelling**: Pair a storybook with a related recipe. Read a story set in another country and then make a dish from that culture, combining literacy with culinary exploration.
- **Edible Art**: Create artworks using food items, like making faces on pancakes with fruit or building structures with vegetables and toothpicks.
- **Blind Taste Test**: Prepare different foods and have a blindfolded taste test. This can be a fun way to introduce new foods and discuss flavors and textures.
- **Cookie Cutter Creations**: Use cookie cutters to make fun shapes out of sandwiches, pancakes, or even large fruit slices. This adds a playful element to ordinary foods.
- **Recipe Reconstruction**: Taste a dish and try to figure out the ingredients together. Then, attempt to recreate it, encouraging problem-solving and sensory skills.
- **Create a Cooking Show Video**: Record your cooking session as if hosting a cooking show. This can build confidence and make the activity exciting.
- **Recipe Book Project**: Start a family recipe book where you document each cooking adventure. Let your child draw pictures or take photos of the dishes to include in the book.
- **Science in Cooking**: Incorporate simple science experiments into your cooking to teach your child about scientific concepts in a fun way. For example, make bread to demonstrate yeast fermentation, or turn heavy cream into butter by shaking it in a jar for 10 minutes to show how liquids can become solids. Note: For best homemade butter results, the cream should be around 62°F and the jar should be no more than half-filled.
- **Cooking for a Cause**: Bake treats to share with neighbors, family, or a local charity. This teaches generosity and the joy of giving to others.

Benefits:

- **Enhances Literacy Skills**: Reading recipes and ingredient labels improves reading skills and comprehension, reinforcing literacy in a practical setting.
- **Promotes Mathematical Understanding**: Following recipes involves counting, measuring, and understanding proportions, introducing basic math concepts in a practical, hands-on way.
- **Encourages Healthy Eating Habits**: Involving children in cooking increases their interest in different foods, promoting a willingness to try new, healthy ingredients and understand nutrition.
- **Introduces Scientific Concepts**: Observing how ingredients change

when mixed or heated introduces basic science concepts like states of matter and chemical reactions in an engaging context.

- **Teaches Problem-Solving Skills**: Encountering and overcoming challenges in cooking, like adjusting a recipe or fixing a mistake, develops critical thinking and problem-solving abilities.
- **Strengthens Bonds:** Cooking together creates opportunities for meaningful conversations and teamwork, deepening connections through shared moments of creativity and success.
- **Boosts Confidence:** Successfully creating a dish fosters a sense of accomplishment and self-reliance, encouraging children to take on new challenges with confidence.

29

PHOTO BOOTH SHENANIGANS

Transform your living room into a lively photo booth! With a few fun props and a backdrop, you and your child can capture silly, creative photos that will become cherished memories. Imagine the joy on your kid's face as they pick out goofy hats, colorful glasses, and quirky accessories, ready to strike a pose. This activity not only fosters creativity but also brings endless laughter and bonding moments.

As the flash goes off and the camera clicks, you'll find yourselves immersed in a world of fun. Whether you're making funny faces or reenacting scenes from their favorite movies, the shared moments of joy will be priceless. Plus, decorating the backdrop together adds an extra layer of creativity, making the experience even more personal and engaging.

Materials Needed:

- ☐ Camera or smartphone
- ☐ Backdrop (could be a decorated sheet or curtain)
- ☐ Fun props (hats, scarves, glasses, wigs, boas, etc.)
- ☐ Construction paper, markers, and scissors to make DIY props (e.g., mustaches or speech bubbles; optional)
- ☐ Photo booth app or printer (for instant prints; optional)

Step-by-Step Instructions:

1. **Choose a Location:**
   - Select a well-lit area in your home with enough space for posing and moving around. Natural light is ideal, but you can also use lamps to enhance the lighting.
2. **Set Up the Backdrop:**
   - Hang a colorful sheet or curtain in the chosen location to create your backdrop. Secure it with tape, tacks, or a curtain rod to ensure it stays in place throughout the activity.
   - Add decorations to the backdrop to make it more festive and fun. You can use streamers, balloons, banners, or themed decorations depending on the occasion.
3. **Gather Props:**
   - Collect a variety of fun props such as hats, glasses, wigs, and other accessories.
   - **Optional:** Gather some paper, markers, and scissors to make custom props. You and your child can draw and cut out fun accessories like mustaches, speech bubbles, or crowns. This adds an extra layer of creativity and excitement!
   - Arrange the props in a basket or on a table for easy access during the photo session.
4. **Create the Photo Booth Area:**
   - Set up a designated area near the backdrop where you can easily switch props and take photos. Ensure there is enough room for playful movement and different poses.
5. **Position the Camera:**
   - Place the camera or smartphone on a tripod or stable surface to keep it steady.
   - Adjust the angle and distance to capture the entire backdrop and ensure good framing.
6. **Strike a Pose:**
   - Encourage your child to pick their favorite props and maybe even mix and match to create the goofiest look possible.
   - Pick out props for yourself too and let your child suggest what you should wear for the next shot.
   - Set the camera or smartphone on a timer or take turns being the photographer.
   - Strike fun, silly, or creative poses, from funny faces to reenacting

scenes from their favorite movies. Encourage your child to use their imagination—perhaps they want to be a superhero, a movie star, or a pirate!

7. **Review and Edit Photos:**
    - After the photo session, sit together and scroll through the pictures. Pick your favorites, laugh at the funny moments, and talk about which ones to save or print for an instant keepsake.
    - **Optional:** Add fun filters, effects, or frames using editing software or a phone app to make the photos even more personalized.

Safety Considerations:

- Keep cords, cables, and props organized and off the floor to prevent tripping. Use cord covers or tape down loose wires if necessary.

Troubleshooting Tips:

- **Poor Lighting:** Adjust the lighting to avoid shadows and ensure clear photos. Use additional lamps if needed.
- **Blurry Photos:** Use a tripod or a steady surface for the camera to keep it stable. Utilize the camera's timer function to avoid shaking.
- **Prop Overload:** Too many props or decorations can be overwhelming. Simplify the setup to keep the focus on fun and reduce clutter.

Cleanup Tips:

- Gather all props and return them to a designated box or basket. Encourage your child to help sort and put away each item to make cleanup faster.
- If you used a photo booth app, organize and save the photos to a dedicated folder on your device. Delete any unwanted photos to keep your storage space organized.

Variations and Adaptations:

- **Themed Photo Booth:** Choose a specific theme like ninjas, mermaids, or astronauts for your props and backdrop. Decorate accordingly to enhance the theme.
- **Face Painting Fun**: Add face painting to the mix. Paint simple designs or characters on each other's faces before taking photos to add a creative twist.
- **Emoji Expressions:** Try mimicking emoji faces and see who can capture the expressions best. This can lead to lots of giggles and funny photos!
- **Decade Dress-Up**: Choose a decade (like the '60s, '70s, or '80s) and dress up in styles from that era. Play music from the time period to enhance the atmosphere.

- **Silly Costume Relay**: Turn dressing up into a game where you race to put on as many costume pieces as possible within a time limit before snapping a quick photo.
- **Glow-in-the-Dark Party**: Use glow sticks, neon face paint, and black lights to create a glowing photo experience. This works best in a darkened room for maximum effect.
- **Family Heritage Theme**: Incorporate elements from your family's heritage or traditions into the photo booth. Wear traditional clothing or use meaningful props.
- **Comic Strip Series**: Take a series of photos that tell a joke or a funny story, then compile them into a comic strip format.

Benefits:

- **Enhances Creativity:** Designing props, choosing costumes, and inventing poses stimulate your child's imagination and artistic expression.
- **Boosts Confidence:** Performing in front of the camera helps your child become more comfortable expressing themselves, boosting their self-esteem and public speaking skills.
- **Enhances Planning and Organization Skills**: Preparing for the photo booth—gathering props, setting up scenes—develops organizational skills and attention to detail.
- **Strengthens Bonds:** The shared joy of pulling faces, dressing up, and creating silly photos creates moments of laughter and connection, strengthening the bond through lighthearted fun.
- **Enhances Emotional Expression**: Acting out different emotions and characters allows your child to explore and understand various feelings, aiding emotional intelligence.

30

TIME CAPSULE CRAZE

Step into a time-traveling adventure by building a time capsule with your child! Gather items that represent their current interests, achievements, and dreams, and tuck them away for future discovery. Picture the excitement as you both select mementos, write notes to your future selves, and seal them in a container, ready to be unearthed years down the line. This activity is a beautiful way to capture a snapshot of the present while looking forward to the future.

The process of choosing and discussing items to include can spark deep conversations and reflections. Together, you'll decide what memories and hopes to preserve, making this an intimate bonding experience. When the time comes to bury or store the capsule, you'll share a sense of anticipation for the day it will be opened, reconnecting with the past and marveling at how much has changed.

Materials Needed:

- ☐ Sturdy container (metal or plastic)
- ☐ Items to include (photos, letters, toys, etc.)
- ☐ Paper and pens/pencils
- ☐ Sealant or tape for the container
- ☐ Plastic sleeves or resealable plastic bags (optional)
- ☐ Moisture absorbers (e.g., silica gel packets; optional)
- ☐ A shovel (if burying the capsule)

Step-by-Step Instructions:

1. **Select the Container:**
   - Choose a durable container that can withstand time and the elements. Ensure it is large enough to hold all your selected items.
2. **Gather Items:**
   - Collect items that represent current interests, achievements, and memories. This could include photos, small toys, notes, drawings, and other meaningful objects.
   - Encourage your child to think about what items they will find interesting or fun when they open the capsule in the future.
3. **Write Letters:**
   - Write letters to your future selves, including hopes, dreams, and predictions. Encourage your child to share their thoughts and aspirations in their letter.
4. **Seal the Capsule:**
   - Place all the items in the container. For extra protection, consider placing photos or letters in plastic sleeves and adding moisture absorbers, like silica gel packets, to keep the contents dry.
   - Seal the capsule tightly, and label it with a future date to open. Use sealant or tape to ensure the capsule is waterproof and well-protected.
5. **Store or Bury:**
   - Choose a safe place to store or bury the time capsule, ensuring it will be retrievable in the future.
     - If you decide to bury the time capsule, head outside with a shovel and choose a special spot in your backyard. Let your child help dig the hole.
     - If you prefer not to bury it, find a secret place in the house (like a closet or attic) to store the capsule for future discovery.
   - Mark the location or make a note of where the capsule is stored, and agree on a date or event for when you'll open it again.

Safety Considerations:

- If burying the time capsule, choose a location that is safe and free from potential hazards, such as areas with underground utilities or heavy foot traffic. Call utility services to confirm there are no underground cables or pipes where you plan to dig.
- Choose environmentally friendly materials for the container, its contents, and sealants used, especially when burying the time capsule. Opt for biodegradable, recyclable, or safer plastic alternatives whenever possible.

Some plastics, like PET (Polyethylene Terephthalate) and HDPE (High-Density Polyethylene), are more recyclable and have a lower environmental impact compared to others like PVC (Polyvinyl Chloride) and PS (Polystyrene), which can release harmful chemicals and are less eco-friendly.

- Avoid Hazardous Materials: Do not include batteries, electronics with batteries installed, or any items that could leak, corrode, or become hazardous over time.

Troubleshooting Tips:

- **Water Damage:** Use a waterproof sealant to protect the contents from moisture and weather conditions.
- **Potential Item Deterioration**: Include moisture absorbers like silica gel packets and seal photos and papers in plastic sleeves or resealable plastic bags for extra protection.
- **Lost Location:** Mark the burial spot or store a map to avoid losing the capsule. Keep a copy of the map in a safe place.
- **Reluctant to Part with Items**: Reassure your child that the items are not gone forever but will be rediscovered later. Encourage them to choose items they feel comfortable parting with or consider making copies (like photocopies of drawings) to include.
- **Understanding Time**: Young children might struggle with the idea of waiting years to open the capsule. Consider creating a smaller "mini" capsule with a shorter opening date to satisfy curiosity sooner.

Cleanup Tips:

- Ensure that everyone washes their hands after handling the materials, as sealants and adhesives can sometimes cause skin irritation.

Variations and Adaptations:

- **Digital Time Capsule:** Create a digital version using a USB drive or cloud storage. Include photos, videos, voice recordings, and scanned artwork.
- **Themed Capsules:** Focus on specific themes like holidays, birthdays, or family vacations. Include items related to the chosen theme.
- **Annual Capsules:** Make it a yearly tradition to create and store a new time capsule, allowing you to track growth and changes over the years.
- **Soundtrack of Today**: Create a playlist of favorite songs or record your child singing. Music can vividly bring back memories when listened to later.
- **Community Time Capsule**: Collaborate with your child's school or local community to create a larger time capsule. Involving more people can

enhance the experience and teach about collective memory and history.

Benefits:

- **Fosters Reflection:** Encourages thinking about current interests and future aspirations, promoting introspection and self-awareness.
- **Builds Decision-Making Skills**: Selecting meaningful items to include in the capsule teaches children how to make thoughtful choices and prioritize what's most important to them.
- **Teaches Personal Growth**: Revisiting the capsule later allows children to see how much they've grown and changed, reinforcing the importance of personal development over time.
- **Strengthens Bonds:** The collaborative nature of creating a time capsule encourages meaningful conversations and shared experiences between you and your child, deepening emotional connections.
- **Supports Goal-Setting**: Writing letters to their future selves or including predictions helps children practice setting goals, reflecting on their dreams, and evaluating their progress when the capsule is opened.

OUTDOOR FUN

Get ready for outdoor excitement designed for early-elementary explorers! Whether it's setting up a mini golf course in your backyard or creating a bird feeder to attract colorful friends, these activities make the outdoors a playground for creativity and discovery. The adventures range from backyard sports games that get them moving to engaging nature photography sessions, where they capture the beauty of plants, animals, and landscapes through their own lens. Each activity encourages physical play, hands-on creativity, and a deeper connection with nature, creating unforgettable experiences in the fresh air.

31

MINI GOLF MADNESS

Bring the excitement of mini-golf right to your backyard with a DIY miniature golf course. With a variety of household items repurposed as obstacles, you and your child embark on a project to design and build imaginative holes. From creating challenging ramps and tunnels to crafting intricate pathways, each step in setting up the course is an adventure in itself. The anticipation builds as you map out the course, eagerly awaiting the moment when you can finally test your skills.

Once the course is ready, the real fun begins. Taking turns navigating the cleverly designed obstacles, you and your child will delight in the playful competition. Each hole offers a new challenge, and every successful putt is a cause for celebration. The blend of strategic thinking and physical activity makes for an engaging and entertaining experience, turning your backyard into a place of laughter, excitement, and shared enjoyment.

Materials Needed:

- ☐ Toy golf clubs (or a DIY version with sticks or pool noodles)
- ☐ Golf balls or small foam balls
- ☐ Household items for obstacles (boxes, tubes, buckets, etc.)
- ☐ Cups or small containers for targets
- ☐ Chalk or tape to outline holes and boundaries
- ☐ Paper and pen for scorekeeping (optional)

Step-by-Step Instructions:

1. **Plan the Course:**
   - Start by brainstorming with your child how many holes you want to create (start with 3–6 for a manageable course).
   - Let your child suggest ideas for challenges like ramps made from cardboard, tunnels out of boxes, or zig-zag paths marked with chalk.
   - Sketch out the course on a piece of paper, discussing where you'll place obstacles, ramps, and tunnels.
2. **Set Up Obstacles:**
   - Use household items like boxes, books, tubes, and buckets to create obstacles for each hole.
   - Get creative with ramps, tunnels, and tricky turns to make the course more exciting. Encourage your child to add their own imaginative ideas.
   - Tape down any items that may shift during the game, like ramps or small objects.
3. **Mark the Boundaries:**
   - Use chalk or tape to outline the boundaries of each hole and the starting points. This step can involve creating winding paths, straight shots, or tricky turns to keep it interesting.
   - Clearly mark where each hole begins and where the target (cup or container) is located.
4. **Place the Targets:**
   - Place cups or small containers at the end of each playing area to serve as the targets.
   - Ensure they are stable and securely positioned so they don't move or roll away when the ball enters.
5. **Play the Course:**
   - Once the course is built, grab your clubs (or makeshift clubs) and start the game! Take turns trying to navigate each hole by tapping the ball toward the goal, avoiding obstacles along the way.
   - Encourage your child to count how many strokes it takes to sink the ball in the hole and cheer each other on after every successful shot.
   - Encourage your child to experiment with different techniques to overcome obstacles.
6. **Keep Score (Optional):**
   - Keep track of the number of strokes for each hole and see who has

the lowest score at the end.

- Use a simple scorecard to tally up points and declare a winner.

Safety Considerations:

- Teach your child to be mindful of where others are standing before swinging the club, and establish a "no-swing" zone to prevent accidental hits.
- Supervise your child to prevent any rough play or accidents with the golf clubs.
- Ensure your child is wearing appropriate sun protection to prevent sunburn during extended play.

Troubleshooting Tips:

- **Limited Space:** Get creative by designing vertical obstacles or using the same space for multiple holes by reconfiguring the layout after each round.
- **Obstructive Yard Fixtures:** Incorporate immovable yard features like benches, fire pits, or garden beds as creative obstacles for your course. Use ramps and angled surfaces to navigate around or over these features, turning them into exciting challenges.
- **Ball Bouncing Out of Boundaries**: If the ball frequently bounces out of bounds, build barriers along the edges of the course using soft materials like cardboard or pool noodles to keep it in play. Alternatively, set up the course on grass or other soft surfaces to make the game more forgiving if the ball bounces or rolls unexpectedly.
- **Obstacles Too Difficult:** Simplify the course by removing obstacles, reducing the height of ramps or widening tunnels. Keep the game fun by ensuring obstacles match your child's skill level.

Cleanup Tips:

- Turn cleanup into a fun game by assigning points for different tasks—e.g., 5 points for collecting all the golf balls or 10 points for disassembling an obstacle. The goal is to accumulate as many points as possible.

Variations and Adaptations:

- **Ball Swap:** Use different types of balls (tennis balls, rubber balls) to vary the difficulty and add an element of surprise.
- **Themed Course:** Design the course based on a theme, such as "Unicorn Quest", "Alien Invasion", or "Wild West Adventure." Design obstacles and holes that match the theme, using props like sparkly rainbow bridges, space ships, or cowboy hats and cacti to add extra excitement.
- **Obstacle Workshop**: Make part of the fun designing and building the

course itself! Give your child a set of materials and challenge them to build the most creative or difficult obstacle, turning construction into part of the game. For example, paper towel rolls and tape can be used to create winding tunnels.

- **Multilevel Mini Golf**: Get creative with ramps, stools, or boxes to create a multi-level course where the ball moves between different heights. This adds complexity to the game and encourages more strategic thinking.
- **Night Golf:** Turn the course into a nighttime adventure by using glow-in-the-dark balls, paint, and tape to illuminate the obstacles. Add glow sticks or battery-operated lights to enhance the ambiance further.
- **Giant Mini Golf**: Scale up the game by using larger objects for obstacles and balls (like beach balls). Use a broom or large stick as a putter to create a hilarious, larger-than-life mini golf experience.

Benefits:

- **Improves Hand-Eye Coordination**: The act of aiming and hitting the golf ball helps children develop their hand-eye coordination, improving their precision and control.
- **Promotes Creativity**: Building the DIY course encourages children to think creatively, using everyday objects in imaginative ways to design unique obstacles and create fun, engaging challenges.
- **Develops Problem-Solving Skills:** Navigating different obstacles requires children to strategize and think critically about how to best approach each challenge, fostering creative problem-solving abilities.
- **Boosts Focus and Concentration**: Successfully putting the ball into the hole requires concentration and patience, helping children practice their ability to focus on a task for extended periods.
- **Introduces Basic Physics Concepts**: As children play, they naturally start to understand concepts like force, angle, and motion, introducing them to basic principles of physics in a hands-on way.
- **Strengthens Bonds:** Working together to build the course and play the game strengthens bonds by encouraging teamwork, open communication, and joint decision-making throughout the process.
- **Teaches Sportsmanship**: Mini golf provides a fun way to introduce children to the concept of fair play, taking turns, and celebrating others' successes, all of which promote good sportsmanship.

32

SIMPLE BIRDIE BUFFET

Turn your outdoor space into a lively bird sanctuary, where every flutter and chirp brings a new sense of wonder. This delightful activity starts with a simple pinecone, transforming it into a feeder that will attract colorful birds to your yard. Each step is a mix of giggles and concentration, as they eagerly prepare a treat for their feathered friends.

Once the bird feeder is ready, the adventure continues as you search for the perfect spot to hang it. The anticipation builds, and soon, the first birds arrive, creating a scene of natural wonder and discovery right outside your window. Watching the birds enjoy the feeder is a source of endless fascination and delight for your child. This simple project fosters a love for nature and teaches the joy of giving back to the environment, turning a small craft into a gateway to a world of outdoor exploration and appreciation.

Materials Needed:

- ☐ Pinecone
- ☐ Peanut butter (or vegetable shortening for nut allergies)
- ☐ Birdseed
- ☐ Large bowl
- ☐ String or wire
- ☐ Butter knife
- ☐ Scissors or wire cutters
- ☐ Bird identification book or app (e.g., Merlin Bird ID [free]; optional)

Step-by-Step Instructions:

1. **Gather Supplies:**
   - Collect a large pinecone and ensure it's clean and dry.
   - Set up the work area with peanut butter, a bowl of birdseed, and string.
2. **Prepare the Pinecone:**
   - Tie a piece of string or wire around the top of the pinecone to create a hanger.
   - Make sure it's secure and long enough so the feeder can hang easily from a tree branch.
3. **Apply Peanut Butter:**
   - Use a spoon or butter knife to spread peanut butter evenly over the pinecone.
   - Encourage your child to get their hands a little sticky and really press the peanut butter into the crevices.
   - Ensure all the nooks and crannies are covered to hold the birdseed.
4. **Add Birdseed:**
   - Roll the peanut butter-covered pinecone in the bowl of birdseed until it's thoroughly coated.
   - Press the seeds gently to ensure they stick well.
5. **Hang and Observe:**
   - Together, head outside to find the ideal location to hang your bird feeder, preferably near a window for easy viewing.
   - Look for a tree or a spot where birds often visit. Let your child help you pick the spot.
   - Tie the string around a tree branch or hook, securing the bird feeder in place.
   - Watch with your child as birds come to enjoy the feast. You can make this a daily activity, checking back to see which birds visit.
   - Be patient! Birds may find your feeder within a few hours or it might take a day or two. Encourage your child to check back in the mornings or late afternoons, when birds are most active.
   - **Optional:** Add an extra layer of excitement by using a bird identification book or app (such as Merlin Bird ID) to help you and your child discover which species visit your feeder. It's a fun way to learn about your local birdlife while turning birdwatching into an interactive adventure!

Safety Considerations:

- Be mindful of any peanut allergies; use vegetable shortening if necessary.
- Ensure the feeder is hung securely to prevent it from falling.
- Hang bird feeders away from areas frequented by pets to avoid potential conflicts with wildlife.

Troubleshooting Tips:

- **Seeds Not Sticking:** Add more peanut butter to the pinecone for better adhesion and press the birdseed firmly into the sticky surface to help it adhere.
- **No Birds Visiting:** Try moving the feeder to a different location or be patient as birds discover it.
- **Birds Ignoring the Feeder**: Try using a variety of birdseed types to attract different species of birds. Offering seeds like sunflower seeds or millet can appeal to a wider range of birds.
- **Squirrel Trouble:** If squirrels are raiding the feeder, try hanging it in a spot that's harder for them to reach, such as from a high branch with a longer string or using a squirrel baffle to deter them.
- **Unwanted Insects**: If the feeder attracts ants or other insects, try moving it to a different location, preferably away from dense foliage or high-traffic areas for bugs.

Cleanup Tips:

- Lay down a tray, cookie sheet, or newspaper under the work area to catch any spills and make cleanup easier.

Variations and Adaptations:

- **Observation Journal:** Keep a journal with your child to note down the different bird species that visit. Your kiddo can draw birds, note their colors, track how often they visit, and describe their behaviors. They can even add stickers or use binoculars for a more interactive experience.
- **Decorated Feeder:** In addition to birdseed, your child can collect small bits of nature like moss, dried flowers, or twigs to decorate the pinecone feeder, making it a more creative project.
- **Fruit and Nut Mix:** For a more diverse buffet, mix in some small pieces of dried fruit, nuts, or sunflower seeds along with the birdseed.
- **Pinecone Variety Pack**: Instead of using just one type of birdseed, create multiple feeders with different types of seeds to attract a wider variety of birds. Have your child observe which birds are attracted to each feeder.
- **Edible Garland:** String popcorn, cranberries, apple slices, and other bird-

friendly fruits along with the feeder for added bird treats. **Caution:** Avocados are toxic to birds, so do not include them.

- **Peanut Butter Roll**: Use a paper towel or toilet paper roll instead of a pinecone. Have your child spread peanut butter over the roll, roll it in birdseed, and then string it up in the yard for a simple, fun alternative.
- **Recycled Bottle Feeder**: Create a bird feeder using a plastic bottle. Cut openings on the sides, fill it with birdseed, and insert perches made from sticks or pencils.
- **Fruit Cup Feeders**: Hollow out halves of oranges or pineapples, scoop out the insides, and fill them with birdseed. Hang the fruit cups from a tree branch using string or twine. Birds will enjoy the seeds, as well as the leftover fruit.
- **Cookie Cutter Seed Blocks**: Press birdseed and peanut butter into shaped cookie cutters to make birdseed blocks. Let them harden for a bit, then tie a string through them to create fun-shaped feeders that attract birds in a unique way.
- **Birdseed Ice Wreath**: Freeze birdseed, water, and berries in a Bundt pan or round mold to create a birdseed ice wreath. Hang it outside during colder weather and watch as the birds pick at the seeds as the ice slowly melts.

Benefits:

- **Develops Wildlife Knowledge:** Educates children about different bird species, their behaviors, and feeding habits, fostering a deeper understanding of local wildlife and ecosystems.
- **Encourages Creativity**: Decorating and assembling the bird feeder gives children a chance to express their creativity through the choice of materials, design, and placement.
- **Introduces Basic Scientific Concepts**: Observing bird species and their behaviors introduces children to basic concepts of biology, ecology, and environmental science in an accessible way.
- **Strengthens Bonds:** Collaborating to design and create the bird feeder fosters meaningful interactions, allowing for shared moments of learning and fun that deepen emotional connections.
- **Promotes Environmental Awareness:** Instills a sense of responsibility towards nature by encouraging children to actively care for wildlife and understand the importance of conservation.

33

BACKYARD SPORTS SPECTACLE

Get ready for a day of action-packed fun with backyard games that will have you and your little one laughing and cheering. Organize a series of fun and friendly competitions like soccer, sack races, and Frisbee, creating an atmosphere of joy and healthy competition. Imagine the thrill of setting up goals with cones, lining up for a sack race, or perfecting a Frisbee throw. Your backyard becomes a bustling arena where every corner offers a new challenge and every game brings a wave of exhilaration.

As the games unfold, you and your child will find yourselves immersed in the fun of physical activity and the joy of playing together. Cheer each other on, celebrate victories, and learn the art of good sportsmanship along the way. The day culminates in a playful awards ceremony, where homemade medals or simple prizes add a touch of magic to the event. This energetic and engaging day strengthens not just muscles, but also the bond between you and your child, creating memories of fun-filled competition that will last a lifetime.

Materials Needed:

- ☐ Various sports equipment (e.g., soccer ball, Frisbee)
- ☐ Outdoor game equipment (e.g., sacks for racing—old pillowcases work great)
- ☐ Cones or markers for goals
- ☐ Whistle (optional)
- ☐ Stopwatch or timer (optional)
- ☐ Prizes (e.g., stickers, small toys, or homemade medals; optional)

Step-by-Step Instructions:

1. **Plan Activities:**
   - Decide on the games you want to include in your backyard sports day. Some simple ideas could be:
     - **Soccer Match:** Set up a friendly father-child soccer game where you both can dribble, pass, and shoot goals.
     - **Sack Race:** Hop to the finish line while inside a sack or pillowcase—who will win?
     - **Frisbee Throw:** See who can throw the Frisbee the farthest or aim it through a designated target (like between trees or goalposts).
   - Explain each event to your child and let them help decide the order in which you'll compete.
2. **Set Up Stations:**
   - Choose an area in your backyard that is flat and safe for running, jumping, and playing. Clear away any obstacles that could cause tripping.
   - Set up "goals" using cones or markers for soccer. You can also use chairs or other backyard items if cones aren't available.
   - Mark a starting and finish line for the sack race using chalk, tape, or simple visual markers like sticks or shoes.
   - Designate zones for Frisbee throwing or any other games you plan to include. Make sure there's enough space between each activity area.
3. **Play and Compete:**
   - Start with a fun warm-up, like stretching or a short run.
   - Dive into the first event on your schedule. Play each game with enthusiasm and encouragement. Whether it's a competitive soccer match or a silly sack race, be sure to keep the energy high and the laughter flowing.
   - Let your child take turns as the "coach" or referee, giving them a fun sense of responsibility and involvement.
   - Cheer each other on throughout the games and make sure to emphasize fair play and enjoyment over winning.
4. **Keep the Fun Going with Challenges:**
   - For soccer, set up mini-challenges like dribbling around cones or scoring from farther distances.
   - For Frisbee, challenge your child to land it in a specific zone or pass it between two markers.

  - For the sack race, you can try variations like a backwards race or a partner relay where you both race together.

5. **Awards Ceremony:**
  - Celebrate the day with a small awards ceremony. You can give homemade medals, ribbons, or simple prizes (like a special snack or a hand-drawn certificate) to celebrate wins and recognize efforts like "Most Determined Athlete," "Fastest Sack Racer," or "Longest Frisbee Catch."
  - Encourage your child to appreciate the fun and effort more than the results.

Safety Considerations:

- Ensure the play area is safe and free from obstacles that could cause injury.
- Schedule regular water breaks, especially on warm days, to ensure your child stays hydrated and avoids overheating during the physical activities.
- Ensure adequate sun protection with sunscreen and hats during outdoor activities to prevent sunburn.
- Have a basic first aid kit nearby in case of minor scrapes, bumps, or falls during the games, allowing for quick treatment if needed.

Troubleshooting Tips:

- **Uncooperative Weather:** Have a backup plan for indoor games and modify the activities. You can play a mini basketball game with rolled up socks and a laundry hamper or have a paper airplane race inside, ensuring the fun doesn't stop.
- **Different Skill Levels:** Adjust the rules or provide assistance to level the playing field. For example, you can add fun handicaps, like having the more skilled player kick the soccer ball backward!
- **Equipment Malfunctions**: If a Frisbee, ball, or other equipment gets damaged, improvise with items from around the house. A paper plate can serve as a temporary Frisbee, or a sock can be used as a ball for light games.

Cleanup Tips:

- Make cleanup a scavenger hunt by assigning points for finding and collecting left-behind items or trash in the yard.

Variations and Adaptations:

- **Water Games:** On a hot day, turn the event into a water-based competition. Use water balloons for tossing games, have a sponge relay race, or create a slip-and-slide course for a refreshing twist on backyard games.

- **Personal Best Challenges**: Instead of competing against each other, make it all about achieving "personal bests" in various activities—like the farthest Frisbee throw, fastest 100-meter dash, or most consecutive jumps. Each player tries to beat their own record throughout the day.
- **Cultural Sports:** Introduce games from different cultures, such as bocce ball, cricket, or petanque, to add variety and educational value.
- **Sports Tournament with a Twist**: Organize a mini sports tournament, but with unusual rules for each game. For example, play soccer with only your non-dominant foot or have a Frisbee toss where players must spin before each throw.
- **Sports Day Undercover**: Introduce secret challenges for each event. Before starting the day, secretly write down additional bonus objectives (e.g., "throw the ball underhand" or "finish the race in slow motion"). Reveal them only when the game starts to add an element of surprise and creativity.
- **Fitness Circuit:** Set up a series of fitness stations with activities like jumping jacks, sit-ups, and push-ups to create a fun workout routine.
- **Trick Shot Challenge**: Have a special event where you try creative trick shots with Frisbees, balls, or bean bags. Set up crazy obstacles, like shooting through hoops, bouncing off walls, or hitting moving targets. Bonus points for style!
- **Double Dare Challenge**: For each game, add a fun and messy challenge halfway through, like running with whipped cream on your head or hopping through a small pool of water.
- **DIY Trophy Craft**: Before the games begin, have a craft session with your child to make trophies or medals from recyclables or craft materials. Award them at the end of the sports spectacle to celebrate each event.

Benefits:

- **Promotes Physical Fitness:** Engaging in a variety of sports and physical challenges boosts endurance, strength, coordination, and flexibility, helping children develop a healthy and active lifestyle.
- **Encourages Healthy Competition:** Encourages a healthy competitive spirit, helping children learn to compete and strive for improvement.
- **Builds Sportsmanship:** Teaches the importance of fair play, respect, and graciousness in both victory and defeat.
- **Strengthens Bonds**: The collaborative and competitive nature of the games fosters meaningful connections between you and your child, deepening emotional bonds as you work together, cheer each other on, and celebrate achievements.

- **Boosts Confidence:** Successfully completing challenges or learning new sports skills builds a child's confidence, helping them feel proud of their abilities and willing to take on new challenges.

34

NATURE PHOTOGRAPHY ESCAPADE

Introduce your child to the art of photography with a delightful nature photo session. Equip them with a simple camera or smartphone and set off on an adventure through your backyard, a local park, or a nearby nature trail. Each step is filled with excitement and discovery as your child learns to observe the world through the lens, capturing the beauty of plants, animals, and landscapes. The process of framing a shot and choosing subjects becomes a creative journey, fostering an appreciation for nature's intricate details.

As you review the photos together, the conversation flows with reflections on what they captured and why. Celebrate their unique perspective and encourage them to experiment with different angles and lighting. This activity not only nurtures creativity but also deepens their connection to the natural world. Each photograph becomes a memory, a moment frozen in time, and a testament to the shared experience of exploring and appreciating the beauty around you. Nature photography turns a simple walk into a rich, educational adventure filled with artistic expression and bonding.

Materials Needed:

- ☐ Simple camera or smartphone
- ☐ Comfortable walking shoes
- ☐ Water, snacks, and sun protection (for extended outings)
- ☐ Notebook and pencil (for notes; optional)
- ☐ Tripod (optional)
- ☐ Bug repellent (optional)

Step-by-Step Instructions:

1. **Choose a Camera:**
   - Select a simple camera or smartphone with a good camera function for your child to use. If possible, strap it to a lanyard or provide a small case to make it easier to carry.
   - Ensure the device has enough battery life and storage space for photos.
2. **Start Your Adventure:**
   - Visit your backyard, a local park, or a nature trail. Opt for a spot with varied plants, trees, and maybe even a few animals.
   - Encourage your child to take their time as they look around for interesting subjects. Remind them to notice details they might normally miss—like tiny flowers, insects, or the way the sunlight filters through the trees.
   - Invite your child to jot down simple notes or sketch drawings about their observations, the locations of interesting subjects, and any thoughts they have about the shots they want to capture.
   - Teach your little one to avoid touching or disturbing wildlife while taking photographs.
3. **Take Photos:**
   - Show your child how to frame a shot, focusing on their chosen subject.
   - As your child snaps pictures, encourage them to try different angles—lying on the ground for a bug's-eye view, looking up at the trees, or getting close-up shots of leaves and flowers.
   - You can join the fun by taking a few pictures yourself, showing your child how you frame certain scenes. This can lead to a conversation about what you each find fascinating and why.
4. **Review and Reflect:**
   - After your walk, sit down together and scroll through the photos. Ask your child to explain what inspired them to capture each shot, encouraging reflection and conversation about their creative choices.
   - Highlight the unique elements of their photos, such as interesting lighting, textures, or composition. Praise their artistic eye and encourage them to keep experimenting next time.
   - Once back home, print out some of the photos or use a digital device to create a slideshow. Let your child pick their favorite shots to display on the fridge or in a special album.

Safety Considerations:

- Be mindful of any plant or insect allergies and avoid areas that may trigger them.
- Supervise your child closely to prevent wandering off or accidents.
- Ensure your child stays hydrated, especially on longer outings.
- If you anticipate being out for an extended period or exploring remote areas, carry a basic first aid kit and have an emergency plan in place. Know the nearest location to seek help if needed. Keep a charged mobile phone and inform someone of your location and expected return time.
- Be mindful of potential hazards such as steep slopes, poisonous plants, bodies of water, and dangerous wildlife, and supervise closely in these areas.
- If you're exploring areas with tall grass or wooded regions, regularly check for ticks during and after the activity. Promptly and properly remove any that are found. Wear long sleeves and tuck pants into socks to minimize exposure.

Troubleshooting Tips:

- **Blurry Photos:** Teach your child to hold the camera steady by keeping elbows close to their body, bracing against a solid surface, or using a tripod if available.
- **Uncooperative Subjects:** Encourage patience when photographing animals or wait for better lighting conditions for plants and landscapes.
- **Uncooperative Weather:** If the weather turns bad, bring nature inside by photographing houseplants, flowers, or even natural objects like shells or rocks. If you prefer to wait out the weather, seize the opportunity to capture post-rain reflections, snowflakes, or interesting light patterns as the weather clears, turning the conditions into a creative opportunity.

Cleanup Tips:

- Opt for eco-friendly and biodegradable materials to minimize environmental impact. Bring reusable bags to easily collect and carry waste, making cleanup more efficient.
- Collect all trash or packaging materials you brought along, and gather any litter you come across to leave the environment clean and pristine.
- Take a final walk around your photography area before leaving to ensure no items or litter have been left behind.
- Make cleanup a fun and educational activity by involving your child. Turn it into a mini scavenger hunt to teach them the importance of environmental stewardship.

Variations and Adaptations:

- **Photo Themes:** Choose themes like "Close-ups," "Colors of Nature," or "Textures" for focused photo sessions.
- **Seasonal Photo Collage**: Encourage your child to take photos of nature in different seasons, then create a collage showing how the landscape changes over time. This teaches them about the cycles of nature.
- **Animal Action Shots**: If possible, encourage your child to capture animals in motion—birds flying, squirrels climbing, or insects moving—teaching them patience and observation in photography.
- **Photo Story Sequence**: Turn the outing into a storytelling challenge. Ask your child to capture a series of photos that tell a story, like the journey of a leaf falling from a tree or the life of a flower throughout the day.
- **Reflection Photography**: Introduce your child to the art of reflection photography by finding ponds, lakes, or even puddles to capture mirrored images of trees, skies, or themselves.
- **Editing Fun:** Teach your child basic photo editing techniques, such as cropping and adjusting brightness and contrast, using free apps or software.

Benefits:

- **Encourages Creativity:** Nature photography allows children to express themselves artistically by experimenting with angles, framing, and lighting, fostering their creative thinking and aesthetic appreciation.
- **Enhances Observation Skills:** Capturing specific subjects through photography trains children to pay close attention to details, honing their ability to observe small elements in nature like textures, colors, and patterns.
- **Improves Organizational Skills**: Planning which subjects to photograph and deciding how to capture them helps children develop organizational skills, learning to prioritize tasks and arrange their approach logically.
- **Strengthens Bonds:** Sharing the experience of exploring nature and reviewing photos together strengthens the bond between you and your child, encouraging communication and collaboration.
- **Encourages Exploration and Discovery**: Photography motivates children to explore their surroundings in search of interesting subjects, inspiring a sense of curiosity and wonder about the world around them.

35

BACKYARD CAMPING GETAWAY

Create an unforgettable adventure by transforming your outdoor space into a cozy campsite perfect for a night filled with wonder and discovery. Set up a tent together and fill it with sleeping bags and cushions, crafting a snug retreat that brings all the excitement of camping right to your home. As you gather around a portable fire pit to toast marshmallows, giggles and warmth fill the night air, with each glowing ember, each whispered tale bringing an element of enchantment to the evening.

The night is packed with classic camping activities, like telling captivating stories, playing flashlight tag, and singing familiar campfire songs. Wrapped in blankets and surrounded by the comforting sounds of the evening, you'll experience a perfect blend of adventure and convenience, where each shared moment turns into a lasting memory filled with wonder, laughter, and the simple joys of being together.

Materials Needed:

- ☐ Tent and sleeping bags
- ☐ Portable fire pit (many affordable options available online or at big box retailers)
- ☐ Roasting goodies (foil-packets, veggie skewers, bananas)
- ☐ Roasting skewers (metal forks, tongs, and wooden chopsticks work too!)
- ☐ Marshmallows, graham crackers, and chocolate for s'mores (optional, but delicious)
- ☐ Flashlights or lanterns
- ☐ Camping chairs or blankets
- ☐ Bug repellant (optional)

Step-by-Step Instructions:

1. **Set Up Camp:**
   - Start by setting up your tent in a flat, open area of the backyard. Let your child help with assembling the poles and arranging the sleeping bags inside.
   - Bring out extra blankets and pillows to make the tent cozy and comfortable. Invite your child to arrange their space inside the tent however they'd like—it's their own little camping haven!
   - Set up camping chairs or blankets around the tent for a cozy seating area.
2. **Campfire Fun:**
   - Gather marshmallows, graham crackers, and chocolate for making s'mores, along with any other snacks and meals you plan to prepare during your camping adventure.
   - Set up a portable fire pit or use a grill for your "campfire." This is a perfect time to teach your child about fire safety.
   - Show your child how to safely roast marshmallows over the fire using skewers (or improvised skewers). Let them assemble their own s'mores and enjoy the sticky, delicious fun together!
   - Prepare your other chosen meals or snacks over the fire, then sit back and enjoy your tasty creations together under the stars (see the end of this activity for simple yet delicious campfire recipes, like Banana Boats and Campfire Nachos).
3. **Enjoy Camping Activities:**
   - Gather around the fire and share stories, either classic campfire tales or your own made-up adventures. Let your child take a turn telling a story too!
   - Use flashlights for fun shadow games, flashlight tag, or a nighttime scavenger hunt.
   - Play classic campfire games like "I Spy" or "20 Questions."
   - Sing some classic campfire songs together—songs like "The Lion Sleeps Tonight," "She'll Be Coming 'Round the Mountain," "Bingo" (B-I-N-G-O), or any family favorites.
4. **Tuck Into the Tent:**
   - When you're ready to settle down, climb into the tent and get cozy. Share a few more stories or talk about the fun things you did during the day before drifting off to sleep.

Safety Considerations:

- Check your local ordinances and regulations regarding making fires in the backyard to ensure compliance with fire safety guidelines.
- Teach your child fire safety rules before starting the fire—like staying a certain distance away, not throwing items into the fire, and using fire responsibly, especially when roasting marshmallows. Always supervise your child around the fire.
- Keep a bucket of water or a fire extinguisher nearby when using a portable fire pit.
- If you have pets, make sure they are kept away from the fire and any small camping tools.
- Ensure the fire is completely extinguished and the area is safe before leaving it unattended.

Troubleshooting Tips:

- **Uncooperative Weather:** Have a backup plan ready in case of bad weather. Move the camping setup indoors to the living room or a covered porch to keep the adventure going. You can still enjoy activities like storytelling and campfire games to maintain the camping spirit.
- **Child Scared of the Dark**: If your child feels uneasy in the dark, use soft lanterns or string lights around the campsite for extra comfort. Keeping flashlights close by should also help them feel more secure.
- **Difficulty Sleeping**: If your child is having trouble falling asleep outdoors, encourage them to listen to the calming night sounds (like crickets or the breeze) and tell a soothing bedtime story to help them relax.
- **Noise from Neighbors**: If outside noise (like neighbors or street sounds) disrupts the camping mood, try playing ambient nature sounds on a speaker to create a calming, immersive atmosphere.

Cleanup Tips:

- Make cleanup a game by assigning roles like "Chief Organizer" and "Master Collector" to make it feel like a mission.
- Practice leave-no-trace principles with your child by packing out all trash, including food wrappers and biodegradable waste.
- Dispose of campfire ashes in designated fire pits or bins following local regulations and guidelines.

Variations and Adaptations:

- **Themed Camping:** Create themes like "Jungle Safari" "Pirate Adventure," or "Space Camp" for added fun. Decorate the campsite to match the theme, and incorporate themed activities like storytelling, costumes, or themed games.

- **Tent Decorating:** Let your child decorate the tent using whatever they like—fairy lights, nature items they collect, or even their favorite toys and crafts—to create a cozy, one-of-a-kind camping hideaway.
- **Outdoor Craft Station:** Gather leaves, twigs, and stones to make simple nature-inspired crafts like leaf rubbings, pinecone animals, or twig sculptures, adding a creative touch to the camping night.
- **Nature Detective**: Turn the camping night into a nature detective adventure. Equip your child with a magnifying glass, flashlight, and notebook, and go on a night-time exploration to observe plants, insects, and nocturnal animals.
- **Breakfast Outdoors:** Extend the adventure with a simple outdoor breakfast the next morning. Set up a picnic-style meal with fresh fruit, cereal, or pancakes, and savor the morning air while reflecting on the night's camping experience.

Benefits:

- **Provides a Digital Detox:** Encourages time away from screens and technology, promoting face-to-face interactions and outdoor enjoyment.
- **Inspires Adventure:** The adventure of camping, even in the backyard, sparks curiosity and a love for exploration and discovery.
- **Encourages Outdoor Play:** The activity inspires a love for the outdoors by creating an adventure in your own backyard, encouraging children to spend more time outside and develop a positive relationship with nature.
- **Strengthens Bonds:** Spending an immersive night camping together fosters deep connection, creating meaningful conversations, shared experiences, and lasting memories that strengthen the parent-child relationship.
- **Encourages Teamwork and Cooperation**: Setting up the campsite and working together on camping tasks teaches children the value of cooperation and teamwork, strengthening their ability to work alongside others toward a shared goal.

Campfire Nachos

Campfire nachos are a fun and easy-to-make camping treat where you layer tortilla chips with cheese, beans, veggies, and other toppings, then heat them over a campfire until the cheese is melted and everything is warm. They're completely customizable, so you and your child can each create your own unique version. Here's a basic idea of how to make them:

Ingredients:

- ☐ Tortilla chips
- ☐ Shredded cheese
- ☐ Black beans or refried beans
- ☐ Diced tomatoes
- ☐ Sliced jalapeños
- ☐ Corn
- ☐ Diced onions
- ☐ Olives
- ☐ Salsa
- ☐ Sour cream
- ☐ Guacamole
- ☐ Any other favorite nacho toppings

Instructions:

1. **Prepare the Foil:**
   - Tear off a large piece of heavy-duty aluminum foil. Lay it flat and slightly fold up the edges to create a shallow tray.
2. **Layer Ingredients:**
   - Place a layer of tortilla chips on the foil. Add layers of cheese, beans, and your desired toppings. Repeat until you have several layers.
3. **Seal the Packet:**
   - Fold the foil over the top of the nachos to create a sealed packet. Make sure the edges are tightly sealed to prevent any ingredients from spilling out.
4. **Cook:**
   - Place the foil packet on the campfire grill or on hot coals. Cook for about 10-15 minutes, or until the cheese is melted and the toppings are heated through.
5. **Serve:**
   - Carefully remove the foil packet from the fire (use oven mitts). Open the packet and enjoy your campfire nachos.

Campfire Popcorn:

For a classic campfire snack that's both fun to make and delicious to eat, try making Campfire Popcorn. This simple treat requires just a few ingredients and can be prepared right over the fire. The aroma of fresh popcorn popping and the thrill of opening the foil packet to reveal perfectly popped kernels make this a favorite for all ages. Customize it with your favorite seasonings for a tasty, crunchy snack that's perfect for any camping adventure.

Ingredients:

- ☐ Popcorn kernels
- ☐ Oil (vegetable or canola)
- ☐ Salt or other seasonings

Instructions:

1. **Prepare the Foil Packet:**
   - Tear off a large piece of heavy-duty aluminum foil. Add a tablespoon of oil and a handful of popcorn kernels. Fold the foil into a loose packet, leaving enough room for the popcorn to pop.
2. **Cook:**
   - Place the foil packet on the campfire grill or hot coals. Shake the packet occasionally. Cook until the popping slows down.
3. **Season and Serve:**
   - Carefully open the packet (be cautious of steam), season with salt or your favorite seasonings, and enjoy.

Banana Boats:

For a fun and delicious campfire dessert, try making Banana Boats. This easy treat combines gooey chocolate and marshmallows with the natural sweetness of bananas, creating a decadent combination that's perfect for any camping night. Banana Boats are simple to prepare and can be customized with your favorite toppings, making them a hit with both kids and adults alike.

Ingredients:

- ☐ Bananas
- ☐ Chocolate chips or small chocolate pieces
- ☐ Mini marshmallows
- ☐ Crushed graham crackers or your favorite nuts (optional)

Instructions:

1. **Prepare the Bananas:**
   - Slice each banana lengthwise, being careful not to cut all the way through. Open the banana slightly to create a pocket.
2. **Fill the Bananas:**
   - Stuff the pocket with chocolate chips and mini marshmallows. You can also add crushed graham crackers or nuts if you like.
3. **Wrap in Foil:**
   - Wrap each banana in aluminum foil.
4. **Roast:**
   - Place the foil-wrapped bananas on the campfire grill or directly on hot coals. Roast for about 10 minutes, or until the chocolate and marshmallows are melted and the banana is warm and soft.
5. **Enjoy:**
   - Carefully unwrap the foil and enjoy your gooey, sweet banana boat.

LATE-ELEMENTARY

TRAILBLAZERS

INDOOR ADVENTURES

Indoor activities for late-elementary trailblazers are all about creativity, curiosity, and exploration! This section includes a Literary Adventure Lab that unleashes the inner author, Shake-and-Make Ice Cream for delicious DIY fun, and the Artisan Soap Craft Central that lets them become creative chemists. Whether crafting a custom board game, experimenting with soap making, or enjoying a Mystery Box Challenge, these activities are designed to build skills, inspire creativity, and foster a sense of accomplishment—all while sharing memorable experiences together.

36

LITERARY ADVENTURE LAB

Unleash your child's inner author with a creative writing workshop right at home. This activity is perfect for sparking imagination and honing writing skills. Imagine the excitement in your child's eyes as they sit down with a fresh notebook or their favorite tablet, ready to transform their ideas into words. Provide fun prompts like "A day in the life of a superhero" or "The secret door in the attic," and watch their creativity flow as they craft short stories, poems, or even comic strips. This workshop becomes a magical space where their thoughts come to life, and the joy of storytelling takes center stage.

As they write, you'll find the room filled with the sounds of scribbling pens or the click-clack of a keyboard, each moment a step in their creative journey. Share and discuss their creations together, offering positive feedback and constructive suggestions to boost their confidence and improve their storytelling abilities. The sense of accomplishment they feel as they read their work aloud is unmatched, fostering a love for writing that goes beyond the workshop. This activity not only encourages creative expression but also enhances literacy and communication skills, all within a fun, supportive environment where their imagination can soar.

Materials Needed:

- ☐ Notebook, paper, laptop or tablet
- ☐ Pens, pencils, or stylus (if using a tablet)
- ☐ Writing prompts or themes
- ☐ Colored pencils, markers, or stickers for decoration (optional)

Step-by-Step Instructions:

1. **Provide Prompts:**
   - Start by brainstorming fun and exciting prompts together. You can write down some ideas on paper or let your child choose from options like "A day in the life of a superhero" or "If animals could talk."
   - Suggest different types of writing methods they can explore, such as short stories, poems, plays, or even song lyrics.
2. **Write and Create:**
   - Encourage your child to start writing based on the provided prompt, letting their imagination guide them. Remind them that their first draft doesn't need to be perfect—just get their ideas down on paper or the screen.
   - Sit nearby and offer gentle guidance and support, offering help with spelling, grammar, and developing ideas if asked. You can ask questions like, "What happens next?" or "How does your character feel?" to keep their ideas flowing.
   - If your child gets stuck, suggest adding more details to the story, like describing what the characters see, hear, or feel.
   - Promote a positive and encouraging atmosphere, celebrating their effort and creativity throughout the process.
3. **Take Breaks to Share and Discuss:**
   - After writing for a while, take a short break and ask your child to read what they've written so far. Be sure to show excitement and curiosity about their story.
   - Offer positive feedback first, focusing on what you love about their story. Then, if appropriate, provide gentle suggestions like, "What if the character had a surprising twist in the story?" to help them improve their writing skills.
4. **Add the Final Touches:**
   - Once the story is finished, let your child decorate the pages with illustrations, stickers, or colorful doodles if they wish. If using a tablet or laptop, they can add digital drawings or pictures to enhance their story.
   - If your child enjoys performance, invite them to read their story aloud in a fun and engaging way, using different voices for characters.
5. **Celebrate the Accomplishment:**
   - After finishing the writing and any illustrations, celebrate the creation! You can create a "literary corner" where your child's story is displayed on a special shelf or framed, or compile it into a family storybook for

future reading.

Safety Considerations:

- To keep those creative juices flowing without any eye strain, try the 20-20-20 rule: every 20 minutes, take a 20-second break to look at something 20 feet away. It's a simple way to give your eyes a little rest, especially when working on digital devices.

Troubleshooting Tips:

- **Writer's Block:** Offer additional prompts or story starters if your child gets stuck. You can also encourage brainstorming or use visual aids like pictures or toys to spark creativity.
- **Short Attention Span**: If your child loses focus, break the activity into shorter sessions with mini-goals. Incorporating movement breaks or switching to a different type of writing, like drawing comic strips, can help keep their attention.
- **Confidence Issues:** Remind them that there are no wrong answers in creative writing; it's all about expressing their unique ideas.
- **Too Focused on Perfection**: If your child is hesitant to finish because they want their story to be perfect, encourage them to complete a rough draft first. Remind them that they can always edit and revise later.

Cleanup Tips:

- If your child used a tablet or computer, create a special folder to store their stories. Make sure to back up their work on cloud storage or an external drive, so their creations are safe and easily accessible.

Variations and Adaptations:

- **Word Limit Challenge**: Give your child a word limit (e.g., a 100-word story). This helps them practice being concise and encourages creativity as they work within constraints.
- **Story Dice Roll**: Create or use pre-made story dice with pictures of characters, settings, and plot points. Have your child roll the dice to randomly generate story elements and challenge them to create a story based on what they roll.
- **Collaborative Story:** Take turns writing with your child. You can write one sentence or paragraph, and they write the next. This can lead to unexpected twists and adds a fun, collaborative element to the storytelling process.
- **Sensory Story Writing**: Encourage your child to focus on sensory details by having them incorporate elements of sight, sound, touch, taste, and smell into their story. This adds depth to their descriptions and makes the

stories more immersive.

- **Found Object Story Prompts**: Gather random household objects or toys and have your child pick a few to incorporate into their story. This challenges them to think creatively and weave unusual items into their narrative.
- **Interactive Story Adventure**: Turn the story into a "Choose Your Own Adventure" format, where your child writes multiple possible paths or endings. This allows them to explore different outcomes and add an element of surprise to their storytelling.
- **Reverse Storytelling**: Start with the end of the story, and challenge your child to write the events that led to that ending. This unique twist helps them think critically about plot structure and cause and effect.

Benefits:

- **Enhances Literacy Skills:** Through regular practice, children develop better sentence structure, grammar, and vocabulary, helping them become more confident and articulate writers.
- **Promotes Reading Comprehension**: Engaging in storytelling helps children better understand narrative structure, character development, and themes, improving their ability to comprehend and analyze what they read.
- **Encourages Self-Expression**: Writing gives children an outlet to express their thoughts, feelings, and ideas, fostering emotional development and helping them articulate their inner world.
- **Builds Confidence:** Sharing and discussing their work gives children a sense of accomplishment, reinforcing their self-confidence and pride in their creative abilities.
- **Strengthens Communication:** As they share and discuss their stories, children learn how to express their ideas clearly and effectively, improving both their oral and written communication skills.
- **Strengthens Bonds:** Collaborating on story ideas, offering feedback, and discussing their creations fosters open communication and shared creative experiences, deepening the emotional connection through meaningful interaction.
- **Boosts Critical Thinking**: Crafting a story requires logical thinking as children must consider plot progression, character motivation, and cause-and-effect relationships, helping them think critically and make connections.

Instant Inspiration: Writing Prompts to Get You Started

Every story needs a spark! These prompts are here to help, giving you a ready-made springboard to kick off your child's storytelling journey.

1. **A Mysterious Message:** Imagine finding a mysterious message in a bottle on the beach. What does it say, and who is it from?
2. **A Visit to Another Planet:** Describe a trip to an alien planet. What do you see, who do you meet, and what adventures do you have?
3. **Time Travel Trouble:** Write about a time machine that goes haywire, sending you to unexpected places in history.
4. **The Magic Pen:** Write about discovering a pen that brings anything you draw to life. What do you create, and what happens next?
5. **Life as a Pet:** Imagine waking up as your pet for a day. What adventures do you experience from their perspective?
6. **The Day Everything Changed:** Describe a day when something extraordinary happens, altering your everyday life.
7. **The Robot Helper:** Write a story about a robot built to help with everyday tasks. What goes right and what goes wrong?
8. **The Mysterious Neighbor:** Describe the strange activities of a new neighbor who might be a secret agent, a wizard, or something else entirely.
9. **The Floating City:** Imagine a city that floats in the sky. What is life like there, and how do people travel between the floating city and the ground?
10. **A Letter from the Future:** Write a letter to your future self and then imagine receiving a response back.
11. **The Inventor's Workshop:** Create a story about a young inventor who creates something amazing that changes their world.
12. **A World Without Rules:** Envision a world where there are no rules. How does it function, and what are the consequences?
13. **The Enchanted Object:** Write a story about discovering an everyday object that has magical properties. What powers does it have, and how do you use it?
14. **The Secret Society:** Imagine you find an invitation to join a secret society. What is their purpose, and what adventures do you have as a new member?

Challenge Prompt

#15: The Mysterious Melody

One day, you discover a strange, old music box in your attic that plays a mysterious melody you've never heard before. Every time you wind it up, the music changes slightly and reveals a new clue about a hidden secret. What secrets does the music box hold, and where do the clues lead you?

Example:

As you wind up the music box, it begins to play a soft, enchanting melody. You notice that the melody contains a sequence of notes that seem familiar, almost like a pattern you've heard before. Intrigued, you decide to play the melody again, but this time, you record the sequence of notes.

Clue through Musical Notes: You carefully transcribe the notes onto a piece of paper and realize that the sequence spells out a message using musical notation. For instance, the notes C, A, B, and B correspond to the letters C, A, B, and B, spelling out "CAB." You start to wonder if "CAB" is a clue, perhaps leading you to a taxi service, a location, or even an acronym for something important.

Clue through Lyrics: On another occasion, as the melody plays, you hear faint, whispering lyrics accompanying the tune. The lyrics are cryptic, mentioning a "hidden key beneath the old oak tree." You realize that the music box might be guiding you to a physical location where something is hidden.

Clue through Rhythm Patterns: You notice that the rhythm of the melody changes every time you play it. One night, the rhythm mimics the Morse code pattern for "SOS." This pattern leads you to believe that someone or something is calling for help, prompting you to investigate further.

These are just a few examples of how the music box could reveal clues through its melodies. Each clue can be designed to lead the protagonist on a new part of their adventure, making the story engaging and full of surprises.

37

SHAKE-AND-MAKE ICE CREAM

Who needs an ice cream maker when you can whip up delicious, creamy ice cream with just a few simple ingredients and some good old-fashioned elbow grease? The excitement begins as you mix the heavy cream, sugar, and vanilla, watching with anticipation as the ingredients come together. As you start shaking the bag, the kitchen fills with laughter and eager anticipation.

The real reward comes when the ice cream solidifies, and you scoop out the creamy goodness. Each bite is a testament to your teamwork and patience, enhanced by the delightful addition of mix-ins like chocolate chips or sprinkles. Sharing this homemade treat not only satisfies sweet cravings but also creates a sense of accomplishment and joy, turning an ordinary day into a delicious, refreshing memory.

Materials Needed:

- ☐ 1 cup heavy cream or half-and-half
- ☐ 3 tablespoons sugar
- ☐ 1/2 - 1 teaspoon vanilla extract
- ☐ Ice
- ☐ 1/3 cup salt (rock salt or table salt)
- ☐ 1 gallon-sized resealable plastic bag (heavy duty, name brand)
- ☐ 1 quart-sized resealable plastic bag (can use two gallon bags instead if quart size is not available)
- ☐ Towels or oven mitts (for shaking)
- ☐ Toppings or mix-ins (e.g., chocolate chips, crushed cookies, sprinkles, fruit pieces; optional)
- ☐ Ice cream cones (optional)

Step-by-Step Instructions:

1. **Prepare the Ingredients:**
   - Ensure you use high quality, name brand resealable bags to prevent leaks.
   - In the quart-sized bag, combine the heavy cream, sugar, and vanilla extract.
   - Seal the bag tightly, ensuring there is no trapped air inside.
2. **Prepare the Ice Bag:**
   - Fill the gallon-sized bag halfway with ice.
   - Add 1/2 cup of rock salt (or table salt) to the ice. Let your child help with this step by measuring out the salt. Explain that salt lowers the freezing point of ice, which makes it melt but also absorb more heat from the surroundings—helping the ice cream freeze faster—an early science lesson in action!
3. **Combine the Bags:**
   - Place the sealed quart-sized bag inside the gallon-sized bag with ice and salt.
   - Seal the gallon-sized bag tightly.
   - Make sure both bags are sealed properly, especially the small one, so no saltwater leaks into the ice cream mixture.
4. **Shake, Shake, Shake:**
   - Now comes the fun part! Wrap the large bag in a towel or have your child wear oven mitts to protect their hands from the cold. Shake the bag vigorously for about 5–10 minutes. The more shaking, the faster the ice cream will form!
   - Encourage your child to take turns with you, making it a team effort. You can even turn it into a fun game by shaking to the beat of a song or having a little dance-off while shaking.
5. **Serve and Enjoy:**
   - Once the ice cream is ready, carefully remove the small bag from the ice and salt mixture.
   - Wipe off any saltwater from the outside of the bag before opening.
   - For an extra touch of decadence, offer mix-ins like chocolate chips, nuts, or fruit to customize their ice cream creation. Add them to the bag, reseal, and gently knead the ice cream until evenly distributed.
   - Let your child help scoop out the creamy goodness into bowls.
   - Sit down together and enjoy the fruits of your labor! Share a high-five

over your delicious creation and savor every bite, celebrating the fun you had making it together!

Safety Considerations:

- Use towels or oven mitts to shake the bag, as the salt can lower the temperature of the ice, making the bag extremely cold and potentially causing discomfort or mild frostbite if held for too long.

Troubleshooting Tips:

- **Ice Cream Not Hardening:** Add more salt to lower the temperature of the ice, which helps the mixture freeze faster. Also, ensure you're shaking the bag for the full recommended time (about 5-10 minutes).
- **Leaking Bags:** Double-check the seals on both bags to prevent leaks and salt mixing with the ice cream. For added security, double-bag the inner mixture or use a more durable bag. If leaks occur, transfer the mixture to a new bag and continue shaking.
- **Not Enough Ice Cream:** If you need more ice cream, you can easily double or triple the recipe. Just ensure you have enough ice and salt to maintain the freezing process effectively.

Cleanup Tips:

- Safely dispose of the ice and salt mixture. Do not pour it down the sink as it can be too cold and salty for pipes. Instead, let it melt completely and then pour it into a drain.

Variations and Adaptations:

- **Plant-Based Version:** Replace the heavy cream with full-fat coconut milk or another plant-based milk for a dairy-free option.
- **Healthier Option:** Substitute heavy cream with Greek yogurt or regular yogurt for a tangy, lighter version of ice cream. Mix in honey, granola, or fresh fruits for a healthy twist.
- **Ice Cream Sandwiches**: Once the ice cream is ready, scoop it between two cookies or graham crackers to create homemade ice cream sandwiches.
- **Flavor Explosion:** Experiment with different extracts or syrups for unique flavors like mint, almond, or hazelnut.
- **Savory Ice Cream**: For an adventurous twist, try savory flavors like adding a small pinch of sea salt and drizzling olive oil or balsamic glaze for a more gourmet, experimental version.
- **Simon Says Shake**: Add a fun twist by incorporating "Simon Says" into the shaking process. For example, "Simon says shake the bag while spinning in a circle" or "Simon says shake it above your head."

- **Ice Cream Math:** Make the process educational by incorporating math into the measuring and mixing. Have your child practice fractions by adjusting the recipe for larger or smaller portions, or turn it into a game where they must solve simple math problems to "unlock" the next ingredient.
- **International Ice Cream**: Research how ice cream is made or served in different countries, and try to recreate a version inspired by a specific culture's tradition, like Italian gelato, Japanese mochi, or Turkish dondurma.
- **Ice Cream Tasting Journal**: After making different batches or variations, have your child keep an "ice cream journal" where they rate the flavors, textures, and favorite mix-ins. This encourages critical thinking and helps them reflect on their creations.

Benefits:

- **Boosts Patience and Persistence**: The shaking process requires persistence and patience as children wait for the mixture to freeze, helping them understand the value of effort in achieving a reward.
- **Teaches Scientific Concepts**: Making ice cream provides a hands-on way to learn about freezing points and states of matter, giving kids a fun and memorable introduction to science.
- **Encourages Physical Activity**: The act of vigorously shaking the bag keeps children physically active, turning the kitchen into a space for movement while creating a delicious treat.
- **Strengthens Bonds**: Collaborating to measure, shake, and mix the ingredients fosters teamwork, while the shared reward of enjoying the ice cream together strengthens emotional connections through fun and accomplishment.
- **Improves Math Skills:** Measuring ingredients introduces children to practical math skills, like understanding fractions and proportions, in a fun and hands-on way.

38

ARTISAN SOAP CRAFT CENTRAL

Channel your inner artisan and embark on a soap-making adventure right in your kitchen! This DIY project involves using a melt-and-pour soap base, combined with different scents and colors, to create unique bars of soap. The excitement builds as you and your child pick out molds, mix in vibrant dyes, and choose aromatic scents to craft personalized soap creations. This hands-on activity is not only a creative outlet but also a fantastic way to learn about the science of soap making.

As you melt the soap base and mix in various ingredients, you'll see your child's curiosity and creativity come to life. The process of selecting and blending scents and colors fosters a sense of artistic expression and experimentation. Once the soap is set, the satisfaction of unmolding and using their own handmade soap adds an extra layer of achievement. This activity is perfect for bonding, learning, and creating something useful together.

Materials Needed:

- ☐ Melt-and-pour soap base
- ☐ Soap molds (silicone molds work best)
- ☐ Soap colorants (liquid or mica powder)
- ☐ Essential oils or soap fragrances (e.g., cedar, lavender, or fun options like fruity cereal)
- ☐ Microwave-safe bowl or double boiler
- ☐ Mixing utensils (spatulas, spoons)
- ☐ Rubbing alcohol in a spray bottle (to remove bubbles)
- ☐ Enhancements (e.g., dried flowers or exfoliants like oatmeal, coffee grounds, or poppy seeds; optional)
- ☐ Cutting board and knife

Materials Note: *All the materials needed for this project, including the melt-and-pour soap base, silicone molds, soap colorants, and essential oils, are readily available at craft stores or online.*

Step-by-Step Instructions:

1. **Prepare Your Soap-Making Station:**
   - Cover your workspace with newspaper or a plastic tablecloth to make cleanup a breeze.
   - Lay out all the materials so they're within easy reach for you and your child.
2. **Cut and Measure Soap Base:**
   - Using a cutting board and knife (handled by the adult), cut the soap base into small, even chunks.
   - Measure out the amount needed according to your mold size and desired number of soap bars.
3. **Melt the Soap Base:**
   - Place the soap chunks in a microwave-safe bowl.
   - Microwave in 30-second intervals, stirring between each interval until completely melted.
   - Alternatively, use a double boiler for a more controlled melt: Place the soap chunks in the top pot or bowl over simmering water in the bottom pot, stirring gently until fully melted.
4. **Add Color and Scent:**
   - Once the soap base is fully melted, let it cool for a couple minutes. This cooling period is important because adding color and fragrance while the soap is too hot can weaken their effectiveness.
   - Let your child choose the color and fragrance they want for each bar of soap. Help them measure out a few drops of soap dye and fragrance oil (1-2 drops for a light scent, 3-4 for stronger).
   - Once the soap has cooled slightly, add the fragrance oil and soap dye.
   - Stir the mixture gently until the colors and scents are fully blended, using a slow and smooth motion to minimize air bubbles.
5. **Customize with Enhancements (Optional):**
   - Allow your child to sprinkle in your chosen extras like dried flowers, oatmeal, coffee grounds, or poppy seeds for added texture or exfoliation.
   - Stir these enhancements gently into the soap mixture until they are evenly distributed, taking care to minimize air bubbles.
   - Encourage your child to experiment with different combinations and ask them how each enhancement feels or looks.
6. **Pour into Molds:**

- Gently pour the scented and colored soap mixture into your molds, filling each cavity to the top while being careful not to overfill.

7. **Remove Bubbles:**
   - Gently tap the filled molds on the table several times to help bring any trapped air bubbles to the surface.
   - If bubbles do form on the surface, spray a light mist of rubbing alcohol to pop them and create smooth bars.

8. **Let the Soap Set:**
   - Set the molds aside in a safe spot where they can cool and harden. This usually takes about 1-2 hours at room temperature or about 30 minutes in the refrigerator, depending on the size of the mold.
   - During the waiting time, chat with your child about what they want to name their soap creations or ask them to imagine who they might gift the soaps to.

9. **Unmold and Admire:**
   - Once fully set, gently press on the back of the molds to release the soap bars.
   - Have fun admiring each one's unique color, scent, and texture from the enhancements.

Safety Considerations:

- Allow your child to take the lead in adding colors, scents, and mixing, while you handle the cutting, melting, and pouring steps.
- Be mindful of any potential allergies to fragrance oils, dyes, or additives. Use hypoallergenic or natural ingredients when possible, and ensure all ingredients are safe for your child's skin.
- Overheating can cause the soap base to burn or boil, which may release fumes and affect the texture of the soap. Ensure the soap is heated just until melted.

Troubleshooting Tips:

- **Bubbles in Soap:** Spray rubbing alcohol on the surface to remove bubbles before the soap sets.
- **Soap Cracking or Becoming Brittle:** Cracking may occur if too many additives are included. To avoid this, limit the amount of colorants, fragrance oils, and other enhancements for a smoother texture.
- **Soap Doesn't Lather Well**: Use a soap base with added glycerin or experiment with different bases for better lather.
- **Mold Design Not Clear**: Tap the mold gently after pouring to remove

air bubbles and ensure the soap fills all details.

Cleanup Tips:

- Wipe down any surfaces or utensils that have soap residue while it's still warm and soft. Hardened soap can be more difficult to remove.
- Soak mixing utensils in hot water to dissolve any remaining soap residue. Avoid cold water, as it can harden the soap and make it stick.
- If you're not using the soap right away, wrap each bar in plastic wrap or store them in an airtight container to keep them fresh and free from dust.

Variations and Adaptations:

- **Layered Soap:** Create multi-layered soap bars by pouring different colored or scented soap bases in stages. Let each layer partially set and lightly spritz it with alcohol before adding the next for a colorful, striped effect.
- **Scent Layered Soap**: Create a soap bar with different layers, each containing a unique scent. As the soap is used, different aromas are revealed, making each wash a new experience. Experiment with your chosen scent combinations on a cotton ball before adding them to the soap to see how they blend together.
- **Scent-Free Soap for Sensitive Skin**: For those with sensitive skin, omit the fragrances and dyes, and add moisturizing ingredients like shea butter or coconut oil to make gentle, hydrating soap bars.
- **Embedded Objects:** Add small, safe objects into the soap, such as tiny toys, charms, or seashells. As the soap is used, the object is gradually revealed, making it an exciting surprise.
- **Grime Fighter Bar:** Create a tough, grease-busting soap by adding fine sand or finely crushed pumice for strong exfoliation. Use citrus essential oils like lemon or orange to break down grease, and mix in shea butter or coconut oil to keep hands moisturized during and after scrubbing. Embed a loofah slice or scrubber pad into the soap for added scrubbing power.
- **Marble Magic:** Pour multiple colors of melted soap base into the mold and swirl them gently with a toothpick to create a marbled effect. Each bar will have a unique, unpredictable design.
- **Seasonal Suds:** Capture the seasons with fun color and scent combos—warm oranges and cozy vanilla for autumn, cool blues and fresh peppermint for winter, soft pastels and floral scents for spring, and bold citrusy colors for summer.
- **Soap on a Rope**: Add a string or rope to the soap mold before pouring the melted base. This allows you to make "soap on a rope" bars that are perfect for hanging in the shower.

- **Fruit-Inspired Soap**: Use colors, shapes, and scents to make soaps that resemble fruits like oranges, strawberries, or lemons. This adds a fun, fresh twist to the craft.
- **Confetti Soap**: Chop up small pieces of colored soap and sprinkle them into a clear or neutral soap base before pouring. This creates a "confetti" look, perfect for fun or festive occasions.

Benefits:

- **Promotes Hygiene:** Using their own handmade soap encourages kids to be more excited about handwashing and personal hygiene, making cleanliness a fun and engaging habit.
- **Encourages Scientific Thinking**: The process of melting and cooling the soap base offers an engaging way to explore basic science concepts, like phase changes and solubility, fostering curiosity about how things work.
- **Teaches Practical Skills**: Soap-making introduces children to practical life skills, as they learn how to measure, melt, mix, and pour ingredients, gaining confidence in hands-on activities.
- **Strengthens Bonds:** Collaborating on soap-making encourages teamwork and open communication, allowing for meaningful conversations and a shared sense of accomplishment that deepens the connection between parent and child.
- **Boosts Confidence:** Unmolding and using the final soap creation gives children a deep sense of accomplishment and pride in their work, reinforcing the value of effort and creativity.

39

CUSTOM BOARD GAME BUILD-OFF

Bring your imagination to life by crafting a one-of-a-kind board game filled with unexpected twists and creative surprises! This engaging activity allows you and your child to invent unique rules, design the game board, and create personalized playing pieces. The excitement of brainstorming game mechanics and artwork transforms this project into an adventure, where imagination takes the lead. Whether it's a fantasy quest, a race to the finish, or a mystery-solving challenge, the possibilities are endless and uniquely yours.

As you collaborate on designing the game, you'll witness your child's ideas and enthusiasm blossom. The process of developing rules and creating game pieces promotes critical thinking and problem-solving skills. Playing the game together after its completion adds a rewarding element, offering endless hours of fun and bonding. This activity not only fosters creativity but also results in a tangible product that can be enjoyed repeatedly.

Materials Needed:

- ☐ Large sheet of cardboard or poster board
- ☐ Markers, colored pencils, or paints
- ☐ Scissors
- ☐ Glue or tape
- ☐ Construction paper or cardstock
- ☐ Dice (optional)
- ☐ Small objects for game pieces (e.g., buttons, coins, clay figures, or miniatures)
- ☐ Cardboard box or shoebox (to store the finished game)

Step-by-Step Instructions:

1. **Brainstorm the Game Concept:**
    - Sit down together and discuss ideas for the game's theme and objective. Will it be a racing game, a mystery adventure, or a fantasy quest? Let your child's imagination lead, but feel free to offer creative suggestions to guide the brainstorming.
    - Decide on the basic rules and structure, such as how players move, win, and what obstacles they might face. Is it a race to the finish line? Do players need to collect items along the way or solve puzzles? Defining a clear goal helps shape the rest of the game.
    - Start brainstorming potential names for your game. Let your child throw out fun ideas or silly names as inspiration comes to them. Don't worry about settling on the perfect title right away—the best ideas often come once you've immersed yourselves in the game creation, so feel free to revisit the name anytime during the process.
2. **Design the Game Board:**
    - Use a large sheet of cardboard or poster board as the base.
    - Sketch out the layout of the board, including paths, obstacles, and special areas that fit your game's theme.
    - Remember to designate an area for game components like a spinner, cards, or tokens, for easy access during play.
    - Use a ruler to create spaces if the game will involve moving pieces around the board. You can also add areas where players must perform special actions, like drawing a card or skipping a turn.
    - Let your child decorate the board with markers, colored pencils, or paints, and encourage them to add their own creative flair—whether it's drawing mountains, rivers, or magical portals to bring your theme to life.
3. **Create the Game Pieces:**
    - Make the characters or tokens players will use to move around the board. Let your child mold their own pieces using clay, decorate bottle caps, or choose small objects from around the house (like buttons or action figures). The more personal the better!
    - Ensure each piece is unique and easily distinguishable.
    - Name the pieces together to give them personality, such as "Sir Dash" the fast knight or "Detective Dot" the super sleuth.
    - Design cards or tokens if your game requires them, using paper or cardstock. These cards can include fun twists like "jump ahead 2 spaces," "trade places with another player," or even "do a silly dance

before your next turn!"

4. **Write Down the Rules:**
   - Draft a clear and concise rulebook, explaining how to set up the game, how to play, and how to win. Work with your child to come up with rules that are simple enough to follow but still fun to play.
   - Test the rules together, making adjustments as necessary to ensure the game is balanced and fun.
   - Don't worry if the rules change a bit as you playtest the game! The important thing is that you both enjoy the process of figuring out what works best.
5. **Assemble the Game:**
   - Glue or tape any additional elements onto the board, such as card slots or spinners.
   - Add finishing touches to your game by decorating the board and pieces with stickers, stamps, or fun drawings. Let your child personalize it to make it truly theirs.
6. **Design the Game Box (Optional):**
   - Grab a cardboard box or shoebox and transform it into the official storage for your custom game. Use markers, stickers, paints, or any craft supplies you have to decorate the box in a way that matches the theme of your game.
   - Personalize it with fun details like the name of the game and symbols that tie into the game's theme (e.g., wizards' hats for a fantasy game, treasure chests for an adventure game).
7. **Play and Enjoy:**
   - Now comes the exciting part—playing the game you just built! Sit down together and go through a practice round to see how the game flows.
   - Be open to adjusting the rules or adding new elements if you both come up with fresh ideas during play.
   - Use this time to encourage problem-solving and strategic thinking by asking questions like, "What's your plan to win?" or "What should we do if two players reach the finish at the same time?"
   - As you play, take a moment to appreciate the game you've crafted together. The hard work, imagination, and collaboration have led to something truly unique. Each game played will be a new opportunity to create lasting memories, fostering a sense of joy and accomplishment with every turn.

Safety Considerations:

- Ensure small game pieces are kept out of reach of younger children to avoid choking hazards.

Troubleshooting Tips:

- **Ideas Not Flowing:** If brainstorming game concepts is challenging, start by discussing favorite existing games and what elements your child enjoys most. Use these as inspiration to build from, or combine elements from different games to create something new.
- **Unclear Rules:** Playtest the game multiple times to identify and clarify any confusing rules.
- **Overcomplicated Rules**: Simplify the rules by focusing on one core objective. Encourage your child to streamline the gameplay by reducing unnecessary steps or clarifying how to win.
- **Balance Issues:** If one player keeps winning too easily or the game feels too difficult, experiment with modifying the rules. Add power-ups, penalties, or change the game mechanics slightly to create a more balanced experience.
- **Long Play Time**: If the game takes too long to finish, add a timer or set a number of rounds to limit how long each game lasts. This keeps the game fun and fast-paced.

Cleanup Tips:

- Keep all game pieces, dice, and the game board in a designated box or container. Label the box with the game's name for easy identification and storage.

Variations and Adaptations:

- **Educational Games:** Focus on educational themes, such as math challenges or historical adventures, to combine learning with fun.
- **Collaborative Game**: Instead of a competitive game, design a game where players work together toward a common goal. This could be a game where everyone teams up to solve a mystery or complete a task before time runs out.
- **Mystery Box Game**: Include a sealed "mystery box" in the game that can only be opened once players reach a certain point or complete a special challenge. The contents of the box could introduce new rules or game pieces to spice up gameplay.
- **Interactive Story Game**: Build a board game that doubles as a storytelling adventure. As players move around the board, they can encounter events, challenges, or puzzles that progress the game's story. You could even write

small dialogue cards or "choose-your-own-adventure" moments.

- **Family Trivia Game**: Incorporate family history into the game by designing trivia cards with questions about relatives, vacations, or shared memories. This personal touch makes the game meaningful and engaging for everyone.
- **"Infinite Game Board"**: Design a modular game board made up of smaller, interchangeable pieces. This allows players to rearrange and expand the board for different configurations each time, keeping gameplay fresh.
- **DIY Expansion Packs**: After building the main game, create "expansion packs" with new rules, pieces, or additional objectives that can be added later. This gives the game lasting appeal as you can keep evolving it over time.

Benefits:

- **Encourages Creativity:** Designing a game from scratch fosters creativity as children invent game mechanics, rules, and visual elements, helping them explore their imaginative potential.
- **Boosts Strategic Thinking**: Thinking through game mechanics, such as how players win or what obstacles they face, encourages children to develop strategies, sharpening their ability to think ahead and plan.
- **Promotes Resilience and Adaptability**: When parts of the game don't work as intended, children must adapt and revise their designs, building resilience and the ability to adjust their plans when things don't go as expected.
- **Strengthens Bonds:** Working together to build a custom board game fosters meaningful interaction, encouraging collaboration, communication, and shared creative experiences that deepen the connection between parent and child.
- **Introduces Project Management**: By breaking down the game-building process into steps—planning, designing, building, and testing—children learn the basics of managing a project and following it through to completion.

40

MYSTERY BOX CHALLENGE

Step into the world of spontaneous creativity with a Mystery Box Challenge! Fill a box with random craft supplies and challenge your child to create something amazing using only the items inside. This activity sparks imagination and ingenuity, pushing the boundaries of what can be achieved with a limited set of materials. The thrill of discovery and the excitement of crafting something unique make this a fantastic way to spend quality time together.

Watching your child's mind at work as they sift through the box and conceptualize their creation is truly rewarding. The Mystery Box Challenge encourages problem-solving and resourcefulness, as they figure out how to use each item creatively. This activity also fosters a sense of accomplishment and confidence when they transform a jumble of materials into a masterpiece.

Materials Needed:

- ☐ A medium-sized box or container
- ☐ Assorted craft supplies (e.g., pipe cleaners, googly eyes, buttons, popsicle sticks, fabric scraps, glue, tape, string, beads, paper, etc.)
- ☐ Scissors
- ☐ Timer (for added challenge; optional)

Step-by-Step Instructions:

1. **Prepare the Mystery Box:**
   - Secretly gather a variety of random craft supplies and place them in the mystery box. Aim for a fun mix of items to spark creativity—nothing too obvious or ordinary.
2. **Introduce the Challenge:**
   - Explain the rules to your child: they can only use the materials inside the box to create something, and they must incorporate as many items as possible into their creation.
3. **Set a Time Limit (Optional):**
   - For an added challenge, set a timer and see what they can create within a specified time frame, encouraging quick thinking and resourcefulness.
4. **Begin Creating:**
   - **Optional:** Before opening the box, have your child guess what kinds of materials might be inside based on clues you give. Afterward, see how close their guesses were, adding a fun element of prediction.
   - Hand over the mystery box to your child, letting them open it and explore the contents.
   - Encourage them to take a moment to examine each item and think about how it might be used in their creation.
   - Collaborate with them if needed—helping with any tricky cutting or gluing, or working together to bring their vision to life. This is a great chance to share ideas and enjoy problem-solving together.
   - Offer support and encouragement as they work on their creation.
5. **Showcase the Creation:**
   - Once the creation is complete, ask your child to present their masterpiece! Let them explain their thought process, the inspiration behind it, and how they used each item from the box.
   - Celebrate their ingenuity and effort, no matter what the final result looks like—this challenge is all about creativity and resourcefulness!
6. **Bonus Round (Optional):**
   - If you both had a blast with the first round, fill the box with a new set of mystery supplies for a second challenge. This time, you can even switch roles and have your child put together the mystery box for you to tackle!

Safety Considerations:

- If using glue guns, scissors, or other crafting tools, make sure they are appropriate for your child's skill level. Supervise use of any hot or sharp tools to prevent burns or cuts.

Troubleshooting Tips:

- **Limited Inspiration:** Provide gentle prompts or suggestions, such as, "What could you make if this item were the centerpiece?" You can also suggest they start by arranging the materials without a set goal and see what comes to mind.
- **Material Shortages:** Encourage improvisation! Challenge your child to think creatively and find new uses for materials they might not have considered. Allow them to request a few additional items if they feel truly stuck, but keep the main challenge intact.
- **Items Won't Stick Together**: If glue or tape isn't working to hold materials together, try using a stronger adhesive like hot glue (with supervision), or explore other methods like tying items with string or creating joints with twist ties or pipe cleaners.
- **Getting Stuck on One Idea**: If your child becomes fixated on one idea that isn't working, gently suggest exploring a new direction. Encourage them to think outside the box by asking, "What could you do differently?"

Cleanup Tips:

- Instead of discarding smaller, usable materials like buttons or yarn, have a jar or box where your child can store leftover bits for the next crafting challenge.

Variations and Adaptations:

- **Themed Boxes:** Set a theme for the challenge (e.g., "something that flies," "a creature from space," or "a futuristic invention") to inspire a specific direction.
- **Mystery Box Fashion Show**: Challenge your child to create wearable art! Fill the box with fabric scraps, beads, and ribbons, and have them design a piece of clothing, jewelry, or an accessory to model in a "fashion show."
- **Collaborative Mystery Box**: Instead of working solo, create a collaborative version where both you and your child (or multiple children) work together to create something amazing. Take turns adding to the creation, building teamwork and problem-solving skills.
- **Mystery Box Architecture**: Give your child a box full of building materials like cardboard, paper tubes, and glue, and challenge them to build a structure, like a bridge, tower, or house. Test how strong their creation is afterward!

- **Eco-Friendly Challenge:** Fill the box entirely with recycled materials like old cereal boxes, bottle caps, newspapers, and fabric scraps. This adds an eco-friendly twist and teaches the value of reusing items to create something new.
- **Double Trouble Mystery Box**: Include a rule where each participant gets two mystery boxes: one they create from, and one they must swap halfway through. This adds an element of surprise and forces them to adapt to new materials mid-project.

Benefits:

- **Sparks Creativity:** The mystery and spontaneity of the box challenge pushes children to use their imaginations, as they visualize possibilities and stretch their minds to see beyond the obvious use of each item.
- **Enhances Problem-Solving Skills:** The challenge of using limited materials pushes children to think critically and come up with creative solutions, improving their ability to overcome obstacles and adapt to new situations.
- **Boosts Resourcefulness**: Using whatever is available teaches children to be resourceful, helping them understand how to make the most of what they have rather than relying on pre-set solutions.
- **Strengthens Bonds:** The shared experience of working through the unknown together fosters deeper interaction and meaningful conversations, as both parent and child collaborate, offer suggestions, and celebrate each other's creative ideas.
- **Encourages Flexibility:** Working with unexpected materials helps children become more flexible thinkers as they adapt to limitations, modify their approach, and think on their feet to solve problems creatively.

OUTDOOR FUN

Adventure awaits with these outdoor activities for late-elementary trailblazers! From making a DIY wind chime to transforming a backyard into a water balloon battleship arena, these activities mix exploration, creativity, and physical challenges. Enjoy stargazing under a blanket of stars or create sun-powered prints using nature's magic. Each activity encourages an adventurous spirit, a love for nature, and the chance to share incredible experiences outdoors.

41

DIY WIND CHIME WORKSHOP

Let your child's creativity soar with this DIY wind chime project, transforming everyday materials into a beautiful, melodic masterpiece. Begin your adventure by gathering an array of natural and household items like sticks, shells, beads, and old keys, turning each piece into a potential part of your unique wind chime. Imagine the delight on your child's face as they carefully select and arrange their materials, ready to craft a work of art that will sing with the wind. The process of tying strings and arranging decorative items becomes a harmonious blend of creativity and discovery, each step bringing the project closer to completion.

Once assembled, the wind chime becomes a source of pride and joy. Hang it in your backyard and watch as your child's eyes light up every time a breeze sets it into motion, producing soothing, magical sounds. This hands-on project not only engages your child in crafting but also teaches them about different sounds and materials, creating a sensory experience that resonates with the beauty of nature. Each gust of wind becomes a reminder of their creativity and the special moment you shared, turning a simple craft into a cherished memory and a decorative piece that adds charm and melody to your home.

Materials Needed:

- ☐ String or fishing line (Opt for UV- and weather-resistant nylon, polyester, or paracord)
- ☐ Sticks or a wooden hoop (for the top of the wind chime)
- ☐ Decorative items (beads, shells, bamboo, metal spoons, old keys, copper pipe fittings, etc.)
- ☐ Scissors
- ☐ Drill (optional)
- ☐ File or sandpaper (optional)
- ☐ Hot glue gun with weather resistant glue (optional)
- ☐ Clear varnish (for weatherproofing; optional)

Step-by-Step Instructions:

1. **Gather Materials:**
   - Begin by exploring your house or outside with your child for items to use in your wind chime. Consider a mix of natural elements like shells, pinecones, and sticks, and household items like old keys, bottle caps, ceramic shards, or beads.
   - When choosing materials, remind your child that lighter items like shells, beads, or keys will catch the wind better than heavier items. This will help their wind chime create a more melodic sound when the breeze blows.
   - Lay everything out on a table so your child can see the range of possibilities. Talk through the different items and how they might sound when they catch the wind.
2. **Prepare the Base:**
   - Choose a couple sturdy sticks, dowels, or a wooden hoop as the base of your wind chime.
   - If needed, trim the sticks to size and smooth out any rough spots using sandpaper or a file.
   - Optionally, drill small holes along the length of the sticks if you plan to tie strings through them.
   - If using sticks, arrange them in a crisscross pattern and tie them securely together at the intersection with string or fishing line.
3. **Weatherproofing (Optional):**
   - Apply a layer of clear varnish to the wooden pieces or the chimes themselves to protect them from the elements. This step is optional but can help the wind chime last longer in varying weather conditions.
4. **Cut the Strings:**
   - Measure and cut multiple lengths of string or fishing line, each about 12-18 inches long, depending on how long you want your wind chime pieces to hang. The lengths can vary to create different sounds and patterns of movement.
5. **Prepare Decorative Items:**
   - If needed, use a small drill (handled by the adult) to carefully drill holes in items like shells or thick pieces of wood to thread the string through. Use a small drill bit appropriate for the material you're drilling into. For shells, a fine carbide or diamond-tipped bit works best.
     - **Pro Tip:** If drilling shells, you can submerge the shell partially in water while drilling. This keeps the shell cool and reduces the risk

of cracking.

- Use weatherproof hot glue or a similar adhesive for items that cannot be drilled.

6. **Attach Chimes to Strings:**
    - Let your child decide on the order and arrangement of the items, using their creativity to make the wind chime unique.
    - Help your child attach each item to the strings. Alternate between heavier and lighter items to create a balanced wind chime that will move easily in the breeze.
    - Ensure you leave enough string to tie a knot to the base.
    - Make sure all knots are tight and secure so they don't slip or unravel. Use a dab of hot glue to secure the knots in place if needed.
7. **Secure the Strings to the Base:**
    - Tie the other end of each string to the sticks or wooden hoop. Ensure the strings are evenly spaced around the base to balance the wind chime.
    - Adjust the lengths if necessary to create a visually pleasing arrangement.
    - Add a piece of string at the top of the base so the wind chime can be hung up. Tie it tightly or use an eye screw to attach it securely.
8. **Test the Chimes:**
    - Before finalizing the wind chime, gently shake it to ensure the items produce a pleasing sound when they strike each other.
    - Make any necessary adjustments to the spacing or length of the strings to enhance the sound.
9. **Hang the Wind Chime:**
    - Take your finished wind chime outside and find the perfect spot to hang it—somewhere the wind can catch it easily, like a tree branch or the porch.
    - Use a sturdy hook or nail to hang the wind chime securely.
    - After hanging the wind chime, take a moment to step back and admire the final product together. Listen quietly for a minute, waiting for the breeze bring your child's creation to life.
    - Ask your child what they like most about their wind chime and how it makes them feel when they hear its sound. This can be a beautiful opportunity to discuss how the wind chime will remind them of the fun you had together each time it plays its song.

Safety Considerations:

- Allow your child to take the lead in selecting materials and tying strings, while you handle the drilling and hot glue tasks to ensure safety.
- When collecting materials to use for your chime, avoid sharp or fragile materials like glass shards, jagged metal, or items that could break easily. Smooth rough edges with a file or sandpaper before using them.
- Some items, like beads or small shells, could be choking hazards if younger siblings are around. Keep small parts organized and ensure they are used properly during the project.

Troubleshooting Tips:

- **Chime Doesn't Look as Expected**: If your child feels the wind chime doesn't look how they envisioned, encourage them to rearrange the materials before permanently securing them. Offer suggestions for balancing colors or shapes to match their creative vision.
- **Not Producing Sound:** If the items are too far apart to produce sound, shorten the distance between the strings or add more items to create closer contact points. Ensure that the items can move freely and strike each other in the wind.
- **Unbalanced Chime:** Rearrange the placement of the hanging objects or try adding or removing items to even out the weight distribution on all sides.
- **Strings Getting Tangled**: Incorporate a few additional heavier items for stability or increase the space between the strings so each item has room to move freely.
- **Noisy in Strong Winds**: If the wind chime is too noisy or clanging excessively in strong winds, try adding heavier items that won't move as easily, or hang it in a more sheltered area to reduce the impact of the wind.

Cleanup Tips:

- Sort and store any leftover decorative items, string, and other materials in a craft box or container for future projects.

Variations and Adaptations:

- **Themed Chimes:** Create a wind chime based on a specific theme, such as ocean treasures (using shells, sea glass, fish shapes, and driftwood) or a forest theme (using pinecones, pebbles, and small branches). This adds a fun twist to the project and gives the wind chime a cohesive look.
- **DIY Clay Wind Chime**: Make your own clay pieces by shaping and baking air-dry clay. Paint or decorate each piece, then string them together.
- **Musical Metal**: Incorporate copper pipes or toy xylophone bars to turn

the wind chime into a musical instrument. You can experiment with different lengths of pipes to create various tones and pitches, making it both a visual and auditory experience.

- **Seasonal Wind Chime**: Create a wind chime for each season, using seasonal colors and items. For example, spring could feature flowers and pastel colors, while autumn could include leaves and earthy tones. Swap out the chimes as the seasons change.
- **Kaleidoscope Wind Chime**: Use small transparent colored plastic pieces or glass beads to create a kaleidoscope effect when the sun shines through the wind chime. This way, the wind chime not only makes sounds but also casts colorful shadows on sunny days.
- **Light Reflectors**: Use reflective materials like CDs, mirrors, or metal pieces that catch and reflect sunlight. This adds a sparkling visual element to the wind chime, making it both sound- and light-focused.

Benefits:

- **Strengthens Problem-Solving Skills**: Children must decide how to balance the materials, choose proper string lengths, and adjust their design, which builds critical thinking and problem-solving abilities.
- **Supports Environmental Awareness**: Using natural and upcycled materials helps children become more mindful of their environment, teaching them the value of reusing items and appreciating nature's beauty.
- **Introduces Sound Exploration**: As children experiment with different materials and their sounds, they learn about acoustics and how different objects produce various tones, adding an educational aspect to the craft.
- **Strengthens Bonds:** Collaborating on the wind chime allows for shared moments of creativity and problem-solving, deepening the connection between you and your child through teamwork and communication.
- **Builds Confidence**: Successfully designing and assembling a functioning wind chime gives children a sense of accomplishment, boosting their confidence in their abilities to create something meaningful.

42

WATER BALLOON BATTLESHIP

Bring the classic Battleship game to life with a splashy twist by creating a life-size version using water balloons and cardboard targets. This activity combines strategy, teamwork, and a whole lot of fun as you and your child engage in a friendly water balloon battle. The excitement of trying to "sink" each other's ships while dodging incoming attacks makes this game an exhilarating and memorable experience.

Setting up the game involves crafting cardboard ships and filling water balloons for ammunition. Once the battlefield is ready, the strategic planning and quick reflexes come into play. This interactive game promotes physical activity and provides endless laughter and bonding opportunities as you play together.

Materials Needed:

- ☐ Several cardboard sheets or large boxes
- ☐ Scissors or a utility knife
- ☐ Markers or paint
- ☐ Biodegradable water balloons (around 50–100 for a full game)
- ☐ Buckets or large containers
- ☐ Rope or string
- ☐ Wooden stakes (one for each ship; optional)
- ☐ Waterproof sunscreen

Step-by-Step Instructions:

1. **Create the Ships:**
   - Cut cardboard sheets or large boxes into ship shapes or simple rectangular ships. You can create different sizes to represent small and large ships, like in the classic game.
   - You can create 5 ships per side, just like in the classic game, or you can adjust the number based on your space and how long you want the game to last.
   - Let your child decorate the cardboard with markers or paint to resemble ships, adding details like windows and flags.
2. **Prepare the Battlefield:**
   - Choose a large outdoor area where you can set up the game.
   - Use rope, string, or even garden hoses to create a dividing line between the two sides. This will serve as the "ocean" between the opposing ships.
   - Place the ships in the two separate zones to represent each player's fleet.
   - Place the cardboard ships on each side of the battlefield to represent each player's fleet. Stand them up against trees, fences, stakes in the ground, or other small objects.
   - Ensure the ships are spaced out in various positions so they are not all grouped together. This allows for strategic gameplay.
3. **Fill the Water Balloons:**
   - Using a faucet or hose, work together to fill 50–100 balloons (or more, depending on how long you want to play).
   - Make some "extra powerful" water balloons by filling them to the point where they are just about to burst, adding an extra element of excitement!
   - Place the balloons in large buckets or containers on each side for easy access.
4. **Explain the Rules:**
   - Establish the basic rules of the game: each player takes turns throwing water balloons across the dividing line, trying to hit and "sink" the opponent's ships.
   - If a balloon hits a ship and it gets knocked over, that ship is "sunk." The first player to sink all of the other player's ships wins.
5. **Start the Battle:**
   - Take turns launching water balloons at the other side, aiming to sink

your opponent's ships. You can throw from a fixed distance or allow some movement on the battlefield to make things more challenging.
   - Dodging incoming water balloons adds to the excitement, and teamwork between you and your child on strategy and tactics becomes a fun bonding element, even if you're on opposing sides.

6. **Final Splash Round:**
   - Once all the ships have been sunk and a winner declared, finish the game with a playful bonus round where both sides launch their remaining water balloons at each other, no targets needed. This way, everyone gets one last burst of energy and laughter to wrap up the game on a fun, lighthearted note.

Safety Considerations:

- Inspect the play area for any potential hazards such as sharp objects, uneven ground, or obstacles that could cause tripping or injury.
- Emphasize throwing water balloons at the targets or lower body to prevent potential injuries to the face or eyes.
- Keep water available for drinking, apply sunscreen, and consider wearing hats to protect against sunburn and heat exhaustion.
- Use biodegradable water balloons to minimize environmental impact.

Troubleshooting Tips:

- **Unstable Ships:** If the cardboard ships fall over too easily, reinforce the base with heavier objects like small rocks or weights to keep them stable.

Cleanup Tips:

- If available, lay down tarps in the area where most of the balloon action will take place. Once the game is over, just lift the tarp, and all the balloon pieces can be easily gathered.
- If you have a leaf blower, use it to push the pieces into one corner or pile for easier collection. Just be sure it's on a low setting to avoid blowing fragments everywhere.
- Turn cleanup into a treasure hunt by assigning point values to balloon fragments based on their size or color (e.g., small fragments = 1 point, medium = 3 points, rare colors = 5 points). The player who collects the most points wins a small prize, such as a "Balloon Cleanup Champion" title or a small treat, making the process fun and competitive.
- Do a final sweep of the yard to ensure no small balloon fragments are left behind, as they can pose choking risks to small children and be harmful to wildlife or pets if ingested.

Variations and Adaptations:

- **Different Ammo:** Use sponges soaked in water or small water guns instead of water balloons for a less messy version of the game.
- **Different Targets:** Instead of cardboard ships, use other targets like plastic bottles, tin cans, or large inflatable objects. This variation can change the difficulty level and make the game more interesting.
- **Water Balloon Dodgeball Hybrid**: Incorporate dodgeball elements by allowing players to throw water balloons directly at each other (in addition to targeting ships). Players must dodge, dip, and dive while aiming for ships and avoiding incoming balloons.
- **Mystery Ship Cargo**: Add mystery "cargo" to ships, where each ship hit reveals a fun surprise—such as an extra balloon for your team, a time bonus, or even a silly challenge to complete.
- **Obstacles:** Increase the challenge by adding obstacles between players' ships, such as cones or pool noodles, that players must navigate to get a better angle for throwing.
- **Themed Battleship:** Decorate ships to match themes like pirates, naval ships, or space battles. Add props or costumes to immerse yourselves fully in the theme, whether it's treasure maps and eye patches for pirates or shiny foil and helmets for space battles.
- **Scoring System:** Introduce a point system where different parts of the ship have different point values. For example, hitting the "command center" could be worth more points than hitting the "hull."
- **Weather Adaptation:** On colder days, use snowballs instead of water balloons if you live in a snowy area. This makes the game versatile for different climates.

Benefits:

- **Encourages Strategic Thinking:** Planning and executing attacks promotes tactical decision-making as players determine the best way to "sink" their opponent's ships, encouraging them to think critically and adapt their strategies.
- **Promotes Physical Activity:** Running, dodging, and throwing water balloons engages children in physical exercise, improving their overall fitness, coordination, and reflexes.
- **Enhances Coordination:** Aiming and throwing water balloons at targets requires precision, improving hand-eye coordination and motor skills.
- **Strengthens Bonds**: Collaborating on building the ships and engaging in friendly competition helps foster connection between you and your child, as the shared excitement of aiming, throwing, and reacting together leads

to moments of laughter and fun.

- **Teaches Good Sportsmanship**: The game provides an opportunity to learn how to handle both winning and losing graciously, fostering a positive attitude toward competition.

43

BACKYARD STARGAZING ODYSSEY

Turn an ordinary night into a celestial adventure with a stargazing evening in your backyard. Set up a cozy spot with blankets and pillows, and use a star map or stargazing app to explore the night sky. Picture yourself lying back with your child, the cool night air filled with whispers and wonder as you identify constellations and planets. Each star becomes a gateway to stories and science, sparking curiosity and imagination.

The night sky is a vast canvas of twinkling lights, and your child's eyes widen with each new discovery. Share fun facts about the constellations, recount myths from ancient cultures, or simply enjoy the serene beauty of the universe above. This quiet, contemplative time offers a unique opportunity to connect deeply, away from the distractions of daily life. Stargazing becomes a cherished ritual, blending the awe of the cosmos with the warmth of togetherness, creating an unforgettable experience that fosters a lifelong fascination with the stars.

Materials Needed:

- ☐ Blankets and pillows
- ☐ Star map or stargazing app (e.g., SkyView, Star Walk 2; free versions work great)
- ☐ Flashlight with a red filter (to preserve night vision; use a red balloon, cellophane, plastic folder, or marker on clear plastic as DIY filters)
- ☐ Snacks and drinks
- ☐ Astronomy Books (optional)
- ☐ Bug repellent (optional)

Step-by-Step Instructions:

1. **Set the Stage:**
   - Pick a night with clear skies, and find a spot in your backyard that's away from bright lights. The darker the surroundings, the better you'll see the stars.
   - Lay out blankets and pillows to create a cozy stargazing station.
   - Place your child's favorite snacks and drinks within reach to make the evening feel special and relaxing.
   - If your flashlight doesn't have a red filter, you can make one by cutting a piece of red balloon, cellophane, or plastic folder large enough to cover the flashlight lens. If those aren't available, use a red marker to color a clear plastic bag. Secure the filter with a rubber band or tape to create your night vision-friendly flashlight.
2. **Select your Star Guide:**
   - Download a stargazing app or print out a star map that matches your location and season to help identify constellations and planets.
   - Review the basics of the night sky with your child, talking about the difference between constellations, stars, and planets.
   - Explain how to use the map or app to your child, pointing out major features.
3. **Get Comfortable and Adjust Your Eyes:**
   - Once you're outside, lie back and let your eyes adjust to the darkness. This might take 10-15 minutes.
   - While waiting, you can start talking about the stars and planets you're hoping to spot. Let their curiosity guide the discussion by asking what they notice and which stars stand out to them. You can also share how ancient civilizations used the stars for navigation and storytelling, weaving in the fascinating ways the night sky influenced their lives and cultures.
4. **Explore the Sky:**
   - Start by identifying familiar constellations like the Big Dipper or Orion. Point them out to your child and ask them to trace the shape with their finger or try to connect the stars with their imagination.
   - Encourage your child to find other constellations, stars, and planets using the map or app. Show them how to use reference points in the sky to track down specific patterns.
   - Share fun facts about the stars and constellations you observe. Use the app or astronomy books to learn more about the stars, planets, and other celestial objects.

5. **Connect with the Cosmos:**
   - Spend some quiet moments simply lying back and talking about the vastness of space. Share your thoughts or ask your child questions like, "What do you think is out there beyond the stars?" This step opens the door to deeper conversations and reflections.
   - As the evening comes to an end, talk about your favorite parts of the night. Did they discover something new? Which constellation or planet was the most exciting? These closing conversations will help create a lasting memory of your stargazing adventure.

Safety Considerations:

- If you're using a stargazing app, encourage your child to take breaks from screen time to avoid eye strain. Dim the screen brightness and use the "night mode" feature on your phone to reduce strain and preserve night vision.

Troubleshooting Tips:

- **Cloudy Night:** Have a backup plan like watching a space-themed documentary or reading a book about stars. You can reschedule for a clearer night while still making the evening fun with an impromptu indoor "space talk."
- **Difficulty Seeing Stars:** If nearby city lights or streetlights affect visibility, try creating a shaded area by hanging up dark fabric or tarps to block out excess light. You could also use this opportunity to explain the concept of light pollution and how it affects our view of the night sky.

Cleanup Tips:

- If you know the ground is likely to be damp or dewy, lay a large tarp down before placing blankets and pillows. It keeps them dry and makes post-activity cleanup faster and more efficient.
- Do a quick check of the area to make sure nothing is left behind. Encourage your child to be a 'cleanup detective' and find any forgotten items.

Variations and Adaptations:

- **Telescope Target Practice:** If you have a telescope or binoculars, incorporate them into your stargazing session for a closer look at the moon and planets. Create a "target list" of specific stars, planets, or moon craters to find.
- **Astronomy Challenges:** Set up fun challenges such as identifying the most constellations in a set time or finding a specific star or planet.
- **Star-Themed Snacks:** Turn the stargazing session into a "starry picnic."

Pack star-shaped sandwiches, moon pies, freeze-dried ice cream, and other space-themed snacks.

- **Space Playlist:** Add a cosmic soundtrack to your stargazing night. Play real recordings of "space sounds" from NASA, like radio emissions from planets or pulsars, to add a real scientific element and deepen the connection between sound and space. Or, curate a playlist of famous space-themed music, such as *Starman* by David Bowie, the soundtrack from *2001: A Space Odyssey*, or classical pieces like Holst's *The Planets*, to fill the night with the atmosphere of space exploration.
- **Themed Stargazing Nights:** Choose a theme for your stargazing night, such as space exploration or famous astronomers. Share stories and facts related to the theme to make the experience more engaging.
- **Star Stories**: Explore captivating myths and legends about constellations, whether sourced online, in books, or from your own creative storytelling. This journey will ignite their curiosity and spark their imagination, creating lasting memories for both of you.
- **Night Photography:** Try capturing the night sky with a camera or smartphone, experimenting with long exposures. You can even set up a camera or smartphone on a tripod to take time-lapse photos of the stars or moon throughout the night.
- **Astronomy Journal:** Encourage your child to keep a stargazing journal, where they can draw constellations, write down their observations, and note interesting facts they learn. Over time, it becomes a keepsake full of stargazing memories.
- **Celestial Crafting:** Before or after stargazing, engage in related crafts such as making constellation art with glow-in-the-dark paint or creating planet models.
- **Educational Videos:** Watch short, educational videos about astronomy (like clips from Carl Sagan's classic *Cosmos* series) before heading outside to stargaze, setting the stage for what you will observe.
- **Constellation Bingo:** Create Bingo cards with different constellations that are visible in your area, and challenge your child to find them in the sky. Use a star map or stargazing app to help, and mark off each constellation as you spot it. The first one to complete a row wins!
- **Cosmic Trivia Night:** Bring a small collection of astronomy facts or trivia questions and quiz each other throughout the night to make it more interactive.
- **DIY Constellation Projector**: Use a flashlight and a piece of paper to create a DIY constellation projector. Let your child poke small holes in the paper that represent different constellations, and shine the light

through it onto a wall or ceiling. This fun project can bring the stars indoors after the outdoor stargazing session.

- **Meteor Shower Party:** Research dates and times for upcoming meteor showers and plan your stargazing nights around the events for an added spectacle. Encourage your child to make a wish for every meteor they spot.

Benefits:

- **Fosters a Sense of Wonder**: Stargazing sparks curiosity about the universe, encouraging children to ask questions and explore the mysteries of space, which helps develop an inquisitive mindset.
- **Improves Observation Skills**: Searching the night sky for stars and constellations trains children to pay attention to detail and improves their ability to recognize patterns in the vastness of the sky.
- **Encourages Reflective Thinking**: Contemplating the vastness of space often leads children to think deeply about big concepts, such as their place in the universe or the possibility of life on other planets, fostering reflective thinking.
- **Strengthens Bonds:** Sharing the peaceful and awe-inspiring experience of stargazing offers a unique opportunity for meaningful conversations, deepening the emotional connection between you and your child.
- **Expands Vocabulary and Knowledge**: Discussing constellations, planets, and space introduces new vocabulary and concepts, expanding children's understanding of the world and their communication skills.

44

SUN-POWERED PRINTS

Harness the power of the sun to create stunning nature-themed art with sun print paper. This activity involves placing leaves, flowers, and other natural items on special sun print paper and exposing it to sunlight to develop beautiful prints. The magic of watching the sun transform ordinary objects into intricate designs captivates the imagination and fosters a love for both art and nature.

As you and your child explore the outdoors to collect items for your prints, you'll enjoy the beauty of the natural world and the thrill of discovery. The process of arranging the items on the sun print paper and observing the transformation encourages creativity and scientific curiosity. This activity is perfect for bonding, learning, and creating lasting memories together.

Materials Needed:

- ☐ Sun print paper (also known as cyanotype paper; available online)
- ☐ Leaves, flowers, and other natural items
- ☐ Sheet of glass or acrylic (included in most sun print kits)
- ☐ Piece of cardboard or tray slightly larger than the paper
- ☐ Sunny outdoor area
- ☐ Large bowl of water

Step-by-Step Instructions:

1. **Prepare Your Workspace:**
   - Set up in a sunny area outdoors, like the backyard or a park. Make sure you have everything ready before you open the sun print paper, as it will start reacting once exposed to sunlight.
   - Place all your materials nearby so they're easy to grab once you start.
2. **Explore and Collect:**
   - Go on a nature walk with your child, exploring the backyard or nearby areas to collect small, flat items like leaves, flowers, or other unique objects. Encourage them to think creatively about what might look interesting as a silhouette.
   - Choose items with distinct shapes and patterns for the best prints.
   - Chat as you explore—talk about the different plants and shapes you find, asking questions like, "How do you think the veins on this leaf will show in the print?"
3. **Prepare the Sun Print Paper:**
   - Take out a sheet of sun print paper from its packaging, keeping it away from direct sunlight until ready to use.
   - Place the paper on the cardboard or tray in a shaded area.
4. **Arrange the Natural Items:**
   - Help your child arrange the natural items on top of the paper in a way that they think will look good. Encourage them to experiment with spacing, layering, and positioning to create unique designs.
   - Once you're happy with the arrangement, carefully place the glass or acrylic sheet over the items to hold them in place and ensure good contact with the paper.
5. **Expose to Sunlight:**
   - Carefully pick up the tray or cardboard to carry the prepared paper to a sunny area.
   - Expose the paper to sunlight for about 2-5 minutes, or until the paper turns a lighter shade – almost white.
   - Leave the paper exposed to the sun for about 2-5 minutes. Keep an eye on it as the sunlight works its magic! The blue color will start to fade to almost white where the sunlight hits, leaving shadows where the natural items are blocking the light.
   - This step is a perfect opportunity to talk about how the sun's rays interact with the chemicals in the paper, giving your child a mini science lesson in a fun, hands-on way.

6. **Rinse and Reveal:**
   - Once the exposure time is complete, carefully remove the acrylic sheet and natural items from the sun print paper.
   - Submerge the sun print paper in a bowl of water for about a minute to stop the developing process. For a richer, deeper blue, you can extend the submersion time up to 5 minutes.
   - Watch the colors reverse as the print develops into a beautiful blue and white design.
7. **Dry and Display:**
   - Remove the paper from the water and lay it flat on a towel or drying surface to air dry. Once it's dry, the design will be fully developed and ready to display.
   - Once the prints are complete, spend time together examining the final product. Discuss how each item turned out, pointing out the intricate details left behind by different leaves and flowers. Ask your child which part of the print is their favorite and why. This encourages observation and reflection, which can deepen the connection through conversation.

Safety Considerations:

- Supervise the use of glass or acrylic sheets to prevent breakage and injuries.

Troubleshooting Tips:

- **Not Enough Sunlight**: If it's a cloudy day, extend the exposure time to compensate for less direct sunlight. Alternatively, you can wait for a sunnier day or use a UV light to create the prints indoors.
- **Faint Prints:** Ensure the items are in good contact with the paper and that the exposure time is sufficient.

Cleanup Tips:

- Store unused sun print paper in a dark, dry place to preserve its quality.
- If you're making multiple prints, set up a simple drying rack using clothespins and a line to hang the wet prints while they dry. This speeds up the drying process and keeps the prints in good condition.

Variations and Adaptations:

- **Pressed Flower Prints**: After creating your sun prints, collect more flowers and press them into books. Use these pressed flowers to decorate the sun prints by attaching them to the print itself, combining real flowers with the print design.
- **Seasonal Prints**: Create prints based on the changing seasons. For

example, in the fall, use leaves and pinecones; in the spring, focus on fresh flowers. Over time, you'll build a seasonal art collection that reflects the beauty of nature throughout the year.

- **Textured Prints**: Add an extra dimension by combining natural objects with textured materials like lace, mesh, or fabric. Layer the textures on top of the natural items to create intricate designs when exposed to the sun.
- **Wearable Prints:** Take your sun prints beyond paper by using cyanotype fabric sheets, which are available premade, or create your own with a 2-part cyanotype chemical set (available online and from art stores). Apply the sun print technique to fabric items like tote bags, t-shirts, or scarves for unique, wearable art. This variation allows you and your child to craft something functional and stylish while exploring the magic of sunlight and creativity.
- **Sun Print Adventure Map**: Collect unique natural items from each place you visit with your child—like leaves or flowers—and use them to create sun prints. Over time, these prints form a keepsake "adventure map" that captures memories of your journeys. Add drawn trails or landmarks afterward to complete the story of your outdoor adventures together.

Benefits:

- **Teaches Scientific Concepts:** Observing the chemical reaction that occurs when the sun print paper is exposed to sunlight introduces basic principles of photography and chemistry in a hands-on, engaging way.
- **Encourages Learning Through Experimentation**: The process of testing different items, exposure times, and layouts introduces children to the concept of experimentation, helping them learn through trial and error.
- **Introduces Artistic Techniques**: This activity introduces children to new artistic methods beyond traditional drawing and painting, broadening their understanding of how art can be created through alternative techniques.
- **Strengthens Bonds**: Collaborating on every step—from collecting materials to creating the prints—encourages meaningful conversations, teamwork, and shared excitement. This cooperative process strengthens emotional connections, creating deeper, lasting memories.
- **Promotes Outdoor Exploration:** Collecting leaves, flowers, and other natural items promotes outdoor activity and a connection with nature, fostering a sense of curiosity and appreciation for the environment.

45

ROCK BALANCE MASTERY

Step outside and engage in the tranquil art of rock balancing! With a variety of rocks at your disposal, you and your child can create impressive rock towers, testing your patience and precision. Picture the quiet concentration as you both carefully place each rock, adjusting and readjusting to find the perfect balance. This activity is a fantastic way to spend quality time outdoors, combining creativity with a touch of engineering.

As you work together, you'll experience moments of triumph when a particularly tricky rock finally stays in place. The challenge of building higher and more stable towers fosters a sense of teamwork and shared achievement. The serene setting and the focused task make this activity not only fun but also a great way to unwind and connect with nature.

Materials Needed:

- ☐ Various sizes of rocks
- ☐ A flat, stable surface
- ☐ Closed-toe shoes (to protect feet from falling rocks)

Step-by-Step Instructions:

1. **Collect Rocks:**
   - Head outside to collect a variety of rocks with your child. Look for rocks of different shapes, sizes, and textures. Smooth, flat rocks are great for stability, while rounder ones add a fun challenge.
   - Use this opportunity to discuss the different types of rocks and how their shapes might affect their ability to balance.
2. **Choose a Stable Surface:**
   - Find a flat and sturdy surface for your stacking adventure. This could be a patio, flat stone, or even a patch of even ground. The surface needs to be firm and unmoving for the best results.
   - **Pro Tip:** If the ground is slightly uneven, it adds to the challenge and teaches how to compensate with your foundation rock.
3. **Start with a Strong Base:**
   - Begin with the largest, flattest rock as the base of your tower and place it on the ground or surface.
   - Take your time wiggling your base rock into position to make sure it's stable and not wobbling.
   - While setting your foundation, you can demonstrate how starting with a strong base helps create a stable structure. It's a fun way to incorporate some basic engineering principles as you work together.
   - **Stacking Tip #1:** A secure foundation sets the stage for success. Make sure the first rock is perfectly steady before adding more.
4. **Use the Triple Anchor Technique:**
   - As you place the second rock, focus on creating three distinct points of contact between the two rocks. This creates a strong triangular support structure that keeps the top rock steady.
   - Drag the top rock gently over the surface of the base rock until you feel it "anchor" itself into place using those three points for stability.
   - Encourage your child to experiment with positioning, adjusting each rock until it balances perfectly before adding the next one. Use gentle movements and patience to achieve the right balance.
   - This is a great time to discuss patience and how small changes can make a big difference when building.
   - **Stacking Tip #2:** The triple anchor technique ensures that the top rock stays secure by connecting at three key points, creating a solid foundation for the next layer.
5. **Fine-Tune the Balance:**

  - Continue using the triple anchor technique with each additional rock.
  - Adjust each rock until it balances perfectly before adding the next one. Use gentle movements and patience to achieve the right balance.
  - **Stacking Tip #3:** Rounded rocks can be tricky. Rotate them slowly, feeling for where they naturally catch on three stable points. Let your child take the lead in this discovery process!

6. **Experiment with Counterbalance:**
   - As you continue stacking, try counterbalancing the rocks by placing them off-center. Look for grooves or flat edges where the rocks can rest securely.
   - **Stacking Tip #4:** Small rocks can be used as shims to stabilize larger ones. Experiment with placement to see how balancing weight can prevent the tower from toppling.

7. **Aim High:**
   - Work with your child to build the tallest or most symmetrical tower possible. Don't worry if it falls—each attempt helps you learn and improve! Share laughs and teamwork as you adjust and rebuild.
   - **Stacking Tip #5:** Alternate between large and small rocks for added stability. Placing smaller rocks between bigger ones often adds both height and strength.

8. **Wrap Up and Reflect:**
   - Once you've completed your rock tower, take a moment to admire your hard work! Snap a picture before the inevitable collapse. Use this as a chance to reflect on how patience and teamwork made the structure possible.
   - If you've built your tower in a public or natural area, take a moment to carefully dismantle it, returning the rocks to their original spots. This helps maintain the balance of the ecosystem, allowing wildlife to continue benefiting from the resources these rocks provide, while also preserving the natural beauty for others to enjoy. If you're at home, feel free to leave it standing for as long as you'd like!

Safety Considerations:

- Avoid setting up rock towers near steep slopes or uneven terrain where rocks could roll or fall dangerously.
- Before you start collecting rocks, encourage your child to carefully check under each rock before lifting it, looking for any wildlife that may be hiding underneath. This helps ensure that both you and the animals can stay safe and undisturbed.
- Ensure that the rocks you and your child are using are not too large or

heavy to handle safely. Avoid rocks that are too big for your child to lift or manipulate without strain.

- As your child balances rocks, encourage them to place their fingers carefully to avoid pinching or crushing them between heavy rocks. A slow and mindful approach helps prevent accidents.
- Keep an eye on your child at all times, especially if the towers get tall or wobbly. If a stack begins to lean precariously, help guide your child in dismantling it safely before it falls.

Troubleshooting Tips:

- **Toppling Towers:** Start with a stable base and ensure each rock is securely balanced before adding more. Use wider rocks at the base for better stability.
- **Wobbly Rocks:** Use flatter rocks for the base and more irregular ones as you build higher. Adjust the position until you find the perfect balance.
- **Limited Rocks:** If you have a limited supply of rocks, get creative with the arrangement by incorporating natural elements like twigs and leaves, or try building a miniature landscape with your rocks to create a fun scene.

Cleanup Tips:

- Teach your child the "leave no trace" principle by ensuring the area looks just as it did when you started. This reinforces environmental stewardship while encouraging mindfulness about cleaning up.

Variations and Adaptations:

- **Timed Challenge:** Add a competitive edge by using a timer to see who can create the tallest or most complex balanced tower within a set time. This brings excitement and pushes creativity under pressure.
- **Blindfolded Balance:** Take turns balancing rocks while blindfolded, relying on touch, precise descriptions, and teamwork to guide each other.
- **Miniature Balancing:** Use small pebbles and stones to create miniature rock towers. This variation requires fine motor skills and precision, adding a new layer of challenge.
- **Rock Balance Dice Game**: Turn the activity into a game where each roll of the dice dictates what kind of rock you must balance next (e.g., flat, round, large). The goal is to balance the rocks in a particular sequence without toppling the tower.
- **Color-Coordinated Towers**: Instead of focusing on height or stability, challenge yourselves to build towers with rocks grouped by similar shades or hues. Create gradients with rocks going from dark to light or mix and match complementary colors for an artistic touch.

- **Educational Twist:** Incorporate a lesson on geology by identifying and learning about the different types of rocks you are using. Discuss their properties and how they affect balancing.

Benefits:

- **Enhances Patience and Focus**: Carefully balancing rocks requires sustained attention and patience, helping children practice concentration and perseverance as they work toward achieving a stable structure.
- **Builds Problem-Solving Skills**: Children must figure out how to balance each rock by experimenting with placement and adjusting their approach, sharpening their critical thinking and creative problem-solving abilities.
- **Fosters Creativity and Imagination**: The open-ended nature of rock balancing allows children to explore different designs and structures, encouraging creative thinking and the freedom to experiment with their ideas.
- **Teaches Structural Engineering Concepts**: As children experiment with balance and weight distribution, they naturally learn basic concepts of physics and structural engineering, gaining an intuitive understanding of how forces and gravity work.
- **Strengthens Bonds:** Working together to create rock towers fosters collaboration and teamwork, providing quality bonding moments between you and your child as you strategize, celebrate successes, and overcome challenges together.
- **Boosts Emotional Regulation**: The calming, meditative aspect of rock balancing helps children learn to manage frustration, stay calm, and regulate their emotions, especially when a tower collapses and they need to try again.

MIDDLE SCHOOLERS

ON THE

RISE

INDOOR ADVENTURES

Middle schoolers thrive on challenges, and these indoor activities are made to inspire! Dive into creative projects like Stop Motion Storycraft, where storytelling comes alive through animation using toys and clay. Fictional World Building lets imagination soar as you and your child create entire worlds filled with unique landscapes, cultures, and histories. For those with a flair for visual storytelling, Epic Comic Book Studio offers the perfect outlet, combining writing and art to bring new heroes and tales to life.

46

STOP MOTION STORYCRAFT

Get ready to dive into the fascinating world of stop motion animation with your kiddo. Using toys, clay, or even household items, you can create a short film that brings their wildest ideas to life. Imagine the excitement as you sit together, planning a story, and setting up scenes with their favorite toys or hand-crafted clay figures. This activity not only flexes their creative muscles but also introduces them to the basics of filmmaking and storytelling. Each small movement captured by the camera contributes to the magic of animation, and the sense of achievement they feel when they see their creations come to life on screen is truly priceless.

As the project unfolds, you'll see them engaging deeply, from carefully positioning figures for each frame to eagerly anticipating the next shot. A stop motion app helps simplify the process, allowing them to compile frames into a smooth animation and add special effects. This collaborative effort not only strengthens your bond but also nurtures patience, attention to detail, and a sense of humor. By the end of the project, the look on their face when they watch their animated story is one of pure delight, making all the effort worthwhile.

Materials Needed:

- ☐ Toys, clay, LEGO bricks, or household items
- ☐ Smartphone or camera
- ☐ Stop motion app (e.g., Stop Motion Studio; free version works fine)
- ☐ Additional lighting (optional)
- ☐ Tripod or stable surface for the camera
- ☐ Table or desk space for setting up scenes
- ☐ Background materials (e.g., poster boards, colored paper)

Step-by-Step Instructions:

1. **Plan the Story:**
   - Sit down together and brainstorm a short, simple story. Encourage your child to let their imagination run wild, whether it's a superhero showdown, a fantastical adventure, or a silly household item escapade.
   - Sketch out a simple storyboard to map the sequence of events. Keep it short and sweet to maintain interest and ensure a manageable project length.
2. **Set the Scene:**
   - Find a stable, well-lit area to serve as the "set" for your story. If needed, set up additional lighting to enhance the scene.
   - Use poster boards, colored paper, or even household items as a backdrop.
   - Let your child arrange the setting, adding props and characters to bring the scene to life. Encourage them to add personal touches, like crafting trees from paper or using household items as unexpected props.
3. **Create Characters:**
   - Select toys, action figures, or create clay characters to act as the stars of the story. If your child wants to craft their own characters, help them mold simple figures using clay or modeling dough.
4. **Set Up the Camera:**
   - Secure your smartphone or tablet on a tripod or stable surface to ensure steady shots. Make sure the angle captures the entire scene. Most stop motion apps will allow you to check framing before you start shooting.
   - Open the stop motion app and explore the basic functions together. Familiarize yourselves with how to capture frames, adjust playback speed, and review the sequence, so you're ready to start animating.
5. **Capture Frames:**
   - Begin shooting the first frame by taking a picture of the scene in its starting position.
   - Move the characters or props ever so slightly for each frame to simulate motion. Each movement should be small and deliberate—this is where patience comes in! Work together, taking turns moving characters and snapping pictures.
   - Capture a new frame after each adjustment. Continue this process until you've finished your scene. Depending on the complexity, you'll

need 10-12 frames for every second of your final animation.

6. **Edit and Compile:**
   - Once you've captured enough frames for your story, use the app to compile the photos into an animation. Adjust the playback speed to see how smooth the animation looks.
   - Encourage your child to make edits or reshoot certain sections if needed. This part can be just as fun as watching the final product come together!
   - Use the stop motion app to add special effects, filters, voiceovers, or soundtracks to the animation. Let your child experiment with different sounds, voices, or music to enhance the story.
7. **Add Closing Credits (Optional):**
   - Use the stop motion app or another editing tool to create a slide listing the "cast" (toys, clay figures, or items used), "directors," and any special thanks. You can keep it simple by typing in names or get creative with hand-drawn credits that reflect the theme of your story.
   - Encourage your child to come up with fun titles, like "Best Toy in a Supporting Role," "Master of Clay Figures," or "World's Greatest Animator." It adds a personal and humorous touch to their project.
   - You could even add a short blooper reel or outtakes for a fun finishing touch, showcasing any funny moments or mistakes made during filming.
8. **Host a Screening Party:**
   - Once the animation is complete, sit down together and watch the masterpiece! Celebrate the accomplishment with a little premiere, whether it's just for the two of you or the whole family.
   - Take turns describing your favorite scenes, moments, or even the funniest bloopers that happened during filming.
   - After the credits roll, give each other a well-deserved round of applause for your teamwork and creativity. Finish the evening by sharing what you loved most about working together on the project, and make plans for your next epic stop motion adventure!

Safety Considerations:

- Ensure the camera or smartphone is mounted on a sturdy tripod or surface to prevent it from toppling over. Consider using a stack of books or a small object to prop up or anchor the device for extra stability.
- If you're using additional lights, ensure they don't overheat and are placed away from flammable materials like paper or fabric. Opt for LED lights that stay cool during use, and keep wires organized to prevent tripping

hazards.

Troubleshooting Tips:

- **Frames Misaligned**: If your frames don't line up, mark both the camera and figure positions with tape to ensure consistency throughout the animation. This prevents unintentional shifts when adjusting or repositioning elements.
- **Unwanted Shadows**: Changing shadows can disrupt continuity, so use fixed artificial lighting rather than relying on natural light. This helps maintain a uniform look between frames, especially during longer shoots.
- **Figures Toppling**: Stabilize characters or props with small amounts of putty or create broader bases for figures to stand more securely.
- **Unsteady Hands:** If the frames are shaky, use a remote shutter or timer function.
- **Blurred Frames**: Blurry shots can break the flow of animation. Set your camera to manual focus and lock it in place before starting, ensuring crisp images without sudden focus shifts.
- **Frame Rate Too Fast or Slow**: If the animation feels too fast or sluggish, adjust the frame rate in your app. Start with 10-15 frames per second for smoother movement and tweak as needed for the best pacing.

Cleanup Tips:

- Make sure your animation project is saved and backed up on multiple devices or cloud storage so you don't lose all your hard work.

Variations and Adaptations:

- **Time-Lapse Animation:** Create a time-lapse animation of a craft or science project, showing the process from start to finish. This can be both educational and visually engaging.
- **Chalkboard Animation**: Use a chalkboard or whiteboard to draw different scenes, erasing and redrawing between shots to create a fluid animation. This is great for adding hand-drawn elements or evolving background landscapes that shift as the story progresses.
- **DIY Special Effects:** Experiment with homemade special effects, such as creating explosions with cotton balls, making objects "fly" with fishing line, or simulating water with cellophane. This adds a dynamic element to the animation.
- **DIY Soundtrack**: Have your child create the sound effects and soundtrack for the movie using their voice or household items like tapping spoons or rattling keys. Record these and sync them to the animation to add an immersive auditory experience.

- **Music Video Mania**: Pick a favorite song, and create a stop motion music video to go along with it. Your child can choreograph the characters' dance moves or animate scenes that match the beat of the music, making a dynamic, rhythmic experience.
- **Household Heroics**: Use everyday household items as characters in a quirky stop motion film. Forks become superheroes, or toothbrushes have a dance-off—this variation encourages creativity by turning ordinary objects into the stars of the show.

Benefits:

- **Enhances Patience and Focus**: The careful, repetitive nature of stop motion animation teaches your child to focus on minute details and sustain attention over longer periods, helping them build patience in a fun, hands-on way.
- **Promotes Creative Problem-Solving**: Challenges like figuring out how to make objects move smoothly or how to structure the story encourage your child to think creatively and find solutions on their own.
- **Introduces Cinematic Concepts**: Concepts like camera angles, lighting, and shot composition are naturally introduced through this activity, giving children an early understanding of visual storytelling and film techniques.
- **Strengthens Bonds:** Working together on the project builds teamwork as both you and your child contribute to the creative process. This shared effort encourages communication, joint decision-making, and mutual support, strengthening the bond through problem-solving and shared successes.
- **Introduces Sequential Thinking**: Stop motion requires logical thinking about the order of movements and scenes. This helps children grasp the concept of sequencing, which is useful for math, coding, and other logical tasks.

47

FICTIONAL WORLD BUILDING

Enter a universe of endless possibilities by creating a detailed fictional world together! This activity involves developing the history, geography, cultures, and stories of a new world, providing an expansive canvas for creativity and storytelling. From brainstorming the world's landscape and climates to fleshing out its unique cultures and historical events, each step is a journey into creative thinking.

You and your child will sketch maps, write stories, and develop characters that inhabit this fantastical world. Whether it's crafting a mythology for your world's ancient civilizations or drawing the bustling cities and serene countryside, every aspect is an opportunity to let your imaginations run wild. This world-building adventure not only nurtures creativity and teamwork but also weaves together stories and moments that you and your child will treasure long after the final map is drawn.

Materials Needed:

- ☐ Notebook or sketchbook
- ☐ Pens, pencils, and markers
- ☐ Large paper or poster board (for maps and diagrams)
- ☐ Reference books or online resources (for inspiration)
- ☐ Computer for digital world-building (optional)

Step-by-Step Instructions:

1. **Brainstorm the Big Picture:**
   - Sit down together and start brainstorming the basics of your world, such as the world's name, its inhabitants, and its environment. Ask questions like:
     - Is it a fantasy world with magic, a futuristic planet, or an alternate Earth?
     - What type of climate or environments exist (deserts, forests, oceans, space stations)?
     - Are there different continents, countries, or realms?
   - Encourage your child to explore different possibilities and jot down all ideas, even the wild ones. No idea is too big or too small—this is your fictional world!
2. **Develop the Geography:**
   - Once you have a general idea of the landscape, begin sketching a rough map of the world on a large paper or poster board. Think about continents, oceans, mountains, forests, and cities.
   - Don't worry about being an artist—this is all about creativity! As you sketch, discuss where civilizations might form and where natural resources, like rivers or minerals, are located.
   - Label the most important places and discuss how they might interact or be connected, like trade routes or ancient roads.
3. **Create Cultures and Societies:**
   - Now, focus on the inhabitants of your world. Do different races, species, or cultures live in various regions? What are their customs, religions, and traditions?
   - Choose one or two cultures to flesh out in detail. Discuss the following:
     - What do they wear? What do they eat? What does their language sound like?
     - What is their government or social structure like?
     - What is their relationship with neighboring cultures (friendship, rivalry, trade)?
   - Write down key traits for each culture to bring them to life.
4. **Flesh Out the History:**
   - Work together to develop the history of your world. Think about:
     - Have there been wars, peace treaties, discoveries, or natural

disasters that shaped the way societies function?

    - Are there historical figures or events that everyone in the world knows about?

- Discuss how these past events affect the present-day world.
    - How do they shape the political landscape or relationships between different regions? Are there long-standing tensions or alliances that still matter?
- Create a timeline with key events that shaped the world. Your child can use their imagination to determine what the most dramatic or significant turning points were.

5. **Introduce the Characters:**
    - Create detailed profiles for key characters in your world. These could be leaders, adventurers, or ordinary citizens with interesting stories. Describe their backgrounds, personalities, and roles in the world.
    - Encourage your child to create a hero and a villain. Develop backstories for these characters:
        - Where were they born? What do they want? What motivates them?
        - How do their actions affect the world around them?
    - Sketch or write descriptions of your main characters, and if you'd like, give them unique powers, weapons, or skills to make them stand out.
6. **Build Myths and Legends:**
    - Work together to create myths and legends that took place in the ancient past of your fictional world. These could explain the origins of key landmarks, the rise and fall of civilizations, or the deeds of legendary heroes.
    - Use these narratives to bring depth and richness to your world. These stories can reveal how certain cultures came to be, the significance of specific symbols or rituals, and the mysteries behind sacred places or ancient ruins. Let your child's imagination guide the creation of these epic tales.
7. **Write a Short Story:**
    - Now that your world has geography, culture, history, and characters, work together to write a short story set in your world. This can be a thrilling adventure, a political intrigue, or even a quiet day in the life of one of your characters.
    - Let your child lead the plot, but offer guidance in structure and pacing. Have fun bringing your world to life through this collaborative storytelling!

8. **Reflect and Expand:**
   - Once your story is written, take time to reflect on your world-building process. Talk about what you enjoyed and what could be added.
   - Feel free to keep expanding your world with new stories, maps, or characters. You could even turn this into a long-term project where you revisit and add more to the world as you continue exploring it together.

Safety Considerations:

- Set up comfortable and ergonomic workspaces to avoid strain or injury during prolonged creative sessions.
- If using digital tools for world-building, monitor screen time to prevent eye strain and encourage regular breaks to stretch and move around.

Troubleshooting Tips:

- **Writer's Block:** Try using prompts, reference materials, or random generators to spark new ideas. You can also revisit favorite books, movies, or games for inspiration without copying directly.
- **Conflicting Ideas**: When different ideas emerge, blend concepts where possible to create a unique result, or compromise by exploring both ideas in different parts of the world. Open discussions can lead to richer world-building.
- **Too Many Details:** If you or your child feel overwhelmed by the scale of world-building, focus on one area at a time. Start small—perhaps with a single city or region—and gradually expand the world as you build confidence.
- **World Feels Inconsistent**: Keep notes organized to maintain consistency in your world-building. If the elements of your world (geography, culture, history) don't seem to fit together, revisit the foundation and ask clarifying questions about how different aspects interact. Consider the cause-and-effect relationships in the world's design to bring everything into harmony.

Cleanup Tips:

- Store any physical maps, drawings, and notes in a dedicated binder or folder to prevent them from getting damaged or lost. Label sections for easy reference during future world-building sessions.
- Save any digital documents, sketches, and maps in organized folders on your computer or cloud storage. Use clear file names and back up your work to avoid losing important progress. Periodically go through digital files to delete unnecessary drafts or duplicates, keeping your digital workspace clutter-free.

Variations and Adaptations:

- **Dice-Rolling Decisions**: Add a random element to the process by rolling dice or using a random number generator to make key decisions about the world. For instance, a roll might determine the size of a city, the outcome of a historical event, or even the climate of a region. This keeps the process fresh and unpredictable.
- **Visual Art:** Bring the world to life by drawing or painting scenes and characters, or by using 3D materials like clay, cardboard, or Legos to build cities, mountains, and landscapes.
- **Multimedia World Building:** Use various media forms, such as creating a short film, a song, a comic book, or a digital animation based on your fictional world.
- **Custom Board Game Adventure:** Once your world is built, bring it to life as a board game! Use the geography, history, and cultures you've created to design the game's rules, objectives, and characters. Players can explore different regions, encounter unique challenges, and battle foes as they journey through the world you've crafted. (For detailed steps, see the Custom Board Game Build-Off activity on page 197!)
- **LARPing Quest:** Turn your world into a live-action role-playing adventure (LARPing) where players take on the roles of its characters! With quests to complete, conflicts to resolve, and mysteries to uncover, players navigate their way through the world, interacting with its lore and cultures as they go. This immersive experience invites everyone to think, act, and even speak like their character, deepening their connection to the world you've created together.
- **Fictional World Debate**: After building the world, you and your child defend a different aspect of it in a friendly debate—perhaps about a major historical event or cultural practice. This adds a fun, competitive twist while exploring different perspectives within the fictional world.

Benefits:

- **Enhances Creativity:** Building a fictional world from scratch sparks expansive imagination, encouraging your child to think outside the box and explore new ideas that push creative boundaries.
- **Develops Critical Thinking**: Creating a complex world requires considering how different elements—geography, history, culture—interconnect. This helps hone the ability to think critically and make thoughtful decisions as they design a cohesive universe.
- **Encourages Flexibility and Adaptability**: As the world-building process evolves, earlier ideas may need to be adjusted or adapted to fit new developments. This builds flexibility and adaptability in thinking,

encouraging a willingness to change and improve ideas.

- **Strengthens Bonds:** Working together to create a world fosters a deeper connection, as you and your child share ideas, solve challenges together, and celebrate the creative process as a team.
- **Introduces Project Planning Skills**: World-building requires coordinating multiple elements, such as geography, culture, and history, into a cohesive whole. This process helps develop the ability to plan and execute complex, multi-phase projects with greater organization and foresight.

48

EPIC COMIC BOOK STUDIO

Turn your living room into a comic book studio where imagination runs wild and anything is possible. This DIY comic book activity lets your child step into the shoes of a writer and artist, crafting their own superheroes, villains, and epic tales. Picture the excitement as you develop characters, plot twists, and captivating storylines together, all while expressing creativity through vibrant illustrations. It's a fantastic blend of art and storytelling that will have them grinning from ear to ear when they see their finished product.

Throughout the process, you'll experience the joy of bringing ideas to life on paper. From planning the storyline and sketching rough drafts to creating detailed comic panels, each step is a journey into your imaginations. The end result is a personalized comic book that showcases their unique vision and storytelling skills. This activity not only provides hours of creative fun but also enhances literacy and artistic abilities, making it a perfect blend of education and entertainment.

Materials Needed:

- ☐ Blank paper or a sketchbook
- ☐ Pencils and erasers
- ☐ Colored pencils, markers, or pens
- ☐ Ruler
- ☐ Stapler or binding clips
- ☐ Computer or tablet (optional for digital comics)

Step-by-Step Instructions:

1. **Brainstorm Characters and Story:**
   - Start by discussing character ideas with your child. Who's the hero? What's their superpower? Who is the villain, and what is their motivation? Encourage your child to think about the hero's weaknesses and strengths.
   - Together, brainstorm the main plot. Is it a battle between good and evil? A quest for a lost treasure? Let your imaginations run wild, and don't worry about making it perfect at this stage.
2. **Create a Rough Story Outline:**
   - On a piece of paper, outline the major events of the story. Break it into sections like "Introduction," "Conflict," "Climax," and "Resolution." Discuss how you want each section to unfold, and decide which parts will get more detail in the comic panels.
   - Sketch a rough storyboard to visualize the sequence of events.
   - **Note:** This is a great opportunity to teach your child about pacing in storytelling and how to build suspense.
3. **Sketch the Panels:**
   - Using a ruler, help your child draw the comic panels in their sketchbook, or use a digital tool if you're opting for a digital approach. Decide on the size and number of panels for each page. Some pages may only have one large, dramatic panel, while others might have several smaller ones to show action and dialogue.
   - Encourage your child to sketch the characters and scenes lightly in pencil first. Remind them it doesn't have to be perfect—it's about getting their ideas on paper!
4. **Add Dialogue and Action:**
   - Once the sketches are in place, work with your child to add speech bubbles, sound effects, and captions. This is where they can experiment with dialogue, catchphrases, and internal thoughts. Let them be as creative as they want with the language and expressions their characters use.
   - Talk about the emotions in each scene. Is the hero excited, nervous, or angry? How can you show that through their facial expressions and words?
5. **Finalize the Artwork:**
   - After the sketches and text are complete, go over the lines with a black ink pen or marker to make them stand out. This step is crucial for giving the comic that professional look.

- Encourage your child to add colors using colored pencils, markers, or watercolors to bring their world to life. Discuss color schemes and how certain colors can evoke different moods (e.g., red for danger or excitement, blue for calm or sadness).

6. **Add the Finishing Touches:**
   - Once the comic is complete, review it together. Look for any areas where they want to add more detail, shading, or additional dialogue. Help them make any final adjustments to their artwork or storyline.
   - Create a title page with the comic's name and your child's name as the artist and author. They could also include a "credits" page, just like in professional comic books, to make it even more special.
   - If you've been using loose sheets of paper, bind the pages to create an official comic book. You can staple the pages together along the spine or punch holes and use ribbon or binder rings for a more creative binding. Alternatively, take your comic to a local print shop for professional binding.

7. **Show It Off:**
   - After all your hard work, encourage your child to show off their comic book! You can even make copies for family members or friends, or scan the pages to create a digital version they can share online.

Safety Considerations:

- Take regular breaks to prevent eye strain, especially if your child is working on digital devices. Follow the 20-20-20 rule: every 20 minutes, take a 20-second break to look at something 20 feet away.
- Set up comfortable and ergonomic workspaces to avoid strain or injury during prolonged creative sessions.

Troubleshooting Tips:

- **Writer's Block:** If the story starts to feel stuck, suggest adding a plot twist or introducing a new character.
- **Smudged Lines**: Encourage your child to let ink or markers dry fully before moving on. You can also use smudge-proof pens or place a sheet of paper under their hand to avoid accidental smears.
- **Colors Not Blending Well**: If colors aren't blending smoothly or look messy, suggest using a layering technique. Start with lighter colors and build up darker shades gradually, which often results in smoother transitions.

Cleanup Tips:

- Place finished comic pages in a folder or binder to protect them from damage. If you're working with loose sheets, consider adding page numbers to help keep them in order.

Variations and Adaptations:

- **Super Family Comics:** Create a comic book where you and your child are a dynamic superhero duo, tackling challenges and embarking on thrilling adventures together. This adds a personal and fun twist to the activity, making it even more engaging.
- **Mini Comics:** Focus on creating short three- to four-panel comic strips that can be completed in a shorter time frame. This keeps the stories bite-sized and perfect for experimenting with quick jokes, fun characters, or daily life observations.
- **Fan Fiction Comics:** Create comics based on favorite TV shows, movies, or video games, adding personal twists to beloved characters and stories. You can take existing characters and create new stories or spin-offs with a unique twist.
- **Superhero Origin Stories:** Focus specifically on creating an origin story for a superhero or villain, detailing how they got their powers and what drives them. This can make for a more character-driven narrative and allows for deep storytelling.
- **Historical Comic**: Turn a historical figure or event into a comic book, adding a fun twist or even a fictional character into the mix. This combines creativity with education and can help make learning history more engaging.
- **Silent Comic Challenge**: Create a comic without any dialogue or sound effects. The challenge is to rely entirely on the visuals and character expressions to tell the story, which enhances the ability to communicate visually.
- **Educational Comics:** Create comics that teach lessons or explain scientific concepts in a fun, engaging way. Whether it's breaking down how the water cycle works or exploring math concepts like fractions through colorful characters, turning complex topics into easy-to-follow stories and visuals makes learning both entertaining and accessible.

Benefits:

- **Strengthens Focus and Perseverance**: Completing a full comic book, from rough drafts to final illustrations, requires sustained focus and patience. The process teaches children the value of seeing a project through to completion.
- **Improves Literacy and Language Skills**: Writing dialogue and captions requires careful thought about language, grammar, and punctuation, which naturally strengthens literacy skills in an enjoyable and practical way.

- **Boosts Confidence:** Drawing characters, settings, and action scenes allows children to express their creativity and build confidence in their artistic abilities, encouraging self-expression without fear of judgment.
- **Encourages Personal Reflection**: Developing characters and stories often reflects personal experiences, emotions, or ideas, allowing children to explore their own thoughts and values through their creations.
- **Strengthens Bonds**: Collaborating on creating a comic book provides meaningful opportunities for communication, laughter, and problem-solving. Working side-by-side, discussing characters and stories, and contributing ideas deepens the bond by fostering shared creative experiences.
- **Encourages Creative Problem-Solving**: Plot twists, character challenges, and visual layout issues in comics present opportunities for your child to think critically and solve problems creatively, both in storytelling and artistic presentation.

OUTDOOR FUN

Take learning and fun outside with these activities designed for middle schoolers on the rise! Capture the world around you with Urban Photography Scavenger Hunt, which encourages creativity while exploring the urban environment. For a more tranquil experience, Nature Journey Journaling combines art and mindfulness, letting you record and reflect on the beauty of the outdoors. Dive deeper into history by exploring local Historical Landmarks and learning about the past, or immerse yourselves in the tranquility of Wild Soundscapes, where you record the sounds of nature to create your own personalized sound mix. These activities blend exploration, creativity, and discovery, providing unforgettable moments in the fresh air.

49

NATURE JOURNEY JOURNALING

Begin an enlightening adventure into the great outdoors by starting a nature journal with your child. This activity is all about observing the beauty of the natural world and recording it through notes and sketches. Imagine the serene moments spent together in a local park, your backyard, or on a hiking trail, with your child deeply engaged in capturing the essence of nature. Nature journaling helps foster a deeper connection to the environment, enhances observational skills, and provides a peaceful escape from the hustle and bustle of daily life.

As you explore, take note of everything you see, hear, and feel. Sketch detailed close-ups of leaves, insects, or birds, and write down observations and thoughts. This mindful practice not only nurtures curiosity and appreciation for nature but also blends art, science, and writing into one enriching experience. Each page of the journal becomes a unique reflection of your encounters with nature, creating a lasting keepsake of your adventures.

Materials Needed:

- ☐ Notebook or sketchbook
- ☐ Pencils, pens, and colored pencils
- ☐ A sturdy clipboard (if using loose paper)
- ☐ Backpack for carrying supplies
- ☐ Binoculars or magnifying glass (optional)
- ☐ Field guide books or apps (e.g., Seek, iNaturalist; optional)
- ☐ Comfortable walking shoes
- ☐ Water, packed lunch, and sun protection (for extended outings)
- ☐ Insect repellant (optional)

Step-by-Step Instructions:

1. **Choose a Journal:**
   - Pick a durable notebook or sketchbook that can handle outdoor use. A waterproof cover is a bonus.
   - Encourage your child personalize it with stickers or drawings to make it uniquely theirs.
2. **Choose Your Destination:**
   - Select a nearby park, hiking trail, or even your backyard as the setting for your journaling adventure. Talk with your child about the different locations you could explore, considering their interests (e.g., forested areas, by a lake, or fields).
   - Pack your supplies in a backpack and dress appropriately for the weather.
3. **Set an Intention for the Journey:**
   - Before heading out, discuss with your child what they would like to focus on during the journaling session. Are they particularly interested in trees, birds, insects, or the changing weather? This helps them feel more engaged and adds direction to your exploration.
   - Remind your child that they can draw, write, or do both in their journal.
4. **Explore Nature:**
   - Upon arriving at your destination, encourage your child to take a few moments to absorb their surroundings. Guide them to observe plants, insects, birds, and landscapes, and use all five senses to describe the environment—noting not just what they see, but also what they hear, smell, touch, and even taste (if safe).
   - As you explore, help your child write down quick notes or sketches about what catches their eye, including the colors, shapes, sounds, and smells they encounter. Encourage them to sketch what they find interesting as well.
   - This step is about capturing those first impressions while you're on the move. Share in the experience by jotting down your own observations, sparking curiosity together.
5. **Pause for Sketching and Writing:**
   - Find a comfortable spot, such as a bench or under a tree, to sit and reflect. This is the time to take a closer look and spend time sketching something they find particularly fascinating, like a nearby animal or the veins on a leaf.

- Have your child write down any thoughts or reflections about the environment around them. They could describe how the air feels, what they hear, or how the light changes through the trees.

6. **Encourage Deeper Observation:**
   - Use a magnifying glass (if you have one) to look closer at small objects like insects, moss, or pebbles. This deeper observation can enhance their drawing or writing, adding more detail and encouraging mindfulness.
   - If they struggle to start writing or drawing, ask open-ended questions such as, "What's something that catches your eye right now?" or "How do you think the weather is affecting the environment today?"

7. **Reflect and Wrap Up:**
   - As your journaling session comes to a close, ask your child to review their entries. Talk about what they noticed that was unexpected or interesting.
   - Discuss any new observations or thoughts they might have. Reflect on how different elements of nature interact and encourage your child to think about their role in nature.

Safety Considerations:

- Wear weather-appropriate clothing, including hats, sunscreen, and insect repellent to protect against sunburn and bug bites.
- Familiarize yourself with the area and any potential hazards like poisonous plants, wildlife, or uneven terrain.
- Bring enough water and snacks to stay hydrated and energized, especially if you'll be out for an extended period.
- Identify and avoid plants, insects, or other allergens that might cause reactions.
- Observe animals from a safe distance and avoid feeding or provoking them.
- Keep a charged mobile phone and inform someone of your location and expected return time in case of any unforeseen situations.
- Carry a basic first aid kit to handle minor injuries such as scrapes or insect stings.
- Regularly check for ticks during and after the activity. Promptly and properly remove any that are found. Wear long sleeves and tuck pants into socks to minimize exposure.

Troubleshooting Tips:

- **Weather Interruptions**: Sudden rain or extreme weather can cut a journaling session short. Keep a waterproof pouch or bag handy to protect your journal and pens. If the weather changes drastically, use the time to reflect and write about how the weather affects the environment. Consider having a backup indoor nature-related activity if the weather is uncooperative.

- **Noise Distractions**: Outdoor environments can be full of distractions like noise from traffic or crowds. If the setting becomes too overwhelming, find a quieter spot or focus on journaling about how these sounds interact with the natural environment around you.
- **Lost Interest:** Keep sessions short and varied to maintain enthusiasm. If your child begins to lose interest, try adding a game element. Challenge them to spot specific things like three different types of leaves or listen for distinct bird sounds to bring focus back to the journaling task.

Cleanup Tips:

- Bring a small trash bag to collect any litter or waste you may produce during your journaling adventure.
- Before leaving, do a thorough check of the area to ensure no personal items or litter are left behind. Teach your child the importance of environmental stewardship and involve them in the cleanup process to instill good habits.

Variations and Adaptations:

- **Night Journaling:** Venture out at night with flashlights or headlamps to explore the unique sights and sounds of nature after dark. Observe nocturnal animals, stars, or the moon, and journal about how the environment differs from daytime.
- **Seasonal Journals:** Try journaling at the same location during different seasons. Capture how the environment changes from winter to spring or summer to fall, observing how plants and animals adapt.
- **Eco-Art Journaling**: Incorporate natural materials like pressed leaves, flowers, or bark rubbings into the journal. Collect small, non-harmful items from nature and use them to decorate the pages. This adds a tactile element to the journal and gives your child the chance to create eco-friendly art.
- **Guided Journals:** After observing plants, animals, or insects, use a field guide or app to research their names, habitats, and behaviors. You can add short descriptions of each, turning your journal into a personalized nature field guide.
- **Creative Writing Twist**: Add a creative writing element to the journal by writing short poems, stories, or reflections inspired by nature. This could include imagining what a tree "feels," writing from an animal's perspective,

or creating fictional characters based on the landscape.

- **Map-Making Journaling:** Draw your own maps of the areas you explore, marking significant spots and noting observations about each location, combining geography with nature study.

Benefits:

- **Enhances Observational Skills:** Focusing on small details in the natural world, such as the intricate patterns of leaves or the behavior of insects, helps children develop a sharper eye for subtle differences. This close observation nurtures a deeper awareness of the world around them.
- **Promotes Physical Activity**: Getting outside and walking through different environments to find subjects for the journal encourages movement. It's an active yet peaceful way to combine exploration with fitness.
- **Encourages Mindfulness:** Nature journaling helps children slow down and focus on the present moment, fostering mindfulness while helping reduce stress and anxiety. By observing and documenting small details in their surroundings, they practice being fully engaged in the world around them.
- **Combines Learning with Play**: Nature journaling seamlessly blends science, art, and writing into one engaging experience. Children gain knowledge about the natural world while developing their creative and analytical skills, making it a holistic learning opportunity.
- **Encourages Scientific Inquiry**: Observing plants, animals, and ecosystems naturally sparks curiosity about how nature works. Children may begin asking questions about biology, weather patterns, or environmental science, nurturing a deeper interest in learning.
- **Builds an Appreciation for Nature**: Journaling about the natural world nurtures a deeper respect and appreciation for the environment. It cultivates a connection to nature that may inspire lifelong interest in conservation and outdoor exploration.
- **Strengthens Bonds:** Journaling together in nature allows for quiet, meaningful moments of connection. As both of you observe and document your surroundings, it fosters a shared sense of discovery and reflection, strengthening your bond through peaceful, shared experiences.
- **Encourages Emotional Expression**: The journaling aspect allows children to express their thoughts and feelings about the world around them, offering a safe and creative space for emotional reflection. This can help them process feelings in a constructive way.

50

HISTORICAL LANDMARK EXPEDITION

Embark on a journey through time by exploring local historical landmarks with your child. This activity combines the thrill of discovery with the enrichment of learning about your community's past. Before your visit, spend time researching the history of the sites you plan to explore, gathering intriguing stories and facts to share. As you wander through these landmarks, you'll weave tales of bygone eras, making history come alive for your child.

Walking through the very places where significant events unfolded offers a tangible connection to the past. From old buildings and monuments to battlefields and museums, each site provides a window into history, sparking curiosity and discussions about different periods and people. This adventure is perfect for fostering an appreciation of history and creating memorable learning experiences together.

Materials Needed:

- ☐ List of local historical landmarks or sites
- ☐ Research materials (books, internet, local archives)
- ☐ Notebook and pen
- ☐ Camera or smartphone
- ☐ Water and snacks (for longer excursions or locations with limited services)

Step-by-Step Instructions:

1. **Select Landmarks:**
   - Together with your child, research local historical landmarks you want to visit. These could include old buildings, monuments, museums, or battlefields.
   - Encourage your child to pick at least one location that interests them. You can guide them by asking if they prefer learning about certain periods or events.
2. **Research History:**
   - Before your trip, sit down with your child and spend time researching the sites you'll be visiting. Share intriguing facts and stories about each location, and let your child take notes or bookmark the most exciting details.
   - Explore the context of the landmarks, such as who built them, what events took place there, and why they are significant.
   - Write down key points in a notebook to refer to during the exploration.
3. **Plan Your Visit:**
   - Map out the locations and create an itinerary for your exploration day.
   - Check the operating hours and any entry requirements for each site.
4. **Explore and Share:**
   - Upon arrival, take a moment to observe the landmark together. Start a discussion by asking your child what they notice or how they think the location has changed over time.
   - Share the stories and facts you researched beforehand. Encourage your child to imagine what life was like when the events you're discussing took place. Engage their curiosity by asking open-ended questions.
   - Consider joining a guided tour to gain deeper insights and anecdotes from knowledgeable guides, enhancing your understanding of the landmarks.
5. **Capture the Experience:**
   - Take photos of the landmark from different angles. Let your child take their own shots of anything they find interesting.
   - Encourage your child to write a few notes or draw sketches about the landmark, capturing their thoughts or what they learned from the visit.
6. **Recap and Reflect:**
   - Once your expedition is complete, sit down together and reflect on

what you discovered. Discuss what surprised them the most or what part of history they found most intriguing.

- For fun, you could create a mini scrapbook with photos and notes from your expedition or start a journal documenting all your historical journeys.

Safety Considerations:

- Check if the historical landmarks have specific guidelines or safety protocols to follow, especially in museums or preserved sites. Adhere to any posted signs or barriers to protect both the site and yourselves, and avoid entering restricted areas.
- Ensure your phone is fully charged and have a backup battery or charger, maintaining communication in case of emergencies.
- Bring sufficient water, particularly if visiting outdoor sites, to stay hydrated throughout the exploration.
- Keep a close eye on your child, especially in crowded areas or places with potential hazards like uneven ground or steep steps.
- Keep personal belongings secure and be aware of your surroundings to prevent theft or loss.
- Teach your child the importance of respecting historical sites, including not touching artifacts or defacing property, to preserve these landmarks for future visitors.

Troubleshooting Tips:

- **Unexpected Closures:** Have backup sites in mind in case of closures or restricted access. Historical towns often have multiple points of interest within a short distance.
- **Limited Information:** If you can't find much information about a specific landmark, try visiting local visitor centers or museums for additional insights. You can also broaden your search to include general history of the area.
- **Disinterest:** Choose landmarks that align with your child's interests to maintain engagement. If interest wanes, try making the exploration more interactive. Turn it into a scavenger hunt or quiz them on fun facts about the landmark. Engaging them through games or storytelling can reignite curiosity.
- **Uncooperative Weather:**
- Check the forecast beforehand, and if bad weather hits, have a backup plan, such as indoor historical sites like museums or heritage centers, to continue the experience without disruption.

- If you're unable to go out, consider virtual field trips. Many museums and historical sites offer free online experiences that are enriching and engaging, providing an excellent alternative to in-person visits. The Smithsonian and Google Arts & Culture are great places to start!

Cleanup Tips:

- Bring a small bag to collect any litter or waste you produce during your visit. Follow the principle of "Leave No Trace" by not disturbing the environment or leaving any trash behind at the landmarks.
- Use hand sanitizer or wipes to clean your hands after touching surfaces or artifacts, especially before eating.
- Do a final sweep of the area to make sure no personal items have been left behind, especially small items like keys or sunglasses.
- Keep the notebook in a place you'll easily remember for future historical adventures.

Variations and Adaptations:

- **Themed Explorations:** Focus each expedition on a specific theme, such as war history, architectural styles, or famous historical figures associated with the landmarks.
- **Landmark Passport**: Create a "passport" where your child gets a stamp or sticker for each landmark they visit. You could set goals to visit all the historical sites in your area, creating an ongoing adventure that extends beyond just one trip.
- **History Detective**: At each landmark, give your child a specific mystery to solve, such as finding the origin of a monument or why a certain event happened at that location. This turns the trip into an investigative mission, making history feel more like an exciting puzzle.
- **Era Explorer Diaries:** As you visit each landmark, write short diary entries from the perspective of someone living in that era—whether it's a soldier, a settler, or a local villager. Add in sketches, personal reflections, or even historical "rumors" about the time period. This makes each landmark visit feel like stepping into history, with a personal twist on the storytelling.
- **Walking Tour Guide**: Have your child pretend to be the tour guide for the day. After researching the landmarks ahead of time, they can "lead" you through the site, sharing facts and stories as if they're the expert. This fun role-reversal boosts their confidence and deepens their understanding, as teaching others is a powerful way to retain what they've learned.
- **Historic Cosplay**: Add an element of role-play by dressing up in simple, themed costumes that reflect the time period of the landmark. Whether

it's colonial attire for visiting an old fort or soldier gear for a battlefield, this adds an interactive and fun element to learning about the past.

- **Soundtrack to History**: Create a playlist of music from different historical periods or songs inspired by the places you'll visit. Play these during the trip to immerse yourselves in the time period while learning about the landmark.
- **Language of the Past**: Learn a few words or phrases in the language or dialect that would have been spoken at the landmark during its peak. Whether it's old English, indigenous languages, or even military jargon, practicing these phrases during the visit helps connect you more deeply with the era.
- **Oral History Recordings**: If the landmark has any local historians or older residents nearby, consider recording their oral histories. To find individuals with firsthand knowledge, reach out to local historical societies, visit community centers, or check out social media groups focused on your area. Interviewing people who know the stories firsthand adds a personal touch to your exploration, preserving the human side of history.

Benefits:

- **Inspires a Love for History**: Exploring real-world historical sites helps history come alive, sparking curiosity and interest in learning about the past in ways that textbooks alone can't achieve.
- **Builds Critical Thinking Skills:** Understanding the significance of landmarks requires analyzing events, cultures, and people from different perspectives, encouraging deeper critical thinking.
- **Strengthens Research Abilities**: Preparing for the trip by researching the history of the landmarks develops skills in finding, evaluating, and synthesizing information.
- **Encourages Physical Activity:** Walking around landmarks, exploring the terrain, and visiting multiple sites promotes physical activity, making learning both mentally and physically engaging.
- **Cultivates Appreciation for Cultural Heritage**: Visiting historical sites fosters a sense of respect for the past and helps develop an appreciation for the cultural and historical heritage of your community and the world.
- **Strengthens Bonds:** As you explore landmarks together, you'll engage in meaningful discussions, solve challenges, and share stories about history. This ongoing interaction strengthens bonds by creating opportunities for teamwork, active listening, and shared curiosity, making each discovery feel like a joint accomplishment.
- **Fosters Respect for Preservation**: Understanding the significance of maintaining historical landmarks cultivates a sense of responsibility for

preservation, encouraging a mindful attitude towards environmental and cultural conservation.

51

URBAN PHOTOGRAPHY SCAVENGER HUNT

Turn your city into a playground of creativity with an urban photography scavenger hunt! This activity challenges you and your child to find and photograph unique items, scenes, or themes around the city. With a list of photo prompts in hand, you'll embark on an adventure, capturing interesting and artistic shots that reflect your perspective on urban life.

This scavenger hunt not only sharpens your child's photography skills but also encourages exploration and observation. Whether it's a colorful mural, an unusual building, or a candid street scene, each photo you take tells a story about your urban environment. This activity is perfect for nurturing creativity, spending quality time together, and seeing your city through a new lens.

Materials Needed:

- ☐ Camera or smartphone (fully charged with ample storage space)
- ☐ List of photo challenges or prompts
- ☐ Comfortable walking shoes
- ☐ Map or GPS (optional)
- ☐ Water, snacks, and sun protection

Step-by-Step Instructions:

1. **Create a Photo Challenge List:**
   - Make a list of unique photo prompts, such as "a unique doorway," "a colorful mural," or "an interesting shadow."
   - Include a mix of easy and challenging items to keep it engaging.
   - Encourage your child to help in choosing or customizing the list. This sets the tone for collaboration right from the start.
2. **Plan Your Route:**
   - Choose a route or neighborhood in the city to explore that covers a variety of locations and scenes. It can be a familiar part of town or somewhere you haven't explored much.
   - Discuss the location with your child, letting them have input in selecting the starting point or destination.
3. **Start the Hunt:**
   - With your list in hand, start walking through your chosen urban environment. Let the scavenger hunt prompts guide your exploration, but encourage your child to keep an open mind about spontaneous photo opportunities that arise along the way.
   - Take turns between you and your child capturing photos, or shoot together and compare how each of you interprets the same scene.
4. **Capture the City Together:**
   - Along the way, take time to stop and observe your surroundings. The hunt is about more than just crossing off items; it's about seeing your city through fresh eyes. Encourage your child to look for small details they might normally miss—a bird perched on a wire, a quirky street sign, or an interesting piece of street art.
   - Have fun with it! You might get silly with some shots or even create stories for the scenes you capture. The goal is to enjoy the experience and deepen your bond through shared creativity.
5. **Explore Creativity:**
   - As you move through the city, discuss the environment and what makes each shot unique. Encourage your child to look for abstract patterns, textures, shadows, or contrasts in the urban landscape. Help them understand how to "tell a story" with their photos.
   - Talk about different photography techniques while you walk. You can introduce simple concepts like framing, lighting, and perspective to enhance the quality of your photos.
   - Take your time to frame each shot creatively and challenge each other

to experiment. Maybe take the same shot from different angles or try using the phone's black-and-white filter for an artsy touch.

6. **Review Your Shots:**
   - Once you've finished the scavenger hunt (or when you decide it's time to wrap up), find a comfortable spot—perhaps a local café or park bench—and review your photos together. Discuss what you liked about each shot, compare perspectives, and reflect on how the photos captured the essence of your city.
   - This review can also include some lighthearted critiques or constructive feedback to help improve each other's skills in future photography adventures.
7. **Preserve the Memories:**
   - When you return home, consider printing your favorite photos or creating a digital photo album to document the scavenger hunt. You can even add captions or short descriptions to remember the day's experience.

Safety Considerations:

- Plan your route in advance and share it with someone else to ensure someone knows your whereabouts.
- Stick to well-populated, well-lit areas for the scavenger hunt. Avoid going into deserted streets, alleys, or unfamiliar neighborhoods, especially if the area feels unsafe.
- Stay aware of your surroundings and keep a close eye on your child, especially in crowded or busy areas.
- Ensure your camera and other valuables are secure and close to you to prevent theft or loss.
- Avoid trespassing on private property and be respectful of public spaces and landmarks.
- Be considerate of people's privacy and avoid taking photos of individuals without their permission.

Troubleshooting Tips:

- **Uncooperative Weather:** Have an indoor backup plan, like visiting a museum or indoor market.
- **Battery Running Low**: Long walks and continuous photo-taking can drain your phone battery quickly. Bring a portable charger or power bank to keep your device charged throughout the scavenger hunt.
- **Weather Challenges**: If the weather becomes too harsh, shoot urban scenes from inside a building, car, or café. Photos taken through windows,

especially in rain, can create interesting effects and perspectives. Modify your photo prompts to match the conditions, using indoor architecture or reflections for creative shots.

- **Crowded Areas:** In crowded areas, be patient and wait for the right moment to take your shot. Try to find less busy times to visit popular locations.

Cleanup Tips:

- Properly dispose of any trash, such as snack wrappers or empty water bottles, and recycle where possible.
- Organize and rename your digital files for easy access later. Create folders based on themes, dates, or locations to keep everything tidy.

Variations and Adaptations:

- **Themed Hunts:** Focus on specific themes like reflections, patterns and textures, or architecture, and center your scavenger hunt around finding subjects that fit the theme.
- **Public Transportation Adventure:** Use the city's public transit system as your guide. Hop on and off buses, trams, or subways at different stops to capture the city from varying perspectives. Each stop offers a new location and unique photo opportunities, turning the journey itself into part of the scavenger hunt.
- **Urban Legends Quest**: Explore locations tied to local myths, legends, or ghost stories. Photograph eerie or mysterious places while learning about the city's folklore. This variation adds a storytelling element, allowing you to weave a narrative into your photos as you uncover the city's hidden secrets.
- **Cultural Exploration:** Dive into the cultural richness of the city by photographing festivals, traditional markets, and ethnic neighborhoods. This variation highlights the vibrant traditions and unique cultural landmarks, offering a deeper exploration of the city's identity through your lens.
- **Mystery Envelope Edition:** Before your adventure, each of you can create sealed envelopes containing secret bonus challenges or photography techniques for the other person. As you explore, open your envelopes at different locations to incorporate the challenges into your photos. The mystery adds suspense and excitement to your hunt as you open your envelopes at different locations.
- **Crowdsourced List**: Instead of creating the photo prompts in advance, ask random people you meet during the hunt to suggest photo ideas. This brings a spontaneous, interactive element to the hunt and makes it unpredictable.

- **Scavenger Hunt with Props:** Each of you can choose a small, quirky prop (like a toy, a funny hat, or a distinctive object) to feature creatively in all your photos. This adds a layer of whimsy and challenges your creativity together.
- **Selfie Challenge**: Along with the scavenger hunt items, you must find creative ways to include yourselves in each photo. This could be through reflections, shadows, or even creative angles where a part of you is included in the scene.
- **Double Exposure Challenge**: Use a camera or editing software that allows double exposure (overlaying two photos on top of each other). The challenge is to find creative ways to blend two different urban scenes into one photo, adding another artistic element to the scavenger hunt.

Benefits:

- **Promotes Physical Activity:** Navigating the city to fulfill various photographic challenges promotes walking and exploration, integrating physical activity with creative pursuit.
- **Strengthens Focus and Attention to Detail**: Searching for specific details or themes to photograph sharpens focus and improves the ability to notice and appreciate small, often overlooked elements in the environment.
- **Sharpens Observational Skills**: The need to find specific items or themes during the hunt trains the eye to notice subtle details, patterns, and contrasts within the environment that might otherwise be overlooked.
- **Enhances Problem-Solving Abilities**: Encountering difficult or abstract prompts promotes critical thinking and encourages creative problem-solving as different approaches to capturing images are explored.
- **Strengthens Bonds:** Collaborating on capturing meaningful or interesting photos fosters deeper connections through shared creative experiences. Working together to complete the scavenger hunt encourages communication, cooperation, and mutual appreciation for each other's unique perspectives.
- **Offers Educational Opportunities**: The scavenger hunt encourages learning about various urban elements, such as architecture, public art, and the history of different areas, providing a hands-on way to explore urban culture and geography.

Urban Explorer's Cheat Sheet

Can't wait to start exploring? Capture the unique sights and hidden gems of your city with these ready-made prompts!

- ☐ **Unique Bench:** Photograph a unique or artistically designed public bench.
- ☐ **Unique Architecture:** Find and photograph a building with unusual or striking architectural design.
- ☐ **Street Art:** Look for interesting graffiti or street art that tells a story.
- ☐ **Reflection in Water:** Capture the reflection of buildings or trees in a puddle, fountain, or pond.
- ☐ **Interesting Street Name:** Photograph a street sign with an unusual or interesting name.
- ☐ **Statue or Monument:** Capture a photo of a statue or monument that represents the city's history or culture.
- ☐ **Green Space:** Find a park or green space nestled within the urban environment.
- ☐ **Street Performers:** Capture a photo of a talented street performer in action.
- ☐ **Bicycle or Scooter:** Find a bicycle or scooter parked in an interesting location.
- ☐ **Colorful Signage:** Look for bright and colorful signs, whether they're advertisements or shop signs.
- ☐ **Public Art Installation:** Find a public art installation and capture its essence.
- ☐ **Iconic Landmark:** Capture a well-known landmark that symbolizes the city.
- ☐ **Food Truck or Street Food:** Find a food truck or street food vendor and photograph their offerings.
- ☐ **Vintage Car:** Look for a vintage car parked on the street and photograph it.
- ☐ **Local Wildlife:** Capture a photo of urban wildlife, such as pigeons, squirrels, or stray cats.

52

WILD SOUNDSCAPES

Immerse yourself in the tranquility of nature by recording its ethereal sounds together. This activity involves venturing into natural settings to capture sounds like bird calls, flowing water, and rustling leaves. Armed with recording devices, you and your child will create a unique nature sound mix, combining the various elements you discover.

Recording the symphony of the outdoors offers a deeper appreciation for the natural world and its diverse soundscapes. Whether you're hiking through a forest, sitting by a stream, or walking through a meadow, each environment provides distinct auditory experiences. This project not only cultivates mindfulness and listening skills but also results in a beautiful, personalized soundscape that you can enjoy long after your outdoor adventure.

Materials Needed:

- ☐ Portable recording device or smartphone with recording app
- ☐ Audio editing software (e.g., BandLab [free], GarageBand [free for Mac and iOS])
- ☐ External microphone (optional for better sound quality)
- ☐ Headphones (for monitoring recordings)
- ☐ Notebook (for jotting down locations and notes)
- ☐ Comfortable walking shoes
- ☐ Water, snacks, and sun protection
- ☐ Insect repellant (optional)

Step-by-Step Instructions:

1. **Plan Your Soundscape Adventure:**
   - Before setting out, decide on a natural setting to explore. This could be a local park, nature reserve, or even your backyard if it's serene enough.
   - Discuss with your child what types of environments interest them—forests, creeks, or open meadows? Each will offer unique soundscapes to capture.
   - Consider the time of day—early mornings or late afternoons often provide the best range of sounds.
   - Pack your gear: make sure your recording device is fully charged, has ample storage space, and test it to ensure it's functioning properly.
2. **Start Your Sound Exploration:**
   - Upon arriving at your location, find a quiet spot to stand still and listen. Take a moment to close your eyes and tune into the soundscape around you.
   - Let your child absorb the natural surroundings and identify some sounds they'd like to capture (e.g., wind through the trees, birds chirping, water flowing).
   - Encourage your child to notice the various layers of sound—the louder, more obvious noises and the softer, more subtle ones.
   - Be sure to select a spot with minimal human-made noise, such as away from roads or heavy foot traffic, to enhance the quality of the recordings.
3. **Start Recording:**
   - Position your recording device and, if possible, use headphones to monitor the sound as you record. Teach your child how to hold the device still, as handling noise can interfere with the purity of the recording.
   - Encourage them to move the device toward the sound they find most intriguing, whether it's closer to the ground to capture rustling leaves or near a water source for the gurgling of a stream.
   - Let your child experiment with different distances to create depth in the recording.
4. **Move Around and Experiment:**
   - Don't limit yourselves to one location! Walk through the environment, stopping at different spots to record new sounds. Try capturing specific noises, like leaves crunching underfoot, water dripping from a branch, or birds singing from afar.

5. **Document Your Findings:**
    - Document the time and place of each recording in your notebook so you can reference it later.
    - Describe the sounds and any interesting observations or notable experiences during the recording process.
6. **Reflect and Discuss:**
    - After recording, spend some time reflecting on the experience with your child. Did anything surprise them? Did certain sounds make them feel calm or more aware of the environment?
    - Jot down your thoughts in the notebook, and take note of the sounds that were particularly memorable.
7. **Create Your Wild Soundscape Mix:**
    - Once back home, upload the recordings to a computer or editing app.
    - Sit down with your child and review the recordings together. Identify which sounds were captured clearly and talk about which ones you find most fascinating.
    - Help them combine the different clips into one continuous soundscape or mix. This could be a calming medley of the day's best sounds, like birds, wind, and water flowing.
    - Let your child experiment with arranging and layering the sounds, fading them in and out, and even looping certain parts to create a unique audio experience.
    - Name your soundscape together and perhaps even create custom covers or titles for different sound mixes based on the locations you explored.
8. **Enjoy and Share Your Soundscape:**
    - After creating your nature soundscape, use it as a calming background for relaxation, meditation, or even as a backdrop for creative activities like drawing or writing. You and your child can enjoy listening to the sounds you captured whenever you need a moment of peace or inspiration.
    - You can even share the mix with friends or family, bringing a piece of the outdoors into their lives.

Safety Considerations:

- Bring enough water for the entire journey to stay hydrated, especially on warm days or long hikes.
- Ensure your phone is fully charged and consider bringing a portable charger. Inform someone of your location and expected return time.

- Wear sunscreen, hats, and sunglasses to protect against sunburn and heat exhaustion.
- Use insect repellent to protect against mosquitoes, ticks, and other biting insects.
- If you or your child have allergies, bring necessary medications and be aware of potential allergens in the area.
- Be aware of your surroundings and any potential wildlife. Avoid disturbing natural habitats and be mindful of your impact on the environment.

Troubleshooting Tips:

- **Battery Drain**: Recording devices can drain batteries quickly, especially when used for extended periods. Bring spare batteries or a portable charger to ensure you don't run out of power in the middle of your session.
- **Wind Noise:** Use a windscreen or foam cover over the microphone. If that's not enough, try shielding the device with your body or find a natural barrier, like trees or rocks, to block the wind.
- **Background Noise:** Select quieter times of day to minimize human-made sounds. Early mornings or more remote locations tend to have fewer interruptions, providing cleaner recordings.
- **Too Quiet:** Encourage your child to create sounds using natural elements like tapping rocks, rustling leaves, or splashing water, and record these interactions.

Cleanup Tips:

- Bring a small bag to collect any litter or waste you produce and dispose of it properly at home or in designated bins.
- Do a final sweep of your recording spots to make sure no personal items or trash are left behind.
- Back up and label your recordings as soon as you get home to keep them organized and easily accessible for editing.

Variations and Adaptations:

- **Night Sound Expedition**: Venture out in the evening or early morning to capture the unique soundscape of nocturnal wildlife. Nighttime offers different sounds like owls, crickets, or the rustling of night animals, providing an entirely different atmosphere.
- **Nature's Rhythm Section**: Record natural, rhythmic sounds like rain hitting leaves, ocean waves crashing, or the repetitive hum of wind through trees. Later, layer these sounds to create a nature-inspired "drum beat" that can be mixed with other recordings.

- **Echo Location Challenge**: Visit areas like caves, canyons, or forests where echoes are prominent, and record the way sounds bounce off natural surfaces. Experiment with clapping, calling, or playing sounds to capture their echoes for a unique auditory effect.
- **Sound Interviews**: Interview each other about the sounds you hear and your experiences, recording these conversations as part of your soundscape.
- **Sound Map:** Create an interactive online map where each recorded sound is linked to the exact location where it was captured. Upload the sounds to a digital platform (such as Google My Maps, using links from Google Drive or Dropbox) and pin them on a map, allowing you to explore the locations by clicking on the markers to hear the recordings. The map becomes a living, evolving soundscape that you can revisit anytime. For an added twist, invite others to contribute their own recordings, creating a shared auditory experience of different places.

Benefits:

- **Encourages Creativity:** Crafting a unique nature sound mix stimulates creativity and encourages imaginative thinking as children explore and interpret the sounds they capture.
- **Offers Educational Opportunities**: Exploring the science of sound, wildlife, and ecosystems introduces educational topics such as ecology, biology, and environmental science in an engaging, hands-on way.
- **Enhances Mindfulness and Focus**: Actively listening to and recording the natural environment encourages mindfulness, helping to improve concentration and awareness of the surroundings.
- **Fosters an Appreciation for Nature**: Immersing in natural soundscapes deepens the connection with the environment, cultivating a greater appreciation for the beauty and complexity of the natural world.
- **Strengthens Bonds:** The collaborative process of finding, recording, and discussing different sounds deepens the connection, creating lasting memories through teamwork and shared discovery.
- **Promotes Physical Activity**: Exploring outdoor spaces to capture different sounds involves walking, hiking, or moving through natural areas, blending creativity with physical exploration.

HIGH SCHOOLERS

TAKING

FLIGHT

INDOOR ADVENTURES

Indoor activities for high schoolers are designed to ignite creativity and inspire new ideas. Try the DIY Hot Sauce Lab, where you can experiment with flavors and create your own signature hot sauce, or transform a personal space with the Ultimate Room Revamp, turning a room into a haven that reflects unique style and personality. Culinary Showdown invites teens to explore their cooking skills with exciting cooking challenges, while the Cyber Learning Hub offers opportunities to explore new topics through online courses. Whether crafting a tune in your DIY Music Studio or discussing passions through Podcast Production Zone, these activities provide creative outlets that foster independence and self-expression.

53

DIY HOT SAUCE LAB

Spice up your culinary adventures with a DIY hot sauce project that promises both flavor and fun. Begin with fresh chili peppers and a few simple ingredients, embarking on a flavorful journey in your kitchen. As you chop and blend the ingredients, the air fills with the tantalizing aroma of spices, igniting anticipation for the fiery results. The process is as educational as it is exciting, teaching your teen about the balance of flavors and the science of cooking. Experimenting with different types of peppers and ingredient combinations is half the fun, and they can even impress their friends with their own signature sauce.

The moment of truth arrives as you simmer the sauce, watching it transform into a vibrant, aromatic concoction. Bottling the hot sauce and creating personalized labels adds a special touch, turning each bottle into a unique culinary masterpiece. Sharing and tasting the homemade hot sauce brings a sense of achievement and delight, enhancing meals with a burst of flavor and a dash of creativity. It's a fun way to explore the world of cooking together, with a spicy twist!

Materials Needed:

- ☐ Fresh chili peppers (1 ½ lbs; any variety)
- ☐ White vinegar (1 ½ cups)
- ☐ Salt (½ teaspoon)
- ☐ Garlic cloves (2-3 cloves; approximately 1 tablespoon minced)
- ☐ Blender or food processor
- ☐ Small saucepan
- ☐ Bottles or jars for storage
- ☐ Gloves (for handling peppers)
- ☐ Labels (optional)

Step-by-Step Instructions:

1. **Prepare the Peppers:**
   - Together, pick out a variety of chili peppers. Discuss what kind of heat you both prefer—mild, medium, or nuclear—and how you might mix different peppers for a balanced sauce.
   - Wash and chop the chili peppers, removing stems. Remove the seeds if you want to tone down the heat. Wear gloves to protect your hands from the heat of the peppers.
   - Peel the garlic cloves.
2. **Blend the Ingredients:**
   - In a blender or food processor, combine the peppers, vinegar, salt, and garlic.
   - Blend until smooth. Adjust the amount of vinegar for your desired consistency.
3. **Cook the Sauce:**
   - Pour the mixture into a small saucepan.
   - Bring to a boil, then reduce heat and simmer (uncovered) for about 10 minutes, stirring occasionally.
   - As the mixture cooks, talk about how the heat breaks down the peppers, releasing their flavor and intensity. You'll notice the kitchen filling with spicy aromas.
   - Once the sauce is done cooking, it's taste-test time! Discuss with your teen whether to add more salt or vinegar based on the flavor profile you're going for—perfect for teaching about balancing flavors.
4. **Cool and Bottle:**
   - Let the hot sauce cool to room temperature.
   - As your sauce cools, use this time to sterilize the bottles. Boil the glass bottles and lids in a large pot of water for 10 minutes to eliminate any bacteria or contaminants. This ensures that the sauce stays fresh for longer and prevents any unwanted bacteria growth.
   - Strain, if desired, and pour the sauce into the clean bottles or jars for storage. Use a funnel to avoid spills.
   - For a fun touch, design custom labels together. Maybe you'll name the sauce something fierce and creative—this gives your teen a chance to showcase their personality and design skills.
   - **Shelf Life Note:** Once bottled and sealed, homemade hot sauce can typically last for about 3 to 6 months when stored in the refrigerator. For best results, keep it in a cool, dark place, and always refrigerate

after opening. If you notice any changes in smell, color, or texture, discard the sauce to ensure safety.

5. **Enjoy and Share:**
   - Crack open one of the bottles and try the sauce together, adding it to tacos, pizza, or any dish you like.
   - Discuss how it turned out—was it fiery enough? What might you tweak next time?
   - Consider sharing your delicious concoction with family and friends as a unique gift.

Safety Considerations:

- Always wear gloves when handling hot peppers to avoid skin irritation and prevent accidental transfer to the eyes or face. If any chili oil got onto your skin, wash your hands with soap and water and use a little vinegar to help neutralize the heat.
- Open windows or use a fan to ventilate the kitchen while cooking the sauce, as the fumes can be quite potent.

Troubleshooting Tips:

- **Too Hot:** Add more vinegar or a bit of sugar to balance the heat. Diluting with other ingredients such as tomatoes or carrots can also mellow the intensity.
- **Too Mild:** For a quick fix, you can also stir in chili flakes or cayenne pepper to boost spiciness without altering the overall flavor too much. For a serious heat boost without changing the flavor balance, you can add a small amount of hot pepper extract. This will raise the heat level significantly, so use it sparingly.
- **Sauce Too Thick:** Add a bit more vinegar or water to thin it out. Add a little at a time, tasting as you go to maintain the balance of flavors.
- **Sauce Too Thin**: Simmer on low heat a bit longer to reduce and thicken. Alternatively, add ingredients like roasted peppers or onions to thicken the sauce naturally.
- **Overpowering Vinegar Flavor**: If the vinegar is too strong, balance it out with a small amount of sugar or honey. Adding fruits or sweeter vegetables can also help soften the acidity.
- **Flavor Lacks Depth**: If the sauce tastes flat, try adding a pinch of salt or a splash of lime juice to brighten it up. Roasting the peppers and other ingredients before blending can also bring out a richer, more complex flavor.

Cleanup Tips:

- Even if gloves were worn, wash hands with soap and water after handling chili peppers.
- Wash all utensils and surfaces immediately after use to prevent spicy residue from the peppers.
- Ensure bottles or jars are properly sealed and stored in the refrigerator.

Variations and Adaptations:

- **Flavor Profile Experimentation**: Turn the activity into a flavor experiment by dividing the base sauce into smaller batches and adding unique ingredients to each one (e.g., one with chocolate, one with fruit, one with herbs). This adaptation teaches about how different flavor profiles can complement or contrast with heat.
- **Hot Sauce Heat Scale Exploration**: Use this variation to teach about the Scoville scale (the measurement of heat in peppers). Have a lineup of peppers with different heat levels, and taste small bits of each before making the sauce. The challenge is to adjust the recipe based on the desired level of heat while learning about the chemistry behind spiciness.
- **Spice Chemistry Exploration**: Dive into the science behind heat by experimenting with different natural "coolants" like dairy, citrus, or sugar to balance spiciness. This adaptation focuses on understanding how ingredients interact to mellow or enhance heat, adding an educational, science-focused twist to the activity.
- **Hot Sauce Competition**: Turn it into a friendly competition, where each person or team creates their own hot sauce recipe from the same base ingredients. At the end, compare the sauces in a blind taste test to see whose creation packs the best punch.
- **Hot Sauce Taste Test Challenge**: After creating the hot sauce, host a taste test challenge where different family members or friends rate the sauce on heat, flavor, and creativity. Add fun categories like "Best for Tacos" or "Most Unique Flavor." This turns the process into a full-on culinary experience.
- **Sauce and Meal Pairing Challenge**: After making the sauce, create a fun challenge where you have to prepare a meal that perfectly complements the hot sauce. This could be anything from tacos to burgers or even unexpected pairings like grilled fruit or desserts. The goal is to showcase the sauce's versatility.
- **Hot Sauce Cooking Show**: Set up a mock cooking show where the process of making the hot sauce is filmed as though it were a TV segment. This adds an element of performance, creativity, and maybe even a bit of improv comedy, as the "hosts" explain their process and offer fun tips.

- **Pepper Planting and Growing**: As an extension of the hot sauce-making process, begin by planting chili pepper seeds in small pots and growing your own peppers. This way, the adventure starts with cultivating ingredients and leads into harvesting, cooking, and bottling the sauce—a full farm-to-table experience.

Benefits:

- **Teaches Cooking Skills:** This activity teaches your teen valuable cooking techniques and the science behind creating balanced flavors, enhancing their overall culinary skills.
- **Encourages Experimentation:** Customizing the hot sauce with different ingredients encourages a spirit of experimentation and innovation, valuable skills in both cooking and problem-solving.
- **Promotes Healthy Eating:** Homemade hot sauce can be a healthier alternative to store-bought versions, allowing you to control the ingredients and avoid preservatives and additives.
- **Strengthens Bonds:** Working together on the sauce-making process encourages teamwork, communication, and the shared experience of experimenting, tasting, and perfecting the recipe.
- **Boosts Confidence:** Successfully making and bottling their own hot sauce gives your teen a sense of accomplishment and pride, boosting their confidence in the kitchen and beyond.

Get Fired Up with These Hot Sauce Ideas:

Looking to spice up your hot sauce game? Try experimenting with these bold variations:

- **Pepper Variety Mix:** Use a mix of different chili peppers such as jalapenos, habaneros, and serranos to create a complex flavor profile.
- **Smoky Hot Sauce:** Incorporate smoked chili peppers like chipotle or add a bit of liquid smoke to your sauce to give it a rich, smoky flavor.
- **Sweet and Spicy:** Add a tablespoon of honey or brown sugar to your hot sauce for a sweet heat that pairs well with a variety of dishes.
- **Fruit-Infused Hot Sauce:** Add fruits like mango, pineapple, or peaches to your hot sauce for a sweet and spicy twist. Blend the fruit with the chili peppers and other ingredients before simmering.
- **Caribbean-Style Hot Sauce:** Incorporate Caribbean spices like allspice, ginger, and thyme for a tropical flair.
- **Herbal Hot Sauce:** Experiment with adding fresh herbs such as cilantro, basil, or oregano to your hot sauce for a complex, aromatic profile.
- **Extra Tangy Hot Sauce:** Add citrus juice like lime or lemon along with the vinegar for an extra tangy kick.
- **Thai-Inspired Hot Sauce:** Add ingredients like lemongrass and ginger for a hot sauce inspired by Thai cuisine.
- **Creamy Hot Sauce:** Blend in some avocado or sour cream for a creamy hot sauce with a smooth texture.
- **Spicy Ketchup:** Mix your hot sauce with tomato paste or ketchup for a spicy condiment that's perfect for burgers and fries.
- **Fermented Hot Sauce (Peppers First):** For a tangy, complex flavor, try fermenting the peppers before blending.
    1. Place the washed peppers (and optional garlic or other dry ingredients) into a clean jar, and cover with a 5% brine solution (1.5-2 tablespoons of salt per 2 cups of water). Make sure the peppers are fully submerged—place a weight on top, like a small baggie partially filled with water, to keep them below the brine.
    2. Cover the jar loosely to allow gases to escape, and let it ferment in a dark place at room temperature for 1-3 weeks; fermenting longer, even for several months, enhances complexity even further. Stir the mixture daily to ensure even fermentation.
    3. Once the fermentation is complete, blend the fermented peppers with vinegar and other ingredients. You can use some of the brine in the sauce for added tang and complexity. Cook and bottle the sauce as usual.

54

ULTIMATE ROOM REVAMP

Transforming a personal space can be a powerful way for your teen to express themselves while learning valuable life skills. A DIY room makeover allows them to unleash their creativity and showcase their unique style, turning their room into a haven that reflects their personality. This project can be as simple or as elaborate as they desire, from rearranging furniture and adding new decor to painting walls and creating custom artwork. The sense of ownership and accomplishment they'll feel from successfully executing their vision is unparalleled, making this a deeply satisfying experience.

Working together on this project provides a fantastic opportunity to teach essential skills such as planning, budgeting, and time management. Discuss ideas, shop for materials, and tackle tasks side by side, making memories that will last a lifetime. The collaborative effort will foster a deeper connection and create a shared sense of pride in the finished product. Plus, the satisfaction of seeing the final result—a room transformed by your joint efforts—will be immensely rewarding for both of you.

Materials Needed:

- ☐ Paint and painting supplies (rollers, brushes, painter's tape)
- ☐ New decor items (posters, artwork, lights)
- ☐ Furniture (new pieces or items to rearrange)
- ☐ Organizational supplies (bins, shelves)
- ☐ Measuring tape
- ☐ Tools (hammer, nails, screwdriver)
- ☐ Drop cloths, tape, and cleaning supplies
- ☐ Notebook and pen (for planning)

Step-by-Step Instructions:

1. **Discuss Vision and Ideas:**
   - Begin by talking with your teen about their ideas for the room. What vibe or theme do they want? Minimalistic, cozy, artsy, or bold? Use a notebook to sketch out ideas and jot down their preferences for color schemes, decor, or functional changes.
   - Encourage them to browse online or gather images that inspire them. You can even create a collection of these images—often called a mood board—to help guide the overall look and feel of the room.
2. **Assess the Space:**
   - Take measurements of the room and its furniture to ensure any planned changes will fit. Discuss any limitations based on the space or budget.
   - Take a "before" picture of the room to capture its current state and track progress.
3. **Set a Budget and Timeline:**
   - Discuss the total budget for the project. Make a list of must-haves, such as new paint, furniture, or decor, and figure out where to allocate funds.
   - Invest in key pieces that can make a big impact (like a new rug or accent wall color) and save on smaller accessories.
   - Set a realistic timeline for the makeover, breaking the project into manageable chunks, like "Day 1: Paint walls" or "Day 3: Assemble furniture." This keeps both of you on track.
4. **Shopping and Sourcing Materials:**
   - Head to local hardware stores, furniture shops, or thrift stores to gather everything needed. Encourage your teen to consider upcycling or DIY decor ideas to stay within budget.
   - Make this a collaborative experience, with your teen picking out the colors, fabrics, and items that reflect their personality.
5. **Room Prep:**
   - Clear the room of furniture and other items, leaving the space ready for the transformation.
   - If you're painting, lay down drop cloths, use painter's tape to protect baseboards, and gather all your supplies.
   - Encourage your teen to participate in the preparation by handling small tasks like taping edges or cleaning surfaces before painting or rearranging.

6. **Tackle Big Changes First (e.g., Painting):**
   - Start with the major projects, such as painting walls or installing new shelving. Let your teen do as much as possible, such as handling the roller or assisting with measurements and drilling.
   - If painting, apply two coats for a solid finish, allowing proper drying time between coats.
   - For furniture rearrangement, experiment with different layouts until your teen finds one that they love.
7. **Add Personal Touches and Decor:**
   - Once the big changes are complete, move on to decorating the room. Let your teen take the lead in hanging artwork, arranging plants, or setting up the lighting.
   - Encourage them to add personal touches like DIY artwork, photos, or handmade decor. This stage is where their vision truly comes to life.
   - Assemble any new furniture or put together shelving if needed.
8. **Final Walkthrough and Adjustments:**
   - Take a step back and admire the room together. Make any last-minute adjustments or tweaks, such as rearranging small decor items or adding additional storage solutions.
   - Capture the "after" picture to compare with the "before" shot, celebrating the transformation.

Safety Considerations:

- Turn off power at the circuit breaker before doing any electrical work, such as changing light fixtures or outlets. If you encounter issues with the wiring, it's best to consult a professional electrician to ensure safety and compliance with local codes.
- Ensure the room is well-ventilated when painting or using any chemicals to avoid inhaling fumes.
- Use proper lifting techniques to avoid back strain or injuries when moving heavy furniture. Bend at the knees and keep your back straight.
- Anchor heavy furniture to the walls to prevent tipping and potential accidents.

Troubleshooting Tips:

- **Budget Overruns**: If you're going over budget, prioritize key pieces and consider DIY solutions or thrift store finds to save money. Re-evaluate and adjust the plan if necessary.
- **Wall Imperfections:** For uneven or damaged walls, use spackling paste

to fill in holes and sand them smooth before painting. Consider using textured paint or wallpaper to disguise imperfections.

- **Furniture Assembly:** Follow instructions carefully and don't hesitate to look up online guides or videos.
- **Decor Not Matching:** If the new decor items don't seem to match, choose a unifying element like a color or pattern to tie everything together. Consider repainting or repurposing items to better fit the theme.

Cleanup Tips:

- Tidy up after each step of the project to prevent a large mess from accumulating. This makes the final cleanup easier and more manageable.
- Clean brushes, rollers, and paint trays immediately with warm soapy water.
- Store unused paint properly for future touch-ups or dispose of it according to local regulations. Never pour paint down the drain.

Variations and Adaptations:

- **Virtual Design Battle:** Before starting the physical makeover, both participants can compete in a virtual room design challenge using an interior design app or software (e.g., Roomstyler 3D Home Planner [free]). Once the virtual designs are complete, combine the best aspects of both designs to create a hybrid plan for the real-world revamp. It's a great introduction to interior design principles in a digital format.
- **Recycled Materials Only:** As a twist, require that all materials used in the room revamp must be recycled or repurposed from things already in the house. For example, turn an old dresser into a new piece with some paint and new knobs, or repurpose pallet wood or old window frames to create unique decor and furniture pieces. This encourages resourcefulness and creativity, pushing the participants to think beyond traditional shopping and use what's already available in innovative ways.
- **Interactive Wall Art:** Create a feature wall with chalkboard paint, whiteboard paint, or a pegboard, allowing your teen to draw and change designs whenever they like.
- **Sustainable Design:** Incorporate eco-friendly and sustainable materials and practices, such as using non-toxic paint, organic fabrics, and energy-efficient lighting.
- **Themed Makeover:** Choose a specific theme like retro, minimalist, or nature-inspired.
- **DIY Wall Treatments:** Create a mural or accent wall with stencils or freehand designs. Enhance the look further by using painter's tape to create patterns or peel-and-stick tiles to add a fun design element without a permanent commitment.

- **Lighting Overhaul:** Install LED strip lights, string lights, or smart bulbs that can change color to create different moods and atmospheres in the room.

Benefits:

- **Develops Life Skills**: Transforming a room teaches valuable life skills such as planning, budgeting, project management, and even some light DIY work, which are essential for future independence.
- **Enhances Problem-Solving**: Unexpected challenges like limited space or fitting furniture into a certain layout require quick thinking and adaptability, fostering resourcefulness and problem-solving.
- **Provides Stress Relief**: A newly designed, personalized room can serve as a sanctuary for teens, providing a calming and stress-relieving environment.
- **Encourages Responsibility**: Taking charge of a room makeover project encourages teens to take responsibility for their decisions and actions.
- **Strengthens Bonds:** Working together on the room makeover requires open communication and teamwork, fostering a deeper connection as you brainstorm ideas, make decisions, and solve problems together.
- **Offers an Educational Experience**: Learning about design principles, color theory, and DIY techniques provides an educational experience that can spark interest in related fields.

55

PODCAST PRODUCTION ZONE

Immerse yourself in the captivating world of podcasting and embark on a collaborative journey of audio production and storytelling. This project allows you and your teen to explore a shared interest by planning, recording, editing, and publishing podcast episodes. Whether you're discussing books, hobbies, current events, or any other topic that excites you, podcasting provides a dynamic platform to express your thoughts and ideas to a wider audience.

Together, you'll brainstorm episode ideas, create engaging content, and master the basics of audio editing. The process of publishing and sharing your podcast will instill a sense of accomplishment and pride, while also enhancing communication skills, technical proficiency, and a love for storytelling. This activity offers a unique blend of creativity, learning, and bonding, making it an enriching experience for both of you.

Materials Needed:

- ☐ Computer or smartphone
- ☐ Podcast hosting platform (e.g., Spotify for Podcasters, Podbean; both free)
- ☐ Microphone (basic or USB mic)
- ☐ Pop filter for microphone (for clearer sound quality; optional)
- ☐ Headphones (optional)
- ☐ Notebook (for planning episodes; optional)

Step-by-Step Instructions:

1. **Pick Your Podcast Topic:**
   - Start by discussing potential podcast topics. This could be something you're both passionate about, like sports, music, books, or even a personal hobby.
   - Make a list of ideas and narrow it down to one topic that excites you both.
2. **Plan Episodes:**
   - Once the topic is chosen, brainstorm episode ideas. Decide if you'll have a specific theme for each episode or if you'll tackle different subjects within the same genre.
   - Write down a rough outline for the first few episodes to keep things organized.
   - Decide on episode lengths, key discussion points, and how you want the episodes to flow. Will you have guest speakers? Segments? Q&A sessions? Come up with a structure that feels natural and engaging.
3. **Set Up Recording Equipment:**
   - Set up your recording space to ensure good audio quality. Pick a quiet room, away from distractions.
   - If you have opted to use an external microphone and headphones:
     - Connect the microphone to your computer and set up headphones for monitoring audio.
     - Position the microphone with a pop filter to ensure clear sound quality.
   - Do a quick sound check by recording a test run to see if the microphone is picking up your voices clearly and without distortion.
4. **Record Episodes:**
   - Record the introduction and main content of each episode. Keep it natural and conversational, but try to stay on topic. Don't worry if it's not perfect—editing will clean up any mistakes later!
     - **Using Podcast Platform:** Many podcast hosting platforms allow you to record directly through their interface. Explore this option for a seamless recording experience.
     - **Using Recording App:** Alternatively, use your computer or smartphone's recording app and then upload the files to the podcast hosting platform.
   - Engage with each other and make the conversation lively and natural.
   - Speak clearly and maintain a consistent volume throughout the

recording.

- Encourage your teen to take the lead on certain sections or topics to make sure it feels collaborative.

5. **Edit and Produce:**
    - If you used a separate recording app, transfer your audio files to the podcast hosting platform.
    - Use the platform's built-in editing software to edit out any long pauses, background noise, or any bloopers you don't want to include.
    - Add intro/outro music or sound effects to create a polished final product.
6. **Publish and Share:**
    - Craft a catchy episode title and write a brief description to accompany the podcast.
    - Share the episode link with friends, family, or even social media to grow your audience.
    - You could even plan a small listening party or celebrate the launch by creating fun promotional art for the podcast using free design tools like Canva.

Safety Considerations:

- Be cautious about sharing personal information on the podcast. Avoid disclosing sensitive details such as your exact location, full names, or other identifying information.
- If you discuss or mention other people, ensure you have their consent to share their names or stories publicly.
- Use royalty-free music and sound effects or obtain proper licenses for any copyrighted material used in your podcast to avoid legal issues.
- Remember that once published, your podcast content can be accessed by anyone. Consider the long-term implications of the content you share.

Troubleshooting Tips:

- **Microphone Malfunctions**: If the microphone isn't working, check the input settings in your recording software to make sure the correct microphone is selected. Restarting the software or re-plugging the microphone can often resolve the issue.
- **Poor Sound Quality:** Adjust the microphone position and ensure it's not too close or too far from the speaker. Use a pop filter to reduce plosive sounds and minimize background noise by recording in a quiet environment.

- **Echo or Reverb in Recordings**: If the recordings have an echo or sound too "roomy," try adding soft materials like blankets, rugs, or pillows to the recording space to absorb sound and reduce reverb. Recording in smaller, enclosed spaces can also help control this issue.
- **Clipping**: If your audio is clipping or distorted, reduce the input volume on your recording device or software. Ensure you're speaking at a consistent volume without shouting.
- **Difficulty Syncing Audio Tracks**: If recording on multiple devices or with multiple speakers, syncing the tracks may be challenging. Use clap syncing at the start of each recording (clapping once so it creates a spike in the audio wave) to align the tracks easily during editing.

Cleanup Tips:

- Create dedicated folders for each episode, including subfolders for raw recordings, edited files, and final versions. Label files clearly with dates and episode numbers for easy access.
- Regularly back up your recordings, edited files, and notes to an external hard drive or cloud storage to prevent data loss.
- Periodically review your digital files and delete any unnecessary or duplicate recordings to free up storage space.
- Keep your planning notebooks or digital notes organized by episode or topic. Review and consolidate notes after each recording session.

Variations and Adaptations:

- **Interview Series**: Invite guests from various fields to share their expertise, experiences, or stories. This could include local community leaders, authors, musicians, or interesting individuals you know.
- **Listener Q&A**: Dedicate episodes to answering questions from your listeners. Encourage audience engagement by soliciting questions via social media or email.
- **Live Recording Sessions**: Record episodes live with audience participation. This can be done via social media platforms, live-streaming services, or in-person events.
- **Debate Format**: Host friendly debates on various topics, allowing each participant to present their arguments and counterarguments. This format encourages critical thinking and dynamic discussions.
- **Collaborative Projects**: Partner with other podcasters or content creators for crossover episodes, allowing you to reach new audiences and collaborate creatively.
- **Video Podcast:** Record video alongside audio to create a video podcast

(vodcast). Consider recording episodes in various locations, such as outdoors, cafes, or other interesting settings.

Benefits:

- **Enhances Communication Skills**: Planning, recording, and presenting podcast episodes sharpens the ability to articulate ideas clearly and confidently. Regular practice in speaking to an audience helps improve both verbal communication and public speaking abilities
- **Nurtures Creativity:** Producing episodes on topics of interest sparks creativity in storytelling, topic development, and the overall production process, fostering a sense of artistic ownership.
- **Teaches Project Management**: From concept to publication, the step-by-step process of producing a podcast offers hands-on experience in managing a project, including organizing content, scheduling, and meeting deadlines.
- **Promotes Active Listening**: Editing audio and crafting episodes requires careful listening, helping to build active listening skills that are useful in conversations, interviews, and other interactions.
- **Encourages Lifelong Learning**: Researching topics for podcast episodes provides continuous learning opportunities, expanding knowledge on a wide variety of subjects and current events.
- **Strengthens Bonds**: Collaborating on the podcast fosters a sense of accomplishment as both contribute to brainstorming, recording, and editing, creating something meaningful together. The process encourages deeper communication and mutual support, strengthening the relationship through shared creative victories and challenges.
- **Encourages Critical Thinking**: Brainstorming topics and structuring episodes encourages thoughtful discussion, analysis, and the ability to present arguments or ideas logically.

56

CULINARY SHOWDOWN

Bring your kitchen to life with a cooking challenge that's bursting with excitement and culinary creativity. This activity invites your teen to explore their culinary talents, try new recipes, and experiment with different ingredients. Whether you choose a specific theme, like "Comfort Food Classics" or "Dessert Duel", or select a mystery basket of ingredients, the challenge will ignite their passion for cooking and maybe even reveal a hidden culinary talent. It's not just about the final dish but the process of creation, learning, and bonding over shared laughter and teamwork.

Cooking together enhances your relationship as you navigate the kitchen, share tips and techniques, and taste-test along the way. Set up a judging panel with criteria such as taste, presentation, and creativity to add a competitive twist. The friendly rivalry and collaboration will make for a memorable experience, filled with fun and learning. Plus, savoring the delicious results of your efforts together adds a sweet ending to this engaging activity.

Materials Needed:

- ☐ Basic cooking supplies (pots, pans, knives, cutting boards)
- ☐ Ingredients based on chosen theme
- ☐ Recipe books or internet access for inspiration
- ☐ Judging criteria (taste, presentation, creativity)

Step-by-Step Instructions:

1. **Set the Stage for the Showdown:**
   - Decide on a theme for the challenge together, like "Asian fusion," "breakfast for dinner," or "healthy snacks." If you want to add an element of surprise, put together a mystery basket of ingredients to use in your dishes.
   - Prepare the kitchen by laying out all the necessary utensils, ingredients, and workspaces. Make sure both of you have your own areas to cook in for maximum creativity and space.
2. **Define the Challenge Rules:**
   - Set a time limit for the challenge (e.g., 60 minutes to create a dish). Make it realistic, but keep the pressure exciting.
   - Define the criteria you'll use for judging the dishes—focus on taste, creativity, and presentation. You can even include a category for "best improvisation" if things don't go as planned!
3. **Start Cooking!**
   - Let the showdown begin! Each of you can choose your ingredients and dive into creating your dishes. Encourage improvisation and experimentation with flavors, and share quick tips or tricks with each other while you cook.
   - As you work side-by-side, check in on each other's progress—whether you're offering advice or playfully bragging about your soon-to-be culinary masterpiece, the interaction adds to the fun.
4. **Plate and Present:**
   - When the time's up, it's time to present your creations. Take a few minutes to plate the dishes in a visually appealing way. Add any final touches for presentation, such as garnishes or a fun name for the dish.
   - Place both plates side by side and admire the work before the taste test begins.
5. **Judging the Showdown:**
   - Together, taste each other's dishes and evaluate based on your chosen criteria. Give feedback about the flavors, creativity, and overall presentation, but keep it lighthearted and fun. You can either judge each other's dishes or invite a third person to do the honors for an unbiased opinion.
   - Declare the winner of the challenge—but remember, it's more about the fun of the process than who "wins."
6. **Enjoy the Meal Together:**

- After the showdown, sit down and enjoy the tasty creations you've crafted together. Reflect on the challenge, share a few laughs about kitchen mishaps, and celebrate the creativity behind each dish.

Safety Considerations:

- Wash hands thoroughly before and after handling food, especially raw meat, to prevent cross-contamination. Clean surfaces and utensils frequently.
- Wear appropriate clothing, including aprons, and avoid loose sleeves that can catch on pots or catch fire. Tie back long hair to keep it away from food and flames.
- Avoid using water to extinguish grease fires; instead, use a lid to smother the flames or use a fire extinguisher.

Troubleshooting Tips:

- **Dish Too Salty:** Balance the saltiness by adding a small amount of an acidic ingredient like rice vinegar, lemon juice, or tomato sauce. Mix thoroughly and taste before adjusting further.
- **Flavor Issues:** Encourage tasting and adjusting seasoning throughout the cooking process. If the flavor of your dish is unbalanced, adjust seasonings gradually. For example, if it's too acidic, add a pinch of sugar; if it's too bland, add salt or spices incrementally.
- **Baking Mishaps**: If baked goods aren't rising, check that the baking powder or baking soda isn't expired, as old leavening agents lose their effectiveness. Ensure the oven is fully preheated before baking, and avoid opening the oven door too early, which can cause the rise to collapse.
- **Presentation:** Add dimension to your plate by stacking or layering elements to create visual interest. Consider incorporating a variety of colors and textures on the plate to make the dish visually appealing.

Cleanup Tips:

- Clean as you go to avoid a huge mess at the end. Load the dishwasher with used dishes, utensils, and cookware throughout the cooking process to keep the sink clear.
- Keep a bowl on the counter for collecting food scraps and packaging as you cook, making it easy to dispose of waste in one go.
- Split the cleanup duties, with one person washing dishes and the other wiping down surfaces or putting away ingredients.
- Soak pots and pans with stubborn residue in hot, soapy water right after use to make cleaning easier.

Variations and Adaptations:

- **Mystery Ingredient Challenge**: Each participant gets a mystery ingredient that must be incorporated into their dish, adding an element of surprise and creativity.
- **Educational Twist:** Look up some fun and interesting facts about the dish or ingredients you're using. Discuss these facts while cooking to add an educational element and spark conversation.
- **Leftovers Remix**: Use only leftovers and pantry items to create a new, innovative dish.
- **Vegetarian Challenge**: Make it a meat-free cooking challenge, encouraging creativity with plant-based ingredients.
- **One-Pot Wonders**: Limit the challenge to dishes that can be made using only one pot or pan, simplifying cleanup and encouraging efficient cooking.
- **Budget-Friendly Challenge**: Set a budget limit and see who can create the most delicious dish without exceeding the set amount.
- **Farm-to-Table Healthy Twist**: Create dishes using fresh, locally-sourced ingredients from farmers' markets or your own garden, emphasizing nutritious and sustainable cooking practices.
- **International Fusion**: Combine elements from different cuisines to create a fusion dish that blends distinctive flavors and techniques.

Benefits:

- **Fosters Creativity**: The freedom to choose ingredients, plating styles, and flavor combinations encourages out-of-the-box thinking and allows for artistic expression through food.
- **Teaches Life Skills**: Cooking is an essential life skill that promotes independence and resourcefulness, providing a foundation for healthy living and practical self-sufficiency.
- **Encourages Adaptability**: Facing unexpected challenges in the kitchen, such as ingredient shortages or timing issues, builds adaptability and problem-solving skills.
- **Develops Time Management Skills**: Managing cooking times, organizing ingredients, and ensuring everything is plated on time fosters strong time management abilities, especially in a fast-paced setting.
- **Offers Educational Opportunities**: Cooking introduces a range of educational opportunities, from learning about different cuisines and cultures to understanding measurements, ratios, and the science of cooking.
- **Strengthens Bonds**: Collaborating on recipe ideas, taste-testing, and refining dishes together creates meaningful moments that deepen bonds

through shared enjoyment and friendly competition.

- **Builds Confidence:** Successfully creating a dish from scratch boosts self-esteem and fosters a sense of accomplishment, helping to build the confidence needed to tackle challenges in a variety of situations.

57

CYBER LEARNING HUB

Set out on a journey of knowledge and growth by exploring online learning courses with your teen. This activity allows you to tailor the learning experience to your teen's interests, whether it's DIY robotics, photography, 3D printing and modeling, or any other subject they are passionate about. The flexibility and accessibility of online courses make them an ideal way to explore new topics and develop valuable skills from the comfort of your home. By embarking on this educational journey together, you foster a love for lifelong learning and curiosity.

Choosing courses that spark your teen's interest ensures that they remain engaged and motivated. Set up a comfortable learning environment, complete with notebooks and relevant tools, and dedicate time to study and practice together. Encourage discussions about what they've learned, help them with challenging concepts, and celebrate their progress, making the learning experience enjoyable and rewarding for both of you.

Materials Needed:

- ☐ Laptop or desktop computer (or tablet)
- ☐ Stable internet connection
- ☐ Notebook and pens
- ☐ Access to online learning platforms (e.g., Udemy, Craftsy)
- ☐ Relevant software or tools for specific courses (e.g., coding software, camera)

Step-by-Step Instructions:

1. **Choose a Course:**
   - Sit down with your teen and browse through various online learning platforms, such as Coursera, Udemy, or Craftsy. Discuss which subject sparks their interest—whether it's DIY robotics, coding, 3D modeling, or another topic.
   - Look for courses that fit both of your skill levels and make sure the content aligns with their personal interests and goals.
   - Consider free courses to keep costs low.
2. **Create a Learning Plan:**
   - Decide how much time you both want to dedicate to the course each week. Setting specific study times can help maintain consistency and motivation.
   - Develop a learning schedule that works for both of you, setting milestones along the way (e.g., completing a module or building a small project).
3. **Engage in the Course Together:**
   - Watch the course videos or read through the lessons side-by-side. Pause frequently to discuss concepts or ask each other questions.
   - If the course requires hands-on work, collaborate on projects together. For example, if you're learning 3D modeling, try building something together on-screen. If it's a coding course, take turns writing the code and debugging together.
4. **Encourage Open Discussions:**
   - After each session, talk about what you've learned. Encourage your teen to ask questions or share thoughts on difficult concepts. These discussions help reinforce learning and keep them engaged.
   - Use real-life examples to connect what you're learning to practical applications. For instance, if you're studying photography, go on a photo walk and experiment with different techniques learned in the course.
5. **Support and Challenge Each Other:**
   - Be open to helping with any areas your teen might find challenging, but also encourage them to figure things out independently when possible.
   - Take on fun challenges to keep things exciting, like creating a mini-project or testing each other on key concepts.
6. **Celebrate Achievements:**

- Once a milestone or a course is completed, celebrate the achievement! Whether it's by working on a project that applies what you've learned or simply recognizing their hard work with a special reward (like a father-teen movie night or a small certificate you design together), make sure the learning journey feels rewarding.

Safety Considerations:

- Choose reputable online learning platforms to ensure the content is accurate, safe, and appropriate.
- Be aware of any course fees or subscription costs.
- Be aware of the platform's data privacy policies and ensure that your and your teen's personal information is protected.
- Encourage regular breaks using the 20-20-20 rule (every 20 minutes, look 20 feet away for 20 seconds) to reduce eye strain and promote a healthy balance between screen time and breaks.

Troubleshooting Tips:

- **Lost Motivation:** If motivation dips, try mixing up the routine by alternating between different types of courses or including more hands-on, practical tasks related to the subject. Setting smaller, more frequent goals can help maintain engagement.
- **Difficult Concepts:** If a topic proves too challenging, break it down into smaller, manageable parts. Look for additional resources such as YouTube tutorials, discussion forums, or related articles to reinforce the concepts.

Cleanup Tips:

- Regularly organize and back up course materials, notes, and assignments on your computer to keep everything accessible and secure.
- Review any course subscriptions or platform memberships periodically to ensure they are still useful and cancel any that are no longer needed.

Variations and Adaptations:

- **Short Courses:** Opt for shorter, high-impact courses that can be completed in a day or two. After each course, apply the newly acquired skills immediately through a mini project or challenge. This creates a sense of accomplishment while keeping the momentum of learning going, and the quick wins help build motivation for tackling more advanced topics down the road.
- **Skill Sharing Sessions**: After mastering certain skills, take turns teaching each other. For instance, one person might lead a session on video editing, while the other focuses on graphic design. This peer-teaching method deepens understanding and encourages collaborative learning.

- **Certifications and Competitions:** Aim for certifications in the course subject or participate in related competitions to add an element of achievement and motivation.
- **Virtual Field Trips**: Enhance learning with virtual field trips related to the course material, such as virtual museum tours, industry visits, or scientific labs, with many free options available.
- **Virtual Study Groups:** Join or create a virtual study group with friends or peers who are interested in the same course. This adds a social element, and the group can discuss the material, share insights, and motivate each other.
- **DIY Learning Hub**: Instead of relying solely on formal online courses, curate a learning hub at home with a combination of online tutorials, free educational resources, and books. Create your own "curriculum" around a shared interest, blending different learning mediums for a more customized experience.

Benefits:

- **Encourages Lifelong Learning:** By exploring a variety of online courses, this activity nurtures a passion for learning that can continue long after the formal schooling years, fostering curiosity and a drive for personal growth.
- **Inspires Career Pathways**: Online courses can introduce teens to potential career paths and industries, helping them make informed decisions about their future.
- **Introduces Emerging Technologies**: Online courses often cover cutting-edge fields like AI, robotics, or 3D printing. Learning about these areas exposes both learners to emerging technologies, fostering curiosity about the future of innovation.
- **Strengthens Bonds:** Exploring new subjects together fosters a sense of teamwork and mutual support. The process of discussing topics, solving challenges, and celebrating progress creates meaningful connections and shared intellectual experiences.
- **Offers Personalized Learning**: The wide range of online courses allows for personalized learning experiences tailored to individual interests, helping build skills and knowledge in areas that align with personal passions or career aspirations.

58
DIY MUSIC STUDIO

Transform a corner of your home into a DIY music studio where you and your teen can dive into the world of music production. With some basic equipment and a bit of creativity, you can write, record, and produce your own songs. Experimenting with different genres and techniques will not only enhance your musical skills but also provide endless hours of fun and learning. This activity is perfect for nurturing a love for music and fostering a sense of accomplishment.

Setting up the studio involves organizing a space with essential recording equipment, learning to use music production software, and exploring various instruments and sounds. You'll guide your teen through the process of songwriting, recording vocals and instruments, and editing tracks. The end result will be your own original music that you can listen to and share with others.

Materials Needed:

- ☐ Computer with music production software (e.g., Audacity [free], GarageBand [free for Mac])
- ☐ Microphone (USB or XLR with an interface)
- ☐ Instruments (guitar, keyboard, etc.)
- ☐ Headphones
- ☐ Audio interface (for premium sound quality; optional)
- ☐ Pop filter (for microphone; optional)
- ☐ Acoustic foam panels (for soundproofing; optional)

Note: *Many of these items are optional and depend on the level of sound quality you aim to achieve. Basic setups with just a computer, software, and a microphone can still produce great results.*

Gear Considerations: *If using an audio interface, choose one with at least two XLR inputs for flexibility in recording vocals and instruments simultaneously.*

Step-by-Step Instructions:

1. **Create the Studio Space:**
    - Select a quiet, comfortable area in your home where you can set up your music studio. This should be a spot with minimal background noise and good lighting for long recording sessions.
    - If possible, choose a space with carpeting or rugs to naturally dampen sound.
    - Arrange a desk or table for the computer and recording equipment.
    - If available, place acoustic foam panels around the recording area to minimize echo and background noise. Alternatively, use heavy curtains, blankets, or even pillows to dampen sound reflections.
2. **Set Up the Basic Equipment:**
    - Position your computer or laptop as the central piece of your setup. Connect it to power and ensure you have space for other equipment around it.
    - Plug in your microphone (either directly via USB or through an audio interface if using an XLR microphone) and place it in an area where it will capture clear sound, avoiding any direct airflow like a window or fan.
    - If using a pop filter, place it in front of the microphone to reduce unwanted sounds during vocal recordings.
    - Set up headphones so you can listen to recordings without interference from external noise. Test the sound levels with your teen to ensure everything is clear and balanced.
3. **Install Music Production Software:**
    - Download and install the music production software of your choice.
    - Spend some time exploring the basics with your child—create a new project, add audio tracks, and familiarize yourselves with key tools such as mixing, looping, and effects.
    - Encourage your teen to experiment with different virtual instruments and built-in sounds the software offers. This step is where the creative process starts to flourish!
    - Watch beginner tutorials or famous DIY music projects online for inspiration and to learn new techniques.
4. **Start Songwriting and Recording:**
    - Discuss song ideas with your teen. Start with the basics—choosing a genre, picking a chord progression or beat, and brainstorming lyrics.
    - Record instruments or vocals one layer at a time. If you're both playing

instruments, record them separately so you can mix the sounds later.

- Have your teen take the lead on one section of the song, and you can work together to harmonize or layer additional tracks.

5. **Edit and Refine Your Song:**
   - Use the software to edit the recordings. Trim audio clips, adjust volume levels, add reverb or other effects, and experiment with panning to create a dynamic sound. This step can get highly technical, but it's also a great opportunity to learn together about the intricacies of sound engineering.
   - Take breaks during this process to discuss what you like or want to change. This not only refines your song but builds teamwork.

6. **Finalize and Export:**
   - Once you're satisfied with your track, export it in a high-quality format (such as WAV or MP3) to share or listen to on other devices.
   - Celebrate your finished product by listening to the song together on speakers or through headphones.
   - If you feel up to it, share the song with friends and family, or even upload it to a platform like SoundCloud! This final step creates a sense of accomplishment, as both of you have crafted something original and meaningful.

Safety Considerations:

- Ensure all electrical equipment is properly grounded and avoid overloading power outlets. Use surge protectors to safeguard against power surges.
- Monitor volume levels during recording sessions to prevent hearing damage from prolonged exposure to loud sounds.
- Ensure the recording area is free of tripping hazards. Keep liquids away from electronic equipment to prevent spills and potential damage.

Troubleshooting Tips:

- **Fatigue:** Remember to take breaks and keep the atmosphere light and fun. Play some favorite songs for inspiration or have a mini dance session between recording takes.
- **Microphone Not Working:** Many microphones, especially condenser mics, require phantom power to operate. Audio interfaces typically provide this power, ensuring your microphones work correctly.
- **Distorted Sound:** Check the audio levels, ensuring they are not peaking, and adjust the microphone placement. Test different distances and angles to find the best sound quality.

- **Latency**: Adjust the buffer size in your music production software settings to reduce latency. Smaller buffer sizes reduce latency but require more processing power.
- **Unwanted Noise:** Check for any ground loops or interference from other electronic devices. Use shielded cables to reduce noise.

Cleanup Tips:

- Store recording equipment in a safe, organized manner when not in use. Use cable ties or Velcro straps to keep cords tidy and avoid tangling.
- Regularly back up your recordings and project files to prevent data loss.

Variations and Adaptations:

- **Remixes and Covers:** Choose favorite songs and create remixes or cover versions, adding your unique twist and learning from the original artists' techniques. This challenge allows you to deconstruct songs, understand their components, and build your own interpretation from scratch.
- **Genre Mash-Up Creations**: Challenge yourselves to blend two or more musical genres into a single song. Combining elements like jazz and hip-hop or classical and electronic can lead to unique and innovative tracks that push creative boundaries.
- **Music Theory Lessons:** Integrate music theory lessons into your sessions, learning about scales, chords, and harmony while applying these concepts to your compositions.
- **Retro Recording Techniques**: Emulate recording methods from past decades. Use vintage effects, aim for lo-fi aesthetics, or limit yourselves to equipment that was available in a specific era to understand the evolution of music production.
- **Voice Modulation Exploration**: Experiment with voice modulation software to alter vocals in fun and creative ways. Whether it's transforming a voice into robotic tones or creating harmonies, this adaptation adds a playful aspect to recording vocals.
- **Virtual Band Collaboration**: Connect with musicians from around the world via online collaboration tools. Exchange tracks and collaborate virtually, layering your recordings with others to create a global music project.
- **Film Scoring Station**: Explore the art of scoring and thematic composition by creating music and soundtracks for videos, short films, video games, or school projects. Compose original music to fit different scenes, adding sound effects and mood music that align with visual storytelling.
- **Charity Album Project**: Produce an album with the goal of donating

proceeds to a chosen charity or cause. This adds a philanthropic dimension to your work, emphasizing the positive impact of music.

Benefits:

- **Boosts Confidence:** Completing an original piece of music and hearing the final product instills a sense of accomplishment, boosting self-esteem and confidence in creative abilities.
- **Promotes Hands-On Learning**: The activity offers a tangible, immersive way to learn about music theory, songwriting, and production techniques through direct application, making the learning experience engaging and practical.
- **Teaches Patience and Perseverance:** The process of recording, editing, and perfecting music can be time-consuming, teaching the importance of patience, persistence, and attention to detail in achieving a high-quality result.
- **Promotes Collaboration and Teamwork**: Working together to produce songs encourages communication and collaboration, with each person contributing their unique strengths and skills to create something greater than the sum of its parts.
- **Strengthens Bonds:** Creating and producing music together fosters deep, meaningful interaction through problem-solving, sharing creative input, and celebrating the completion of each track. The pride in creating something personal strengthens your connection, turning the creative process into lasting memories.
- **Provides Creative Outlet:** Composing and recording original songs allows for deep creative exploration, helping to channel thoughts and emotions into music, fostering self-expression in a unique way.

59

MOCK MARKET INVESTMENT CHALLENGE

Dive into the thrilling world of stock market investing with your teen by using stock market simulators to create a mock portfolio and track its performance. This educational activity will teach the basics of investing, market trends, and financial management in a hands-on and engaging way. By simulating real-world stock trading, you can explore the principles of buying, selling, and holding stocks without any financial risk.

Together, you'll research different companies, choose stocks to invest in, and monitor the portfolio's performance over time. Discussing market trends and analyzing the results fosters critical thinking and financial literacy. This activity is a valuable opportunity to develop a practical understanding of the stock market and investing strategies.

Materials Needed:

- ☐ Computer or tablet with internet access
- ☐ Stock market simulator platform (e.g., Investopedia Simulator, MarketWatch Virtual Stock Exchange; both free)
- ☐ Notebook or spreadsheet for tracking investments

Step-by-Step Instructions:

1. **Set Up Your Challenge:**
   - Sit down together and agree on the rules for your investment challenge. Decide how long the challenge will last (e.g., one week, one month) and how much "virtual money" each person gets to start their portfolio (simulators typically offer a starting amount like $10,000).
2. **Choose Your Stock Market Simulator:**
   - Select a free online stock market simulator, such as the Investopedia Simulator or the MarketWatch Virtual Stock Exchange. Sign up for accounts and familiarize yourselves with the platform. Let your teen take the lead in setting up their mock portfolio.
3. **Research Companies:**
   - Start by researching companies and industries that interest both of you. Discuss their performance, values, and market trends. You can use financial websites, news outlets, and free stock analysis platforms like Reuters or MarketWatch to help with your research.
   - Discuss ethical investing and the importance of considering the social and environmental impact of investment choices.
   - Encourage your child to write down key information about each company (e.g., its past performance, competitors, or any relevant news). This will help when it's time to make decisions.
4. **Build Your Portfolio:**
   - Once you've done your research, it's time to invest. Select a variety of stocks to create a balanced portfolio. Discuss the strategy behind your choices—whether it's buying established companies (blue-chip stocks) or taking risks on startups. Add the selected stocks to your portfolios in the simulator.
   - Keep a running list of the stocks you've picked and the reasoning behind each one in a notebook or spreadsheet. This helps you track your decisions and reflect on your strategy as you move through the challenge.
5. **Track Performance:**
   - Over the course of the challenge, check in regularly (daily or weekly) to monitor how your investments are performing. Watch how the stock prices fluctuate and take note of news or events that might be impacting your stocks.
   - Have discussions about whether to hold, buy more, or sell certain stocks. This encourages critical thinking and decision-making skills based on real-world financial data.

6. **Compare and Reflect:**
   - At the end of the challenge period, compare your portfolios. Who had the best-performing portfolio, and why? Talk about what you both learned from the experience—such as market volatility, the impact of global events on stocks, and your own investment strategies.
   - Reflect on the risks and rewards of investing and how your decisions impacted your portfolio.

Safety Considerations:

- Clearly distinguish between real and simulated investing to prevent any confusion. Emphasize that the activity is for educational purposes and does not involve real money.
- Talk about the emotional ups and downs of market fluctuations, even in a simulation, and ensure your teen understands that the stock market involves both gains and losses. This discussion helps build emotional resilience for future financial decisions.
- Ensure your teen understands the importance of online privacy and responsible behavior when using stock market simulators and other online platforms.
- Encourage critical thinking and skepticism about investment advice found online. Remind your teen to verify information from multiple sources.

Troubleshooting Tips:

- **Lack of Data:** If you struggle to find information on certain companies, try using multiple stock analysis platforms or financial news websites for a broader range of data.
- **Overwhelming Data:** If tracking and analyzing data becomes overwhelming, focus on key metrics such as overall portfolio value, individual stock performance, and market trends. Simplify your approach to make it more manageable.
- **Poor Performance:** If your portfolio is not performing well, review your investment choices and research why certain stocks are underperforming. Use this as a learning opportunity to understand market trends and improve future decisions.
- **Complex Concepts:** If certain investing concepts are difficult to grasp, break them down into simpler terms and use real-world examples to explain them. Consider watching educational videos together to reinforce learning.
- **Loss of Interest:** If your teen loses interest, try introducing new elements to the activity, such as setting up friendly competitions or exploring different investment strategies. Keep discussions engaging and relevant to

their interests.

- **Impulsive Decisions:** Encourage your teen to avoid making impulsive investment decisions based on short-term market fluctuations. Discuss the importance of a long-term investment strategy and staying calm during market volatility.
- **Frustration with Losses:** If your teen feels frustrated with losses, remind them that simulated trading is a learning experience and that losses are part of the process. Discuss what can be learned from the experience to improve future decisions.

Cleanup Tips:

- Create dedicated folders on your computer for all related documents, spreadsheets, and notes. Keep these organized by date or topic for easy reference.
- Periodically clear your browser cache to ensure optimal performance of online tools and platforms.
- Regularly back up your spreadsheets, notes, and other important files to an external hard drive or cloud storage to prevent data loss.

Variations and Adaptations:

- **Sector-Specific Challenge:** Choose a specific industry, such as technology, healthcare, or renewable energy, and build a mock portfolio based only on stocks from that sector. This focuses the research on understanding the trends, risks, and opportunities unique to that industry.
- **Day Trader's Dilemma**: Simulate a day-trading scenario where investments are made and sold within the same day. Track how high-frequency trading performs versus long-term strategies, introducing the concept of short-term market timing and its risks.
- **The Warren Buffett Challenge**: Limit your investment options to companies that renowned investor Warren Buffett has either invested in or publicly recommended. Research his strategies and see how your mock portfolio performs compared to his philosophies of long-term value investing.
- **Dividend Portfolio Focus**: Create a portfolio that focuses exclusively on dividend-paying stocks. This introduces the concept of passive income and reinvesting dividends to grow wealth over time, adding a long-term financial strategy angle to the challenge.
- **Short Selling Challenge**: Introduce the concept of short selling by allowing a portion of the mock portfolio to be allocated toward betting against certain companies. This variation offers a deeper understanding of advanced investment strategies and market volatility.

- **Historical Market Recreation**: Recreate a famous historical event in stock market history, like the dot-com bubble or the 2008 financial crisis. Use past data to simulate how portfolios would perform under those conditions, sparking conversations about market volatility and the importance of diversification.

Benefits:

- **Develops Financial Literacy**: This activity provides a hands-on introduction to the fundamentals of investing, from reading stock charts to understanding market trends, building a solid foundation in personal finance and financial management.
- **Promotes Strategic Decision-Making**: The challenge helps develop the ability to think ahead, consider long-term outcomes, and make informed decisions based on data, promoting strategic thinking in various areas of life.
- **Fosters Emotional Discipline**: Simulating real market fluctuations allows participants to experience the emotional ups and downs of investing, teaching the importance of staying calm and making rational decisions under pressure.
- **Enhances Research Skills**: Finding, evaluating, and synthesizing information about companies, industries, and economic factors sharpens research skills that are essential for academic success and everyday decision-making.
- **Strengthens Bonds:** Collaborating on investment decisions, discussing market trends, and navigating challenges together creates shared moments of problem-solving and teamwork, which naturally deepens the connection through mutual learning and support.
- **Teaches Risk Management**: Through simulated gains and losses, participants learn how to balance risk and reward, a key aspect of investing that translates into other decision-making processes.

OUTDOOR FUN

Take things to the next level with these outdoor activities for high schoolers! Engage in Community Volunteering Day to give back and make a positive impact, or set up a Backyard Bootcamp to work on fitness together in an encouraging, energetic environment. For nature lovers, dive into the wonders of local biodiversity with a BioBlitz Competition, discovering and documenting plants, insects, and wildlife. Each activity offers meaningful experiences that promote exploration, connection, and a sense of fulfillment.

60

COMMUNITY VOLUNTEERING DAY

Instill a sense of social responsibility and empathy in your teen by engaging in community volunteering activities together. Whether it's cleaning up a local park, helping at a food bank, or participating in a community garden, volunteering offers a meaningful way to give back and make a positive impact. This activity teaches the importance of service and helps your teen develop a compassionate outlook, fostering a deeper connection to their community. The experience of working together for a common good will not only strengthen your bond but also create a lasting sense of fulfillment.

Volunteering provides an opportunity to meet new people, learn new skills, and understand the challenges faced by others in the community. By actively participating in service projects, your teen will gain a sense of purpose and pride in their contributions. Discuss the impact of your efforts and reflect on the importance of helping others, reinforcing the values of empathy and generosity. This shared endeavor will create powerful memories and inspire a lifelong commitment to making the world a better place.

Materials Needed:

- ☐ Comfortable clothing appropriate for the volunteer activity
- ☐ Any necessary forms or waivers from the organization
- ☐ Work gloves (for clean-up or gardening projects)
- ☐ Water bottles
- ☐ Snacks or a packed lunch (for longer volunteer activities)
- ☐ Sun protection (for outdoor activities)
- ☐ Binoculars or magnifying glass (optional for detailed work or environmental projects)

Step-by-Step Instructions:

1. **Choose a Volunteer Activity:**
   - Sit down with your teen and discuss different volunteering options in your area, such as cleaning a local park, helping at a food bank, or joining a community gardening project.
   - Look into the specific needs of your community to choose a meaningful volunteer activity.
   - Let your teen have a say in selecting an activity that aligns with their strengths and passions, ensuring they feel invested in the choice.
2. **Register and Gather Details:**
   - Once you've chosen an activity, find out if registration is required. Some community projects might need you to fill out forms or coordinate with an organizer.
   - Confirm the details, such as the time, location, and any special instructions for the day of volunteering.
   - Make a list of any additional supplies or preparations needed for the activity.
3. **Prepare for the Day:**
   - The day before, gather any necessary items such as gloves, tools, or supplies. Pack a water bottle and snacks to keep you both energized.
   - Talk about what to expect during the day and discuss any goals or personal intentions for the experience, whether it's making a positive impact or meeting new people.
4. **Arrive Early and Meet the Team:**
   - On the day of the event, arrive at the location a little early to meet the organizer and other volunteers. This is a great time to introduce yourselves and get acquainted with the task ahead.
   - Encourage your teen to engage with others and ask questions about the project to better understand its purpose and impact.
5. **Work Together with Purpose:**
   - As you dive into the volunteering activity, work side by side with your teen. Whether you're planting flowers, sorting donations, or picking up litter, focus on completing tasks together as a team.
   - Consider taking before and after photos of your efforts to visually document the impact of your work. This adds a personal element and creates a lasting memory of what you've achieved.
   - Use this time to bond by talking, laughing, and sharing stories about the experience, while also reflecting on the importance of the work

you're doing.

6. **Take Breaks and Stay Engaged:**
   - Throughout the day, take breaks to rest and recharge. During these moments, have brief discussions with your teen about how the experience is going, what they've learned, or what has surprised them so far.
   - Encourage them to observe the impact they're making in real-time, whether it's seeing a clean park or interacting with the people you're helping.
7. **Reflect and Celebrate Your Contribution:**
   - Once the work is complete, take a moment to step back and look at what you've accomplished together. Whether it's a cleaner community space or a food bank restocked with donations, emphasize how your combined efforts made a tangible difference.
   - On the way home or later that evening, engage in a deeper conversation with your teen about the experience. Discuss the value of giving back, the challenges faced, and how these small acts can contribute to a larger societal impact.

Safety Considerations:

- Many volunteering organizations have safety protocols in place, such as proper tool usage or hygiene guidelines when handling food. Be sure to follow all provided instructions carefully.
- Wear clothing suitable for the task, such as sturdy shoes for outdoor work or gloves if handling sharp objects. Protective gear may be needed depending on the project.
- Bring water and take regular breaks, especially if working outdoors or in warm conditions, to avoid dehydration and fatigue.
- Carry a basic first-aid kit for any minor injuries.

Troubleshooting Tips:

- **Task Confusion or Unclear Instructions:** If either of you is unsure about how to complete a task, don't hesitate to ask for clarification from the volunteer coordinator. Clear understanding ensures the work is done safely and effectively.
- **Emotional Impact:** Some volunteer activities can be emotionally challenging; provide support and encourage open discussions about feelings.
- **Low Engagement or Motivation**: If your teen seems disengaged, talk to them about the importance of their contribution. Sometimes, seeing the

impact firsthand or interacting directly with those being helped can reignite motivation.

Cleanup Tips:

- Clean up the volunteer site and ensure all tools and materials are properly stored.
- Thank the organization and any other volunteers for their efforts. Consider writing a thank-you note or providing feedback on the experience.

Variations and Adaptations:

- **Virtual Volunteering:** Participate in online volunteer opportunities like tutoring, transcription, or advocacy work.
- **DIY Volunteer Projects at Home**: If volunteering in-person isn't feasible, consider at-home projects like assembling hygiene kits for shelters or creating blankets for animal rescues. You can still contribute meaningfully while working together in the comfort of your own space.
- **Skill-Based Volunteering:** Tailor your volunteering efforts to highlight your teen's unique skills or talents. If they love technology, consider offering tech support at a senior center. If they're artistically inclined, help paint murals at a community center or create handmade cards for hospital patients.
- **Charity Yard Sale or Fundraiser**: Organize a yard sale or car wash with all proceeds going to a local charity. This allows for both practical business skills and community engagement while helping to support a good cause.
- **Charity Walks or Runs**: Combine physical activity with a charitable cause by participating in charity races or walks. Many events support important causes, and raising funds for a charity while completing a physical challenge can be both rewarding and fun.
- **Skill-Swap Volunteering:** Pair up with another family or group where each member teaches a skill they are good at to others, and then volunteer using those new skills.
- **Volunteering Challenge**: Set specific challenges or goals for your volunteering day, such as collecting a certain amount of trash, planting a set number of trees, or serving a specific number of meals.
- **Volunteering with a Twist**: Incorporate a fun twist, such as dressing up in costumes, creating a themed playlist for the day, or having a friendly competition between family members on who can make the most impact.

Benefits:

- **Builds Empathy and Compassion**: By witnessing and addressing the challenges faced by others firsthand, this activity helps foster empathy, encouraging a more compassionate and understanding attitude towards people from all walks of life.

- **Encourages Active Citizenship**: Participating in volunteer efforts introduces teens to the concept of active citizenship, helping them understand how they can contribute to positive social change and play an active role in shaping their community's future.
- **Builds Community and Networks**: Contributing to community projects strengthens social bonds and a sense of belonging, while also helping to build a network of like-minded individuals and potential mentors.
- **Develops Valuable Life Skills:** Teens learn new skills such as teamwork, problem-solving, and communication, which are valuable for personal and professional growth.
- **Promotes Mental Well-Being**: Engaging in community service has been shown to promote a sense of fulfillment and purpose, which can improve overall mental health and boost self-esteem.
- **Strengthens Bonds**: Working side by side during tasks like planting trees in a community garden or organizing food donations at a local shelter fosters teamwork and mutual support. Sharing these meaningful experiences deepens the connection, as both contribute to a shared goal and reflect on the impact together.
- **Inspires Gratitude**: Seeing the impact of their efforts can inspire teens to appreciate what they have and develop a more grateful attitude.

Impact Initiators

Explore these activity ideas to find inspiration for your community volunteering day. While this list is a great starting point, researching your local community's specific needs will help you decide where your efforts can make the most impact.

Education and Preservation:

- **Seed Library Maintenance:** Assist in maintaining a seed library by organizing seeds and educating the community on the critical role of seed saving and biodiversity. This promotes resilient ecosystems and sustainable agriculture through informative seed exchanges.
- **Library Support:** Help organize books, run reading programs, or assist with events at a local library.
- **Organic Gardening Education:** Join initiatives to educate the community on the importance of organic gardening and lawn care, focusing on sustainable practices that promote healthy ecosystems and reduce chemical use.
- **Dark Sky Preservation:** Participate in dark sky preservation initiatives to reduce light pollution, educating communities about the importance of dark skies for astronomy and wildlife through events and advocacy programs.
- **Historic Site Preservation:** Volunteer at a historic site or museum to assist with tours, maintenance, or educational programs.
- **Historic Cemetery Documentation:** Contribute to the preservation of local history by documenting and cleaning historic cemeteries. This involves recording inscriptions, cleaning headstones, and researching the area's history, promoting respect and awareness of local heritage.

Support and Assistance:

- **Soup Kitchen Assistance:** Volunteer at a local soup kitchen to prepare and serve meals to those in need.
- **Elderly Assistance:** Visit a senior center to spend time with the elderly, play games, or help with daily activities.
- **Youth Mentorship:** Volunteer with organizations that offer mentorship programs for at-risk youth.
- **Animal Shelter Support:** Spend time at an animal shelter walking dogs, cleaning kennels, or helping with adoption events.
- **Volunteer Fire Department:** Support the local volunteer fire department with fundraising events, equipment maintenance, or community outreach programs.

Environment and Beautification:

- **Park Clean-Up:** Join a local park clean-up crew to help pick up litter and maintain the green spaces in your community.
- **Graffiti Removal:** Partner with a community organization to remove graffiti from public spaces.
- **Street Clean-Up:** Join a local initiative to clean up city streets and sidewalks.
- **Neighborhood Beautification:** Join a neighborhood beautification project, including planting flowers or trees.
- **Community Garden:** Join or start a community garden project in an urban or suburban area, involving planting, maintenance, and education.
- **Trail Maintenance:** Help maintain hiking or biking trails in rural areas by clearing debris and marking paths.
- **Wildlife Habitat Restoration:** Participate in projects to restore and protect local wildlife habitats, such as planting trees or building birdhouses.

61

BACKYARD BOOTCAMP

Transform your backyard or a local park into an invigorating outdoor fitness bootcamp with various workout stations designed to challenge and inspire both you and your teen. This activity combines the fun of being outdoors with the benefits of physical exercise, creating a dynamic and engaging workout environment. Set up stations for exercises like push-ups, lunges, planks, sprints, and agility drills, and take turns challenging each other to push your limits. The shared effort and encouragement make this a rewarding way to stay fit together.

Working out side-by-side fosters a sense of camaraderie and motivation, as you cheer each other on and celebrate each achievement. The bootcamp setup allows for a variety of exercises, keeping the routine fresh and exciting. This activity not only promotes physical fitness but also strengthens your bond through shared goals and mutual support, making fitness a fun and integral part of your relationship.

Materials Needed:

- ☐ Exercise mats
- ☐ Cones or markers (for setting up stations)
- ☐ Stopwatch or timer
- ☐ Water bottles
- ☐ Sun protection
- ☐ Towels (for wiping off sweat)
- ☐ Digital or printed exercise guides (optional)

Step-by-Step Instructions:

1. **Plan Your Bootcamp:**
   - Discuss and decide on the exercises you want to include in your bootcamp. Aim for a mix of strength, cardio, and agility exercises.
   - Choose a suitable outdoor location with enough space for multiple workout stations.
2. **Set Up Stations:**
   - Use cones or markers to designate different workout stations. Each station should focus on a specific exercise.
     - **Example stations:** push-ups, squats, planks, jumping jacks, sprints, lunges, high knees, burpees, and agility ladder drills.
3. **Explain the Rules:**
   - At each station, you and your teen will perform the exercise for 30 seconds to 1 minute, depending on your fitness levels. Adjust the time to suit your endurance.
   - Take a short 20-30 second rest between stations, and be sure to cheer each other on as you move from one station to the next.
   - You can either work side by side or take turns so one of you is resting while the other completes the station.
   - Consider setting friendly competitions, like who can do the most push-ups or complete the agility drill fastest.
4. **Warm-Up:**
   - Start with a 5-10 minute warm-up to prepare your muscles and prevent injury. Do a mix of light jogging, arm circles, jumping jacks, and dynamic stretches.
   - Let your teen take the lead here if they want, making it more interactive.
5. **Begin the Bootcamp Circuit:**
   - Move through each station, performing the designated exercises at your own pace. Encourage each other to push through any fatigue with words of motivation.
   - Make adjustments as needed—swap an exercise for something else if one of you finds it too difficult or uncomfortable.
6. **Take Breaks and Hydrate:**
   - After completing one full circuit of all stations, take a longer break (2-3 minutes) to catch your breath, stretch, and drink water.
   - Use this time to discuss how you're both feeling and give each other

feedback on the performance.

7. **Complete Multiple Rounds:**
   - Repeat the circuit 2-3 times depending on fitness levels. Increase the intensity by adding extra stations, reducing rest times, or incorporating weights or resistance bands.
8. **Cool Down and Stretch:**
   - End the workout with a cool-down session that includes light stretching and deep breathing exercises. Focus on flexibility by stretching the muscles you worked (legs, arms, and core).
   - You can even include a guided meditation or mindfulness session to relax and rejuvenate the mind and body.
   - Consider keeping a workout journal to track progress and set new fitness goals together.

Safety Considerations:

- Ensure a proper warm-up before starting the workout to prevent injuries. Simple stretches and light cardio can help loosen muscles and prepare the body for more intense exercises.
- Ensure you both understand the correct form for each exercise to prevent injuries. Consider watching instructional videos if needed.
- Drink plenty of water before, during, and after the workout to stay hydrated.
- Pay attention to any signs of discomfort or pain, and stop immediately if you experience any issues.

Troubleshooting Tips:

- **Varied Fitness Levels**: Adapt exercises to match each person's fitness level. Offer easier modifications (e.g., knee push-ups) or more challenging variations (e.g., plyometric push-ups).
- **Lack of Space**: If space is limited, adapt exercises to require less movement or perform the bootcamp in shifts.
- **Motivational Slumps**: Incorporate fun elements like music, games, or rewards to keep motivation high. Create a playlist of upbeat songs to energize the workout.

Cleanup Tips:

- Check any equipment for signs of wear or damage during cleanup. Repair or replace any broken or worn-out items to ensure safety for future workouts.

Variations and Adaptations:

- **Adventure Bootcamp**: Take your bootcamp to different outdoor locations like hiking trails, beaches, or forests to keep the environment fresh and challenging.
- **Obstacle Course:** Create an obstacle course with various fitness challenges like crawling under ropes, jumping over hurdles, and balancing on beams. Time each other to add a competitive edge.
- **Mind and Body Combo**: Combine physical exercises with mental challenges like solving puzzles or trivia questions during rest periods to engage both mind and body.
- **Themed Bootcamp Days**: Create themed bootcamp days such as "Cardio Blast," "Strength Training," or "Sports Drills." This keeps workouts varied and exciting.
- **HIIT Sessions**: Integrate High-Intensity Interval Training (HIIT) into your bootcamp with short bursts of intense exercise followed by brief rest periods.
- **Water Workout:** Incorporate water-based exercises if near a pool, lake, or beach. Activities can include swimming laps, water aerobics, or resistance exercises in the water.

Benefits:

- **Increases Motivation**: Working out with a partner can increase motivation and accountability, making it more likely to stick to fitness routines.
- **Builds Resilience**: Regularly pushing physical limits and overcoming workout challenges helps build mental and physical resilience.
- **Encourages Goal Setting**: Setting and achieving fitness goals teaches valuable skills in goal setting and achievement, applicable in various aspects of life.
- **Improves Mood**: Physical activity releases endorphins, which can help alleviate symptoms of depression and anxiety, leading to improved mental health.
- **Fosters Discipline**: Establishing a consistent workout routine promotes discipline and helps develop a strong work ethic.
- **Improves Sleep Quality**: Regular physical activity, especially in the fresh air, can improve sleep patterns and overall sleep quality.
- **Strengthens Bonds**: Working out together fosters camaraderie and deepens the bond through shared challenges, mutual encouragement, and celebrating each other's progress.

- **Boosts Immune System**: Regular exercise can strengthen the immune system, helping to ward off illnesses and improve overall health.

62
BIOBLITZ COMPETITION

Uncover the wonders of local biodiversity with a BioBlitz competition, where you and your teen will race against time to identify as many species of plants, animals, and insects as possible within a designated area. Armed with field guides or apps, you'll explore your surroundings, recording your findings and learning about the incredible variety of life that exists in your local ecosystem. This engaging and educational activity not only sharpens observational skills but also fosters a deeper appreciation for nature.

As you move through the competition, the excitement of discovering new species and the challenge of identifying them will keep you both engaged and motivated. The friendly competition will encourage teamwork, critical thinking, and curiosity. At the end of the day, you'll have a comprehensive record of the local biodiversity, along with a shared sense of accomplishment and connection to the natural world.

Materials Needed:

- ☐ Field guides or identification apps (e.g., Seek, iNaturalist)
- ☐ Notebooks and pens (for recording observations)
- ☐ Smartphones or cameras (for documenting species)
- ☐ Binoculars (optional)
- ☐ Magnifying glass (optional)
- ☐ Comfortable outdoor clothing and footwear
- ☐ Water and snacks
- ☐ Sun protection
- ☐ Insect repellent (optional)
- ☐ Basic first aid kit (optional)

Step-by-Step Instructions:

1. **Choose Your BioBlitz Zone:**
   - Together, decide on a specific area for your BioBlitz, such as a local park or nature reserve. The key is to choose a place with a variety of plant and animal life.
   - Decide on the boundaries of the area you will explore and set a specific timeframe for the competition (e.g., 2-3 hours).
   - Agree on the rules, such as how to record observations and what counts as a valid identification.
2. **Prepare Your Tools:**
   - Download a species identification app, like iNaturalist or Seek, which allows you to take pictures and identify plants, animals, and insects in real-time.
   - If you prefer old-school methods, grab field guides that cover your area's local flora and fauna. Or, better yet, use a combination of both for comparison and depth of learning.
   - Collect your notebooks, pens, and other necessary materials.
   - Ensure smartphones or cameras are fully charged for documenting your findings.
3. **Start the Blitz:**
   - Start by walking around the designated area, scanning for anything that moves or stands out. Encourage your teen to check under rocks, leaves, and along trails for hidden creatures.
   - Take clear photos of each species to aid in identification and to keep a visual record of your findings.
   - Use your identification tools—upload your photo to the app and see if you can identify the species. Alternatively, flip through your guidebooks and cross-reference your findings.
   - Record your observations in a notebook or the app, keeping track of the number of species identified. You can also take notes about the habitat or conditions where you found each species for a deeper understanding.
4. **Compete and Collaborate:**
   - Compete to see who can identify the most species within the timeframe, but also help each other with tricky identifications and share interesting discoveries.
   - Take regular breaks to discuss your findings and share knowledge about the species you encounter. This is where you can compare notes

to see who's ahead.

5. **Wrap-Up & Analyze Results:**
   - Once the time is up, gather your findings and take a moment to review the species list. How many unique species did you each find? Did you discover any unexpected plants or animals?
   - Discuss your observations with your child—what did they enjoy most? What was the coolest species they encountered? This reflective moment reinforces connection and gives you a chance to discuss what you've both learned about your local environment.
6. **Create a Biodiversity Report:**
   - After the competition, work together to compile your findings into a simple "BioBlitz Report" to keep as a memento or even share with local wildlife organizations. You can organize your report by category (plants, insects, birds, etc.) or by habitat type.
   - Include photos, observations, and any notes about your experience. This step is not only fun but also educational, allowing you to reflect on the biodiversity you explored.
   - Celebrate your efforts with a small reward or treat, and consider sharing your findings with a local nature group or online community.

Safety Considerations:

- Learn to identify and avoid contact with poisonous plants such as poison ivy, oak, and sumac.
- Be mindful of your physical limits and take breaks as needed to avoid overexertion.
- Be aware of larger wildlife in the area and know what to do if you encounter animals like bears or snakes. Keep a safe distance and do not approach or feed wildlife.
- Have a plan for emergencies and ensure your phone is charged. Know the nearest location to seek help if needed and inform someone of your location and expected return time in case of any unforeseen situations.
- If you're exploring areas with tall grass or wooded regions, regularly check for ticks during and after the activity. Promptly and properly remove any that are found. Wear long sleeves and tuck pants into socks to minimize exposure.

Troubleshooting Tips:

- **Difficulty Identifying Species**: Use multiple sources, like different apps and field guides, for cross-referencing and confirming species identifications.

- **Low Biodiversity in the Area**: If the designated area seems to lack visible species, try focusing on microhabitats such as under logs, leaf litter, or near water sources. Shifting focus to smaller, less obvious organisms can reveal a surprising variety of life.
- **Species Overlap**: If the same species keeps appearing, encourage finding more specific identifying features, such as variations in markings or size. This can turn the overlap into an additional learning experience.
- **Weather Challenges**: If the weather is uncooperative, have a backup indoor activity related to biodiversity, such as watching a nature documentary or researching local species online.

Cleanup Tips:

- Before leaving the area, double-check that you've collected all your personal items, such as notebooks, pens, and equipment.
- Follow the "Leave No Trace" principles by ensuring that you don't leave any marks or traces of your activity. This includes avoiding picking plants or disturbing wildlife unnecessarily.
- Picking up any litter you find, even if it's not yours, not only keeps the environment clean and beautiful for others but also sets a great example for your teen, teaching them the importance of environmental stewardship.
- Organize your notes and photos after the BioBlitz and consider sharing your findings with local conservation groups or online platforms.
- If you identified any invasive species, report them to local environmental authorities or conservation groups.

Variations and Adaptations:

- **Backyard BioBlitz**: Conduct the BioBlitz in your own backyard or a nearby green space, proving that you don't need to travel far to discover amazing biodiversity.
- **Themed BioBlitz**: Focus on specific types of species, such as birds, insects, or plants, to deepen knowledge in that particular area and add a challenging twist to the competition.
- **Nighttime BioBlitz**: Turn the competition into an evening or nighttime adventure by using flashlights and headlamps to observe nocturnal species like bats, owls, or insects that only come out after dark.
- **Sensory BioBlitz**: Focus on using different senses to identify species, such as listening for bird calls, smelling flowers, and feeling the textures of leaves and bark.
- **Seasonal BioBlitz**: Plan a series of BioBlitz competitions throughout

different seasons to observe how biodiversity changes throughout the year.

- **Micro-Habitat Focus**: Focus on a specific micro-habitat, such as a pond, a single tree, or a patch of meadow, and document all the species found within that small area.
- **Citizen Science BioBlitz**: Partner with a local conservation group or participate in a larger citizen science project to contribute your findings to a broader scientific effort.
- **DIY Field Guide**: Create your own field guide by compiling notes and photos from your BioBlitzes over time, building a personalized resource for local biodiversity.

Benefits:

- **Develops Scientific Inquiry**: Engaging in species identification fosters a scientific mindset, encouraging curiosity, observation, hypothesis testing, and data collection.
- **Enhances Observational Skills**: The detailed process of identifying plants, animals, and insects enhances the ability to notice subtle differences and patterns in nature, sharpening attention to detail.
- **Inspires Appreciation for Nature and Conservation:** The activity highlights the rich variety of life that exists in even small, local ecosystems, creating a sense of wonder and respect for the complexity and diversity of nature. This hands-on experience can spark a lifelong interest in nature, science, and environmental conservation.
- **Provides Educational Opportunities**: Exploring local biodiversity offers hands-on learning about biology, ecology, and environmental science, providing educational enrichment that goes beyond classroom lessons.
- **Strengthens Bonds**: Working together to discover and identify species fosters teamwork and deepens the connection between parent and teen. The shared excitement of a rare find can create great moments of bonding and learning.
- **Promotes Outdoor Activity**: Moving through different terrains and exploring outdoor environments during the competition encourages physical activity, making the experience both mentally and physically engaging.

THE

FAMILY

FRONTIER

INDOOR ADVENTURES

Indoor activities for the whole family bring everyone together for creativity, laughter, and teamwork! Enjoy a Family Game-A-Thon, where everyone picks their favorite games and engages in friendly competition, from classic board games to newer favorites. Host a Family Talent Showcase, with each family member taking the stage to share a unique skill or performance, celebrating creativity and individuality. For a more reflective experience, embark on an Ancestor Connection Quest, building a family tree together while uncovering fascinating stories from the past. These activities provide an opportunity for every family member to contribute, fostering unity and shared experiences that will be remembered for years to come.

63

FAMILY GAME-A-THON

Ready for some epic family fun? Dive into a family game marathon and spend the day battling it out in a series of friendly competitions. This isn't just about rolling dice and moving pieces; it's about strategy, laughter, and bonding. Set up a cozy gaming area, stock up on snacks and drinks, and get ready to play everything from classics like Pictionary and Risk to newer favorites like Sushi Go! and Forbidden Island. Your family will love the extended playtime and the opportunity to compete against each other, and you'll cherish the moments of shared excitement and friendly rivalry.

As the day unfolds, watch as the room fills with laughter and animated discussions over game strategies. The friendly banter and light-hearted teasing create a warm atmosphere where everyone feels connected. Each game presents a new opportunity for teamwork, cunning tactics, and, of course, the sweet taste of victory or the chance to laugh off a loss. With every move, card drawn, and dice rolled, the bond within the family strengthens, making memories that will be fondly recalled for years to come.

Materials Needed:

- ☐ A variety of board games, card games, or video games
- ☐ Snacks and drinks
- ☐ Comfortable seating
- ☐ Small prizes or handmade certificates (optional)

Step-by-Step Instructions:

1. **Select Games:**
   - Choose a mix of games that cater to all ages and interests. Include strategy games, luck-based games, and skill-based games.
   - Ask each family member to pick their favorite game to ensure everyone's interests are represented.
2. **Set Up:**
   - Arrange a cozy gaming area with enough seating for everyone. Use cushions, bean bags, or comfy chairs to create a relaxed atmosphere.
   - Set up different stations for each game if you have the space. This allows for a smooth transition between games and keeps the excitement alive.
   - Ensure the area is well-lit, but also consider adding some ambient lighting like fairy lights or a cozy lamp to create a warm atmosphere.
3. **Prepare Snacks:**
   - Whip up some easy snacks like popcorn, veggie platters, nachos, fruit slices, and cookies.
   - Have a variety of drinks handy such as water, juice, soda, and perhaps a special treat like hot chocolate or milkshakes.
   - Set up snack stations around the gaming area so everyone can easily grab a bite without interrupting the flow of the game.
4. **Play and Enjoy:**
   - Start playing, keep score if you like, and most importantly, have fun!
   - Foster supportive atmosphere by encouraging teamwork, strategic discussions, light-hearted teasing, and playful banter.
   - Take breaks between games to snack and chat, or reminisce about previous games you've played together.
   - Rotate games to keep the excitement alive and give everyone a chance to play different types.
   - Celebrate wins with small prizes or fun rewards like choosing the next game or getting an extra snack.
5. **Post-Game Wrap-Up:**
   - After the games, gather for a brief family discussion. Share highlights, favorite moments, and funny incidents from the game-a-thon.
   - Consider tallying up the scores or wins to declare a "Game-A-Thon Champion" and hand out a fun prize (even if it's just a silly homemade trophy or crown).

Safety Considerations:

- Keep small game pieces away from toddlers to avoid choking hazards.
- Schedule regular breaks to stand up, stretch, and move around. This helps prevent stiffness and keeps everyone energized.

Troubleshooting Tips:

- **Game Selection Issues:** If participants can't agree on which game to play, create a game selection jar. Write down the names of all available games on slips of paper and draw one at random to decide.
- **Rule Disputes:** Keep a copy of the rules handy or use game apps for quick rule checks. Designate a "game master" for each game who has the final say on rules. This role can rotate between participants.
- **Game Fatigue:** Keep a variety of games on hand and switch to a new game if interest wanes. Introduce a mix of short and long games to maintain engagement.
- **Overly Competitive Atmosphere:** Emphasize the importance of fun and togetherness over winning. Set up team-based games to foster cooperation instead of competition.
- **Snack Spills:** Keep drinks and snacks on a separate table from the games and have napkins and a small trash can nearby for quick cleanups.
- **Uncooperative Players:** If someone is not enjoying the game, allow them to step out and rejoin later or participate in a different role (e.g., scorekeeper).

Cleanup Tips:

- Allocate specific cleanup tasks to each family member, such as putting away games, collecting snack wrappers, wiping down surfaces, and vacuuming or sweeping the floor.
- Before packing away the games, check under furniture and in corners for any stray game pieces. This ensures nothing is missing next time you play.

Variations and Adaptations:

- **Game Review:** Have each family member write reviews of the games you play, discussing what they liked or didn't like.
- **Game Night Snacks Recipe Book:** Create a mini recipe book with favorite snacks to prepare for the Game-A-Thon. Each family member can contribute their favorite snack recipe.
- **Scoreboard and Trophies:** Create a scoreboard to track wins and scores throughout the Game-A-Thon. Award small prizes or make simple DIY trophies and ribbons for different achievements (e.g., Most Wins, Best

Sportsmanship).

- **Themed Game Night**: Choose a specific theme for your game marathon, such as "Retro Games," "Fantasy Adventure," or "Trivia Games." Decorate the room and select games that fit the theme to create a more immersive experience.
- **Themed Costumes:** Have themed game sessions where everyone dresses up according to the theme of the games being played (e.g., medieval knights for strategy games, superheroes for action games).
- **Game-A-Thon Playlist:** Create a playlist of upbeat and energetic music to play in the background. Family members can take turns adding their favorite songs.
- **Intermission Activities:** Plan short, fun activities for breaks between games. These could include quick stretches, mini yoga sessions, a dance-off, or a snack-building competition.
- **International Game Night:** Explore games from different cultures around the world. Research traditional games from various countries and try playing them together.
- **Educational Games Marathon**: Focus on games that are both fun and educational. Choose games that teach math, spelling, geography, or strategy skills. This way, everyone learns something new while having fun.
- **Game Swap**: Invite friends or neighbors to join in a game swap event. Each family brings their favorite game and teaches it to the others, expanding everyone's game repertoire.

Benefits:

- **Encourages Healthy Competition**: Friendly rivalry during games teaches important lessons about winning gracefully, losing with dignity, and competing with fairness and respect for others.
- **Improves Communication Skills**: Discussing game strategies and negotiating moves enhance verbal communication and listening skills.
- **Teaches Conflict Resolution**: Moments of disagreement during games provide natural opportunities to practice conflict resolution, helping everyone learn to manage disputes calmly and constructively.
- **Strengthens Bonds**: Playing games together fosters communication, teamwork, and a sense of unity, strengthening family relationships. The shared experiences and laughter during game play create fond memories that will be cherished for years to come.
- **Encourages Strategic Thinking:** Whether navigating game rules or deciding the next best move, each game sharpens problem-solving abilities in a playful, engaging environment.

64

FAMILY TALENT SHOWCASE

Turn your living room into a stage and host a family talent show! This exciting event allows each family member to showcase their unique skills and enjoy each other's performances. Whether it's singing, dancing, magic tricks, comedy acts, or any other hidden talents, the talent show is a wonderful way to celebrate each person's individuality and creativity. Preparing for the show involves planning acts, rehearsing, and setting up the stage, making the entire process a collaborative family affair.

The anticipation builds as each family member takes their turn in the spotlight, cheered on by the rest. The talent show encourages everyone to step out of their comfort zones, try new things, and support each other's efforts. It's a perfect activity for family bonding, filled with laughter, applause, and memorable moments that will be cherished for years to come.

Materials Needed:

- ☐ A designated performance area (living room or backyard)
- ☐ Simple stage setup (e.g., a rug or mat to mark the stage)
- ☐ Costumes and props
- ☐ Music player for background music
- ☐ Snacks and drinks for the audience
- ☐ Homemade certificates or trophies
- ☐ Camera or smartphone to record performances (optional)

Step-by-Step Instructions:

1. **Announce the Talent Show:**
   - Gather the family and officially announce the big event: a family talent show! Get everyone excited by explaining that it's a fun and relaxed way to showcase each person's unique talents, whether it's singing, dancing, poetry reading, celebrity impressions, or any other special skills they have.
   - Set a date and time for the talent show to give everyone ample time to prepare.
   - Create a sign-up sheet where each family member can write down what talent they plan to showcase. This helps in organizing the event and ensuring a variety of acts.
2. **Talent Preparation:**
   - Encourage each family member to plan their act. Offer help if needed, especially for younger children.
   - Set aside some time for rehearsals. Offer positive encouragement and support each other's creativity. Emphasize that the talent show is all about having fun, celebrating everyone's unique talents, and enjoying time together, rather than the quality of performances.
   - Assist in gathering any props, costumes, or materials needed for the performances. This can also be a fun craft activity where family members help each other create props and costumes.
3. **Event Organization:**
   - Write down the order of performances and make a program schedule. You can decorate the program and hand it out to the audience members.
   - Assign roles such as the host or MC, who will introduce each act and keep the show running smoothly.
   - Create homemade certificates or trophies for various categories like "Best Costume," "Most Creative," or "Funniest Act." Ensure everyone gets a recognition award to celebrate their effort and participation.
4. **Set up the Stage:**
   - Choose a suitable area in your home or backyard for the performances. Make sure there is enough space for the performers to move around comfortably.
   - Set up a simple stage using a rug or mat, and arrange seating for the audience.
   - Decorate the stage area with a bedsheet backdrop, homemade signs,

banners, or fairy lights to create a festive atmosphere.

5. **Prepare Refreshments:**
    - Make some snacks and drinks to enjoy during the show. Simple treats like popcorn, cookies, and juice can make the event feel like a real theater experience.
6. **Host the Show:**
    - Start the show by welcoming everyone and introducing the first act. The MC can use a microphone or a pretend one to add to the ambiance.
    - Use a spotlight (a flashlight or lamp) to highlight the performer on stage.
    - Encourage loud applause and cheers for each performer and share positive feedback.
    - Optionally, record the performances to create a memorable family keepsake using a smartphone or camera.
7. **Celebrate:**
    - End the event with a fun award ceremony. Hand out the homemade certificates or trophies ensuring each participant is celebrated for their talents and efforts.
    - Discuss the highlights of the show and share your favorite moments.

Safety Considerations:

- Ensure the performance area is free of obstacles, sharp objects, or anything that could cause tripping or slipping.
- Supervise young children closely, especially if their act involves physical activities like dancing or acrobatics.

Troubleshooting Tips:

- **Stage Fright:** If a family member feels nervous about performing, encourage them with positive reinforcement and offer to perform with them or have a practice run first.
- **Forgotten Lines or Moves:** Remind everyone that the focus is on fun, not perfection. Improvise if necessary.
- **Timing Issues**: If acts run longer than expected, be flexible with the schedule. Consider having a brief intermission if the show is lengthy to keep the audience engaged.
- **Technical Issues:** If the music player or any electronic device malfunctions, have a backup ready or be prepared to perform without it. Check all equipment beforehand to minimize issues.

- **Interruptions**: Establish ground rules to minimize interruptions during performances. If interruptions occur, calmly handle the situation and resume the show once everything is settled.

Cleanup Tips:

- Assign specific cleanup tasks to each family member to make the process quick and efficient. For example, one person can take down the stage setup and another can return the seating to its original arrangement.

Variations and Adaptations:

- **Talent Swap**: Pair up family members and have them teach each other their talents. For example, one person can teach another a short dance routine, while the other teaches impressions of famous people. They then perform each other's talents during the show.
- **Family Lip Sync Battle**: Turn the talent show into a lip sync battle where family members perform energetic lip sync routines to their favorite songs. Add costumes and props for extra fun.
- **Interactive Audience**: Involve the audience by having them participate in certain acts. For example, a magic trick where the audience helps choose cards or a dance number that everyone joins in on for the finale.
- **Historical Figures Talent Show:** Each participant chooses a historical figure to represent and performs a talent or act that person might have done, such as Einstein explaining a theory or Leonardo da Vinci drawing a quick sketch.
- **Impromptu Acts**: Add a segment for impromptu performances where family members draw random talents from a hat and have a few minutes to prepare an act. This adds spontaneity and excitement to the showcase.
- **Animal Talent Show:** Focus on animal-themed acts where participants perform animal impersonations for the audience to guess, create puppet shows with animal characters, engage in animal-themed sing-alongs, and present interesting animal facts.
- **Cultural Heritage Talent Show**: Encourage acts that celebrate the cultural heritage of family members. Perform traditional dances, songs, or stories from your cultural backgrounds.
- **Environmental Talent Show**: Incorporate an eco-friendly theme where participants create acts that promote environmental awareness, such as songs about recycling or skits about conserving energy.
- **Virtual Talent Show**: Connect with distant family members via video call and share performances online. This way, everyone can participate and share their talents from afar. Record the session to create a memorable keepsake.

Benefits:

- **Boosts Confidence**: Performing in front of others, even in a supportive family setting, helps build confidence. The positive feedback and encouragement from loved ones can boost self-esteem and encourage further exploration of talents.
- **Strengthens Communication Skills**: Speaking, performing, or presenting in front of an audience helps improve communication and public speaking skills, making it easier to articulate thoughts and ideas in other areas of life.
- **Celebrates Individuality**: Each family member's performance showcases their unique skills and personality, providing an opportunity to celebrate what makes them special and highlighting their personal achievements in a supportive environment.
- **Strengthens Bonds**: Cheering each other on during performances and celebrating everyone's unique talents creates a shared experience of encouragement and laughter, which deepens family connections and fosters a stronger sense of unity.
- **Promotes Teamwork**: Preparing acts together encourages active collaboration, as family members rely on each other for support, whether it's helping with ideas, rehearsals, or stage setup. This shared effort strengthens relationships through mutual assistance and joint creativity.

65

ANCESTOR CONNECTION QUEST

Imagine uncovering tales of bravery, adventure, and love hidden in your family's past. Embark on a journey through time and discover your family's rich history by building a detailed family tree. This collaborative project involves researching ancestors, gathering stories, and creating a visual representation of your family lineage. Using free online resources, you can trace your roots and uncover fascinating details about your heritage. This activity not only educates but also strengthens family bonds as you share and preserve the stories of those who came before.

Gather around the table with laptops, notebooks, and a big sheet of paper, ready to dive into the past. As you work together to piece together your family tree, you'll uncover surprising connections and heartfelt stories that bring your ancestors to life. Sharing these discoveries fosters a deeper appreciation for your family's journey and creates a meaningful legacy for future generations.

Materials Needed:

- ☐ Large sheet of paper or poster board
- ☐ Pens, pencils, and markers
- ☐ Laptops or tablets with internet access
- ☐ Genealogy website (e.g., FamilySearch [free], Ancestry)
- ☐ Notebooks for notes and stories
- ☐ Old family photos and documents (optional)

Step-by-Step Instructions:

1. **Gather Around the Table:**
   - Set up a cozy, collaborative space with enough room for laptops, notebooks, and a large sheet of paper or poster board for the family tree.
   - Encourage everyone to get comfortable and bring any family documents or photos they'd like to include.
2. **Start with What You Know:**
   - Begin by writing down the names and details of immediate family members (parents, grandparents, and siblings) on the large paper or poster board. Let each family member contribute, sharing what they know about their own family connections.
   - If anyone has family photos or stories to share, this is the time to discuss them, bringing a sense of shared history to the process. If your family doesn't have many stories passed down, don't worry! Even small details, like where an ancestor lived, worked, or the challenges they faced, can still be fascinating and help build a rich picture of your family's past.
3. **Dive Into Research:**
   - Using online genealogy tools like FamilySearch or Ancestry, start tracing your family roots. Begin with the oldest relatives you know and search for birth, marriage, or death records, as well as census data and other historical documents, to build a fuller picture of your family tree.
   - Encourage family members to work together to interpret records, piece together clues, and discuss new discoveries.
   - As you research, decide how far back you'd like to trace your family's history. This will help determine how much space you'll need when creating your family tree.
   - As you find new names and details, add them to your tree.
4. **Create the Family Tree:**
   - As you gather more information, continue to build your family tree on the large paper or poster board. Use markers to draw lines connecting different generations, and color-code branches if you'd like (e.g., different colors for maternal and paternal sides).
   - Be mindful of how many generations you're including and leave enough space for names and lines to avoid crowding as you go.
   - Each person can take turns adding their findings to the tree, which ensures everyone has a part in crafting the visual representation of your family's history.

5. **Share Stories and Memories:**
   - Throughout the research process, encourage everyone to share any stories or memories they uncover. Whether it's a tale of migration, adventure, or love, these personal stories help bring ancestors to life and foster meaningful discussions among the family.
   - Emphasize the importance of preserving these stories for future generations by writing them in a notebook or creating a digital document. This ensures that the rich history and personal anecdotes of your family are not lost and can be cherished by future family members.
6. **Decorate and Display:**
   - Decorate the family tree with drawings, photos, and other embellishments.
   - Once your family tree is complete, consider taking photos of it to preserve the project digitally, or create a shared family file where additional details can be added later.
   - Display the completed family tree in a prominent place in your home.

Safety Considerations:

- Be cautious when handling old documents or photos to avoid damage. Use clean, dry hands or consider wearing gloves for added protection.
- Be mindful of privacy settings on genealogy platforms to control who can view and access your family tree information. Avoid posting sensitive information about living relatives without their consent.
- Verify the credibility of sources and websites used for genealogical research to avoid misinformation. Stick to reputable and trusted genealogy sites.

Troubleshooting Tips:

- **Missing Information**: If you hit a dead end with missing information, try alternative spellings of names or search for records in neighboring towns or regions. Check multiple sources to verify details.
- **Record Gaps**: To fill in gaps in your family tree, reach out to extended family members who might have information or documents. Oral histories and personal anecdotes can provide valuable clues and lead to new discoveries.
- **Limited Records**: For ancestors from countries with limited online records, consider reaching out to local archives or historical societies who might have access to private collections.
- **Conflicting Records**: Cross-reference with as many reliable records as possible to determine the most accurate details. Prioritize official

documents over anecdotal evidence as mistakes and assumptions can easily be propagated in online genealogies.

- **Illegible Documents**: For old or poorly scanned documents that are difficult to read, try adjusting the contrast and brightness or using image enhancement tools. Seek help from online genealogy forums where others might have experience deciphering similar records.
- **Duplicate Entries**: When building your family tree, be cautious of creating duplicate entries for the same individual. Verify each new addition carefully and merge duplicates to keep your tree accurate and organized.

Cleanup Tips:

- Store old family photos, documents, and keepsakes in acid-free sleeves or archival boxes to protect them from damage. Keep these items in a cool, dry place. Consider digitizing these items to preserve them and make sharing easier.
- Save and categorize all digital documents, photos, and notes in clearly labeled folders on your computer or cloud storage. This makes it easy to access and continue your research later.
- If you borrowed photos or documents from relatives, return them promptly with a thank-you note to maintain good relationships and encourage future sharing.

Variations and Adaptations:

- **Family Tree Night:** Plan a dedicated evening where everyone shares their findings and stories. This can be a fun and interactive way to celebrate your discoveries and foster a deeper connection to your family history.
- **Themed Research Days:** Dedicate specific days to research different branches of the family or focus on particular types of records, such as military service or immigration documents.
- **Digital Family Tree:** Use a genealogy website to create an interactive digital family tree that includes photos, documents, and stories, allowing easy updates and sharing with family members.
- **Ancestry Scrapbook:** Compile a physical scrapbook filled with photos, documents, and written stories about your ancestors. Include decorative elements and personal anecdotes to make it visually appealing.
- **Video Documentary**: Create a family history documentary by recording interviews with relatives, narrating historical events, and showcasing old photos and documents. Edit the footage into a compelling video.
- **Heritage Recipe Book**: Gather traditional family recipes passed down through generations and create a cookbook. Include stories about the origins of each recipe and photos of family gatherings.

- **Genealogy Road Trip**: Plan a road trip to visit places of significance in your family history, such as ancestral homes, cemeteries, or historical landmarks. Document the trip with photos and notes.
- **Cultural Exploration**: Dive deeper into the cultural heritage of your ancestors by exploring traditional music, dance, language, and customs. Incorporate these elements into your family history project.
- **Ancestral Map**: Create a world map marking the locations where your ancestors lived. Include notes about significant events and historical contexts related to those places.
- **Ancestor Letters**: Write letters to your ancestors, expressing what you have learned about them and how their lives have impacted your family. Share these letters with family members.

Benefits:

- **Builds a Sense of Identity**: Discovering the stories of ancestors fosters a deeper understanding of personal heritage, helping to create a sense of belonging and connection to family roots.
- **Promotes Appreciation for History**: Discovering personal connections to historical events fosters a deeper understanding of how the past shaped both the world and individual family stories, making history feel more relevant and engaging.
- **Enhances Research Skills**: Exploring online databases, archives, and historical records helps develop essential research skills, including critical thinking, organization, and data interpretation.
- **Cultivates Empathy**: Learning about the struggles and triumphs of past generations fosters a deeper understanding and respect for their experiences, encouraging greater empathy and compassion for others.
- **Strengthens Bonds:** Collaborating on building the family tree fosters communication, teamwork, and shared discovery, creating meaningful moments of connection as family members uncover and share stories together.
- **Creates a Lasting Legacy**: Documenting family history creates a lasting legacy for future generations, preserving stories, traditions, and important information that might otherwise be lost.

66

FAMILY MOMENT CHRONICLES

Turn your family memories into a cinematic masterpiece by creating a family documentary! Gather photos and videos from past events and weave them into a heartfelt story that showcases the special moments you've shared. This project involves sorting through old albums and digital archives, selecting the most memorable clips, and editing them into a cohesive documentary. The process of reliving cherished memories and reflecting on your family's journey is as rewarding as the final product itself.

As you work together on this documentary, you'll strengthen your family's bond through shared storytelling. Everyone can contribute by choosing their favorite moments, narrating the story, and even adding personal touches like music and captions. Once complete, gather around to watch the documentary, celebrating the beautiful tapestry of your family's history.

Materials Needed:

- ☐ Computer with video editing software (e.g. OpenShot [free], iMovie [free for Mac])
- ☐ Photos and videos from past events
- ☐ External hard drive or cloud storage (for backing up files)
- ☐ Microphone (recording narration; optional)
- ☐ Music files (for background music)

Step-by-Step Instructions:

1. **Gather Materials:**
   - Set aside time as a family to collect both printed and digital photos, videos, and any other media that represents memorable moments. This can be anything from vacation footage to holiday photos or clips from everyday life.
   - Let each family member pick a few favorite moments they would love to see featured in the documentary.
     - **For physical photos:** Use a scanner to digitize physical photos. Save them in high-resolution format.
     - **For physical videos:** Convert old video tapes or DVDs to digital format using a video capture device that connects your VCR or DVD player to your computer. Alternatively, use a service that specializes in converting old media to digital.
   - Consider filming the documentary-making process itself. Capture behind-the-scenes clips of your family working together, setting up shots, and sharing laughs. These moments can add humor and personality to your film.
2. **Sort and Organize:**
   - Together, go through the collected media and create a timeline or list of key moments you want to include. You can organize it chronologically or by themes, such as "Family Vacations" or "Milestones and Celebrations."
   - Make sure everyone has a say in what goes into the final story. This helps create a documentary that truly reflects the entire family's experiences.
   - Be mindful of the emotional impact of certain memories or events included in the documentary. Ensure the content is respectful and considerate of all family members' feelings.
3. **Create a Storyboard:**
   - With the selected memories in mind, discuss how you want the documentary to unfold. Create a simple storyboard with rough sketches or written notes outlining how each moment will transition to the next.
   - Decide if you want to add narration. Each family member can contribute their voice to narrate different parts of the documentary, adding a personal touch to the story.
   - **Note:** Even simple, short documentaries can be incredibly meaningful. Don't feel pressured to create a lengthy film. A short, 5-

minute video with key highlights and special moments can be just as impactful and enjoyable.

4. **Choose Editing Software:**
   - Select a video editing application that best suits your family's needs and skill level. User-friendly options include iMovie (for Mac) and OpenShot, which are both free.
   - Take a few minutes to familiarize yourself with the basic functions and tools of the software.
5. **Import Media:**
   - Upload all the chosen media files to your computer or tablet, using video editing software. This is where the real fun begins, as you see the clips and photos coming together.
   - Begin arranging the media in the timeline of the video editor, following the storyboard you've created.
6. **Edit and Personalize:**
   - Use editing tools to trim videos, add transitions between photos or clips, and adjust the timing so the documentary flows smoothly.
   - Include fun elements like bloopers or funny moments to add humor and personality to your documentary. These lighter moments can make the documentary more engaging and enjoyable.
   - Add music that your family loves to make the documentary more engaging. You can also include sound effects or theme songs tied to the moments being shared.
   - If using narration, record it and layer the audio into the video. Captions or text overlays can be used to highlight names, dates, or significant quotes.
7. **Add Final Touches:**
   - Review the documentary as a family and make any necessary adjustments. You can add extra fun touches like special effects, or even create an opening title and closing credits to give it a real cinematic feel.
   - Once everyone is happy with the final cut, export the video to a format that can be played on your TV or shared digitally with extended family and friends.
8. **Family Premiere:**
   - Set up a viewing party at home and gather the family around to watch the finished documentary. Make some popcorn, dim the lights, and enjoy reliving those cherished memories together.
   - You can also make it an annual tradition to update the documentary

or create a new one each year, adding new memories to your growing family story.

Safety Considerations:

- Be cautious about including personal information in your documentary that could be sensitive if shared outside the family. Ensure that any shared content is done so with the consent of all involved.
- Handle old photos and videos carefully to prevent damage. Store them in a safe place to avoid loss or deterioration.
- If younger family members are participating, supervise their use of the computer and editing software to help prevent accidental deletions, errors, or changes that might cause frustration.

Troubleshooting Tips:

- **Family Disagreements**: If there are differing opinions on what content to include, hold a family meeting to discuss and reach a consensus. Compromise where possible and ensure everyone feels heard and respected.
- **Emotional Reactions**: Be prepared for emotional reactions when revisiting past events. Create a supportive environment where family members can express their feelings and take breaks if needed.
- **Complex Editing Tools**: If you find the editing software's tools complex or confusing, look for online tutorials or user guides. Many software companies offer free tutorials on their websites or YouTube channels.

Cleanup Tips:

- Once you've finished the documentary, organize all digital files, including photos, videos, and project files, into clearly labeled folders for easy access and future reference.
- Save multiple copies of the final documentary on different storage devices, such as external hard drives, USB drives, and cloud storage, to ensure you don't lose your hard work.
- Return any physical photos, albums, or documents used during the project to their proper storage places. Use archival-quality materials to preserve their condition.

Variations and Adaptations:

- **Interactive Elements:** Conduct interviews with family members, asking them about their favorite memories, significant life events, and personal anecdotes. Incorporate these interviews into the documentary.
- **Children's Perspective**: Let the younger members of the family take the lead in creating a segment, capturing the family moments from their

perspective.

- **Themed Documentary**: Focus on a specific theme such as "Family Vacations," "Holiday Celebrations," or "Milestone Moments" to create a series of mini-documentaries.
- **Generational Stories**: Create separate segments for each generation in your family, featuring stories and memories from grandparents, parents, and children.
- **Family Traditions**: Highlight the family's unique traditions, explaining their origins and how they have evolved over the years.
- **Virtual Family Collaboration**: Involve family members who live far away by having them contribute video clips, photos, and stories digitally. Use video conferencing tools to collaborate in real-time.
- **Pet Chronicles**: Create a special segment dedicated to the family pets, showcasing their antics, personalities, and the joy they bring to the family.
- **Cultural Heritage Focus**: Explore and document the family's cultural heritage, incorporating traditional music, dance, clothing, and customs into the documentary.
- **Letters from the Past**: Include readings of old letters, diaries, or journal entries from ancestors, providing a historical perspective and connecting past and present.

Benefits:

- **Promotes Organizational Skills**: Sorting through photos, videos, and digital files to create a coherent documentary improves organizational abilities, teaching how to manage large amounts of data in a structured and effective way.
- **Facilitates Intergenerational Connection**: This activity creates opportunities for older family members to share stories and memories with younger generations, fostering intergenerational connections and the passing down of family history.
- **Fosters Creative Expression**: Adding personal touches, such as music, captions, or narration, allows for creative expression, turning family memories into an artistic project that reflects each person's unique perspective.
- **Enhances Emotional Intelligence**: By reflecting on past experiences and expressing personal emotions through the documentary, family members can develop greater emotional awareness and empathy for one another.
- **Strengthens Bonds:** As family members contribute their favorite moments to the project, it sparks deeper conversations about personal

experiences, values, and important life events, fostering stronger connections through shared reflection.

- **Encourages Reflection and Gratitude**: Revisiting old memories encourages reflection on shared experiences, personal growth, and family achievements, fostering a deeper appreciation for the journey your family has taken together.

67

FAMILY HEIRLOOM CRAFT-A-THON

Transform an ordinary afternoon into a cherished family memory by creating a unique heirloom together. Whether it's a beautifully decorated box, a handmade quilt, or a collaborative art piece, this project unites the entire family in crafting something special. As you gather materials, the room fills with lively conversations about family history, amusing anecdotes, and shared memories. Each person contributes their own skills and creativity, making the project a true reflection of your family's collective spirit.

The crafting process is a blend of individual artistry and teamwork, where each brushstroke, stitch, or glued piece adds to the communal experience. As the heirloom takes shape, it becomes a lasting symbol of your family's journey. Completing the project marks the beginning of something enduring. Placed in your home, the heirloom serves as a beautiful reminder of the time spent together and the stories shared. Every glance at it will evoke the laughter, creativity, and love that went into its creation.

Materials Needed:

- ☐ A chosen item to create or decorate (e.g., box, quilt fabric, canvas)
- ☐ Craft supplies (depends on the chosen heirloom, e.g., glue, paint, decorative items)
- ☐ Tools (e.g., scissors, rulers, sewing machine, paintbrushes)
- ☐ Family photos and memorabilia (for added personalization; optional)

Step-by-Step Instructions:

1. **Choose the Heirloom Project:**
   - Hold a family meeting to decide on the type of heirloom you want to create. Discuss various ideas like a wooden plaque, a custom mosaic, or a family handprint canvas.
   - Take a vote to select the project that excites everyone the most. This ensures everyone feels included in the decision-making process.
2. **Plan the Design:**
   - Spend some time brainstorming design ideas together. Encourage each family member to share their vision and unique style.
   - Invite everyone to contribute personal stories and memories that are meaningful to them, ensuring the design is a true reflection of your family's collective experiences and creativity.
   - Use these shared stories to guide the design process. For example, if a particular memory is significant, discuss how it might be represented visually, such as through specific symbols, colors, or patterns.
   - Work together to create a rough sketch of the final design.
3. **Gather Materials:**
   - Make a list of all the materials and tools you'll need for the project. Use craft supplies you already have at home, or take a fun family trip to a local craft store to select decorations and tools. Make sure everyone picks at least one material they're excited to work with.
   - Opt for high-quality materials to ensure the heirloom's durability and longevity, allowing it to be treasured for generations.
4. **Start Crafting:**
   - Begin working on the project, with everyone contributing their unique skills and creativity.
   - Encourage each person to take turns adding their touch, whether it's painting, stitching, or decorating. For younger kids, ensure they have simpler tasks, such as painting a base coat or gluing pre-cut shapes.
   - Invite each family member to sign their name or add a personal message somewhere on the heirloom to commemorate their contribution.
5. **Personalize with Photos and Memorabilia (optional):**
   - Consider incorporating family photos, old letters, or other memorabilia into the heirloom for added personalization.
   - Secure these items carefully to ensure they are preserved. For instance, photos can be laminated or placed under a clear protective layer, and

letters can be copied and transferred onto fabric.

6. **Finish and Preserve:**
   - Complete the project, ensuring all elements are securely attached and well-crafted.
   - Consider applying a protective finish, like varnish or a quilt protector, to preserve the heirloom.
7. **Celebrate Your Creation:**
   - Choose a special place in your home to display the heirloom.
   - Celebrate the completion of your project with a special family meal or treat. Take photos of the family with the heirloom to document the achievement.
   - Share the completed project with extended family and friends, explaining its significance and the stories behind it.

Safety Considerations:

- Ensure that everyone knows how to safely use any tools required for the project, such as scissors, sewing machines, glue guns, or paintbrushes. Supervise younger children closely to prevent accidents.
- Choose non-toxic, child-safe materials whenever possible, particularly if young children are involved in the crafting process.
- Keep an eye on small materials like beads, buttons, or needles, especially around younger children, to prevent choking hazards or injury.
- If using paints, varnishes, or adhesives, work in a well-ventilated area to avoid inhaling fumes. Consider setting up a crafting station outdoors or near open windows.

Troubleshooting Tips:

- **Inconsistent Design Elements**: If design elements appear inconsistent, take a step back and assess the overall look. Make adjustments by adding or repositioning elements to achieve a balanced and cohesive design.
- **Running Out of Supplies**: To avoid running out of materials mid-project, gather more than you think you'll need. If you do run out, try to creatively incorporate other available materials or plan a quick supply run.
- **Time Management**: If the project is taking longer than expected, break it into smaller tasks and set realistic deadlines for each. Involve all family members to speed up the process.
- **Safe Material Removal**: If you need to remove glue or paint, use appropriate solvents and follow safety guidelines. Test solvents on a small area first to ensure they won't damage the material.

- **Fatigue**: If family members become tired or frustrated, take a break and return to the project later. Keep the atmosphere light and fun to maintain enthusiasm.
- **Design Conflicts:** If design ideas clash, facilitate a discussion to identify common themes and combine elements from different suggestions into a unified design. Voting on the final design can also help reach a consensus efficiently.
- **Skill Development**: If you have a vision for an heirloom but lack the expertise to make it, explore Youtube videos or online classes on sites like Craftsy to learn new skills and bring your idea to life.

Cleanup Tips:

- Lay down newspapers, plastic sheets, or drop cloths before starting the project to protect surfaces from spills and stains. Dispose of or clean these coverings after use.
- Assign fun roles to each family member for cleanup to make it more engaging: 'Surface Sentry' handles cleaning the workspace, 'Tool Tamer' takes care of washing tools, and 'Material Maestro' organizes supplies.
- Once the project is complete, ensure the heirloom is placed in a safe location where it won't be damaged. Consider applying a protective finish to preserve it.

Variations and Adaptations:

- **Heirloom Auction**: Instead of simply voting on heirloom ideas, hold an auction where family members "bid" with fun tokens to choose the type of heirloom to create. The project with the highest total bids becomes the chosen heirloom to create. This adds an element of surprise and excitement.
- **Evolving Heirloom:** Start the heirloom project during the craft-a-thon, but plan to continue adding to it during future family gatherings, making it an ongoing tradition.
- **Generational Collaboration**: Involve multiple generations in the crafting process by inviting grandparents or extended family members to join the project. Each generation contributes their skills, stories, or memories, making the heirloom a richer reflection of family history.
- **Interactive Heirloom Journey**: Document the entire crafting process with photos or videos, then create a mini-documentary or photo book that chronicles the creation of the heirloom. This can be a fun way to preserve not only the final product but also the memories of making it together.
- **Family Legacy Book**: After completing the heirloom, create a "Legacy Book" that accompanies it. The book contains family members' reflections

on the process, the meaning of the heirloom, and any family history or anecdotes related to it. This becomes a companion piece that future generations can add to.

- **Genealogy Art Heirloom**: Create an art project inspired by your family history, such as a mural, painting, or quilt, that visually represents your family's journey through time. Use old photos, documents, and stories to guide the design, incorporating meaningful symbols and imagery that reflect your heritage.

Benefits:

- **Supports Emotional Expression**: Crafting provides an outlet for emotional expression, allowing family members to convey their feelings and memories through art.
- **Boosts Confidence**: Creating a unique family heirloom instills a sense of pride and ownership, as each family member contributes to something meaningful and lasting.
- **Improves Communication Skills**: Collaborating on a project requires clear communication, whether it's discussing ideas, giving feedback, or solving problems, improving verbal and non-verbal communication
- **Stimulates Cognitive Development**: For younger family members, planning and executing different elements of the heirloom enhances cognitive skills, such as spatial awareness, sequencing, and critical thinking.
- **Strengthens Bonds**: The act of creating something meaningful together deepens emotional ties, as the heirloom becomes a symbol of shared experiences, family love, and support.
- **Teaches Valuable Skills**: The activity provides an opportunity to learn and practice various crafting techniques, improving fine motor skills, patience, and problem-solving abilities.

68

FAMILY CREST DESIGN WORKSHOP

Embark on a creative journey with your family by designing your very own coat of arms! A coat of arms, often referred to as a family crest, is a unique heraldic design on a shield or escutcheon, traditionally used to identify families or individuals. It often includes symbols, colors, and patterns that represent the values, history, and achievements of the family. Creating a family coat of arms is a fantastic way to explore your heritage, express your family's identity, and craft a meaningful piece of art that can be cherished for generations.

In this activity, you'll learn about the different elements of a coat of arms, including the shield, crest, motto, and supporters. Each family member can contribute their ideas and creativity to the design, resulting in a personalized emblem that symbolizes your family's story. This project is a fun and educational way to celebrate your family's uniqueness.

Materials Needed:

- ☐ Large paper or poster board
- ☐ Markers, colored pencils, or paints
- ☐ Ruler and pencil for sketching
- ☐ Decorative items like glitter, stickers, or fabric for added flair (optional)
- ☐ Reference books or online resources on heraldry (optional)

Step-by-Step Instructions:

1. **Introduction to Heraldry:**
   - Begin by describing to your family the concept of a coat of arms and its historical significance, explaining how it was used to identify families and individuals, especially in medieval times. (For a quick yet comprehensive overview, check out the *Crash Course in Heraldry* at the end of this activity.)
   - Discuss how different elements, such as symbols, colors, and mottos, represent various aspects of a family's identity and values.
2. **Define Your Symbolism:**
   - Look up examples of historical coats of arms online or in reference books for inspiration (optional).
   - Discuss as a family what symbols, colors, and themes are important to you and could be included in your design. Encourage each family member to share their ideas and listen to each other's suggestions for a truly collaborative effort.
   - You can refer to the *Heraldry Cheat Sheet* at the end of this activity for examples of traditional symbols (*charges*) and colors (*tinctures*) that represent specific values and meanings in heraldry.
   - Consider incorporating secret symbols or hidden elements within the crest that only family members understand, adding a layer of mystery and family bonding.
   - As you brainstorm, incorporate storytelling sessions where each family member shares a story or memory that relates to the symbols and colors chosen.
3. **Design the Shield:**
   - Sketch the outline of a shield on the large paper or poster board.
   - Divide the shield into sections using a ruler, creating distinct areas (*fields*) for different symbols and colors. Common ways to divide the shield include:
     - **Quartering:** Divide the shield into four equal sections.
     - **Per Fess:** Divide the shield horizontally into two sections.
     - **Per Pale:** Divide the shield vertically into two sections.
     - **Per Bend:** Divide the shield diagonally from the top left to bottom right.
     - **Per Bend Sinister:** Divide the shield diagonally from the top right to bottom left.
     - **Checky:** Create a checkerboard pattern with multiple sections.

4. **Add Symbols and Colors:**
   - Decide which symbols and colors to place in each section based on your family's values and identity.
   - Draw and color these elements within the divided sections, ensuring each section represents a meaningful part of your family's identity.
5. **Design the Crest:**
   - Above the shield, design a crest that represents an important aspect of your family. This could be an animal, object, or another symbol that holds special significance.
   - Decorate the crest with intricate details and patterns, making it a prominent part of your coat of arms.
6. **Incorporate a Motto:**
   - As a family, come up with a meaningful motto that reflects your values, beliefs, or heritage.
   - Write the motto below or above the shield, using a decorative font or style.
7. **Include Supporters:**
   - On each side of the shield, add *supporters* – figures or animals that appear to hold up the shield. These often symbolize qualities or traits admired by the family.
   - Draw and color the supporters, ensuring they complement the overall design.
8. **Finalize and Decorate:**
   - Review the entire design and make any final adjustments or additions. Add any decorative items like glitter, stickers, or fabric to enhance the visual appeal.
9. **Display Your Coat of Arms:**
   - Find a prominent place in your home to display the family crest. You can frame it, hang it on a wall, or even digitize it for other creative uses.
   - Celebrate the completion of your family crest by sharing the stories and meanings behind each element with family and friends.

Safety Considerations:

- Ensure that any sharp tools like scissors or craft knives are used carefully and under supervision, especially by younger family members.
- Small decorative items like glitter, stickers, or beads should be used under supervision to prevent choking hazards for younger children.

Troubleshooting Tips:

- **Design Disagreements**: If family members have different ideas, consider incorporating elements from everyone's suggestions into the design. Hold a vote or rotate design responsibilities to ensure everyone feels included.
- **Color Bleeding**: When using markers or paints, test them on a scrap piece of paper to see how they interact. Use high-quality, bleed-proof paper to prevent colors from running.
- **Smudging and Smearing**: To prevent smudging, allow paint and markers to dry completely before adding more layers or handling the paper. Use fixative spray to set finished drawings.
- **Mistakes or Errors**: Keep an eraser handy for pencil mistakes. For errors with markers or paint, use correction fluid or carefully cover them with additional design elements.
- **Difficulty Drawing Complex Symbols**: Break down complex symbols into simpler shapes and build them step-by-step. Alternatively, print and cut out images to use as stencils to achieve more precise results.

Cleanup Tips:

- Use disposable tablecloths, newspapers, or plastic sheets to protect work surfaces from spills and stains. Dispose of or clean these coverings after use.
- Wash brushes, palettes, and other tools promptly after use to prevent paint and glue from hardening and becoming difficult to remove. Use appropriate cleaning agents for different tools.
- Place the completed family crest in a safe location where it won't be damaged. Consider framing or laminating the artwork to preserve it.

Variations and Adaptations:

- **Digital Family Crest**: Use digital design software or online tools to create a digital version of your family crest. This allows for easy modifications and sharing with extended family members.
- **Crest Design Competition**: Turn the activity into a friendly competition where each family member creates their own version of the family crest. Vote on different categories such as most creative, most traditional, or best use of symbolism.
- **Incorporate Ancestry**: Research your family tree and include elements from different ancestors in the crest, such as symbols representing their professions, hobbies, or notable achievements.
- **Seasonal Workshops**: Hold the crest design workshop seasonally, creating variations that reflect the colors and themes of each season.

Rotate the display of these crests throughout the year.

- **Generational Crests**: Create different crests that represent each generation within your family. Compare and contrast these designs to see how family values and symbols evolve over time.
- **Family Goals Crest**: Design a crest that incorporates family goals and aspirations. Display it prominently as a reminder of your collective ambitions and dreams.
- **Pet-Inspired Crests**: Include symbols representing beloved family pets, past and present, celebrating their role and significance in the family.
- **Collage Crests**: Instead of drawing, use a collage technique with magazine cutouts, fabric pieces, and other materials to assemble the crest. This adds texture and a unique artistic touch.
- **Mini Shields:** Have each family member design their own personal coat of arms. These mini shields will showcase their individual characteristics and passions, intertwined with symbols from the main family crest, highlighting the unique contributions of each person to the family's story.
- **Storybook:** Create a family storybook that explains the meaning and significance of each element in your coat of arms.

Benefits:

- **Builds a Sense of Identity**: Creating a family crest helps to develop a stronger sense of family identity and pride by visually representing the family's values, history, and achievements.
- **Encourages Self-Expression**: Each family member can contribute their personal interests, values, and experiences to the crest, promoting individuality within the family unit.
- **Promotes Teamwork and Communication**: Collaborating on a shared design encourages teamwork as family members must work together to create a unified crest. This promotes decision-making, communication, active listening, and compromise to ensure that everyone's input is considered.
- **Enhances Problem-Solving Skills**: Deciding on the design elements and resolving differences in ideas encourages creative problem-solving and critical thinking.
- **Strengthens Bonds**: Working on the family crest creates a space for storytelling, where family members can share memories, discuss family traditions, and reflect on what makes their family unique. This act of sharing and reflecting strengthens emotional connections and builds a sense of shared identity through the collaborative process.
- **Teaches Historical and Cultural Awareness**: Learning about heraldry

and the historical significance of family crests educates participants about cultural heritage and traditions.

Crash Course in Heraldry

Use this brief guide to introduce your kids to the fascinating world of heraldry, helping them understand the significance of coats of arms before creating your own.

Heraldry is a fascinating and ancient art that dates back to medieval times. The word "heraldry" comes from the word "herald," which was a messenger or announcer in a royal court. Heralds were responsible for organizing tournaments and battles, and they also kept track of the symbols and designs used by knights and noble families on their shields and banners. These unique designs, known as coats of arms, helped identify individuals and families on the battlefield and in tournaments.

A coat of arms is more than just a colorful design; it's a way to tell a family's story through symbols, colors, and patterns. Each element on a coat of arms has a specific meaning. For example, a lion might represent courage, while a tree could symbolize growth or strength. The shield is the main part of the coat of arms, and it can be divided into different sections, each containing symbols that represent the family's values, achievements, and history. Above the shield, there is often a crest, which is another symbol that holds special significance for the family.

Historically, a "coat of arms" includes the entire design—shield, crest, motto, and supporters—while the "family crest" specifically refers to the emblem above the shield. Today, people often use these terms interchangeably, but it's interesting to know their original meanings.

One of the most interesting aspects of heraldry is its use of colors, known as tinctures. Each color has a specific meaning: gold (or yellow) stands for generosity, blue represents loyalty, and red signifies bravery. In addition to colors, coats of arms often feature animals, mythical creatures, and objects. For example, a dragon might represent protection, while a star could symbolize guidance. These symbols are chosen carefully to reflect the unique qualities and history of the family.

Here are a few fun facts about heraldry that might surprise you! Did you know that the unicorn is a popular symbol in heraldry, representing purity and strength? Or that some coats of arms include a "motto" – a short phrase or saying that sums up the family's beliefs or values? Another interesting fact is that heraldry isn't just for knights and noble families. Many towns, cities, and organizations also have their own coats of arms, each with its own unique story to tell. Exploring heraldry is like opening a colorful book filled with tales of bravery, honor, and family pride.

Heraldry Cheat Sheet: Symbols and Colors

Symbols and Their Meanings

- **Lion:** Courage, bravery, strength
- **Eagle:** Leadership, decisiveness, keen vision
- **Bear:** Protection, strength, bravery
- **Stag/Deer:** Peace, harmony, gentle nature
- **Dragon:** Defender of treasure, valor, protection
- **Griffin:** Vigilance, courage, strength
- **Horse:** Readiness for duty, speed, intelligence
- **Dove:** Peace, love, gentleness
- **Owl:** Wisdom, knowledge, keen observation
- **Serpent:** Wisdom, secrecy, immortality
- **Tree:** Growth, strength, endurance
- **Cross:** Faith, service, self-sacrifice
- **Heart:** Love, sincerity, charity
- **Sun:** Glory, brilliance, life
- **Moon:** Serenity, reflection, beauty
- **Star:** Aspiration, divine quality, honor
- **Sword:** Justice, military honor, leadership
- **Book:** Knowledge, learning, wisdom
- **Anchor:** Hope, steadfastness, salvation
- **Tower/Castle:** Safety, protection, home

Colors and Their Meanings

- **Gold/Yellow:** Generosity, elevation of the mind, honor
- **Silver/White:** Peace, sincerity, purity
- **Red:** Warrior, strong, military strength, magnanimity
- **Blue:** Loyalty, truth, strength, steadfastness
- **Green:** Hope, joy, loyalty in love, growth
- **Black:** Constancy, grief, wisdom, prudence
- **Purple:** Royalty, sovereignty, justice
- **Orange:** Worthwhile ambition, social ambition
- **Maroon:** Patient in battle, victorious

69

HISTORICAL REENACTMENT DAY

Travel back in time and immerse your family in the captivating world of history with a Historical Reenactment Day. Choose a historical event or era that fascinates you, and spend the day bringing it to life. From donning period costumes to preparing authentic meals, this activity transforms learning about the past into a vivid, interactive experience that the whole family can enjoy.

With endless eras to explore—whether it's the grandeur of ancient civilizations or the intrigue of more recent historical events—each family member can step into the shoes of a historical figure or everyday person from that time. Together, you'll recreate pivotal scenes, engage in period-appropriate games, and savor dishes that reflect the flavors of the past. This hands-on journey through history not only makes learning fun and engaging but also deepens your appreciation for the people and cultures that shaped our world.

Materials Needed:

- ☐ Research materials on the chosen era or event (e.g., books, websites, documentaries)
- ☐ Costumes or clothing that represent the chosen era (can be DIY)
- ☐ Props and decorations to enhance the setting
- ☐ Ingredients for historical meals

Step-by-Step Instructions:

1. **Choose the Historical Event or Era:**
   - Gather as a family and choose a historical period or event that interests everyone. Consider exploring ancient Egypt, the Renaissance, the American Revolution, or any other fascinating time.
   - Research together using historical reference books, documentaries, and online resources to learn about the clothing, food, customs, and significant events of your chosen era.
2. **Plan the Reenactment:**
   - Let each family member choose a role they are interested in, whether it's a historical figure, an everyday person from the era, or a specific character relevant to your chosen event. Ensure these personas would naturally interact with one another.
   - Outline the day's activities, including specific scenes to reenact, games to play, and meals to prepare. A timeline helps keep the day organized and engaging.
   - Adapt the activities based on the interests and energy levels of the family members.
   - Consider documenting the day with photos or a short video, and perhaps even create a scrapbook page to remember the experience.
3. **Prepare Costumes and Props:**
   - Make costumes by gathering materials from around the house, visiting a thrift store, or making simple outfits that reflect the chosen era. Creativity and resourcefulness are key.
   - Create or collect props to enhance the authenticity of your reenactment. This might include toy weapons, homemade shields, or period-appropriate household items.
   - Transform your reenactment area with decorations that set the scene, like hanging banners, setting up tents, or arranging furniture to mimic historical settings.
4. **Learn and Share History:**
   - Begin the day with a brief presentation or discussion about the chosen era. Share interesting facts, stories, and the significance of key events.
   - Throughout the day, continue to share historical tidbits and encourage questions to deepen everyone's understanding.
   - Encourage everyone to stay in character throughout the day to enhance the immersive experience.
5. **Prepare Authentic Meal:**

- Research and prepare a meal from the historical time period. Use ingredients that would have been available during that era. For example, make a simple medieval stew, ancient Egyptian bread, or a revolutionary-era pie.
- Involve the whole family in cooking and preparing the meal. Enjoy the process of creating and tasting dishes from the past.

6. **Reenact Key Moments:**
   - Reenact pivotal scenes or daily life activities from the chosen time period. Write simple scripts or narrate important events as a family, but feel free to improvise to keep things fun and dynamic.
   - Encourage each person to play their role with enthusiasm, whether it's a famous speech, a historical debate, or a dramatic battle.
7. **Explore Historical Activities:**
   - Integrate crafts and artistic activities from the era, such as making pottery, creating simple textiles, or storytelling and dancing that reflect the culture of the time. These hands-on and interactive elements enhance the reenactment experience, especially for younger children.
   - Play historical games and sports that were popular during the chosen era. This can include activities like medieval jousting with pool noodles or ancient Roman chariot races using toy cars.
8. **Reflect and Discuss:**
   - Conclude the day by discussing what everyone learned and enjoyed the most. Discuss the roles each person played and what surprised them about life in the past, reflecting on the historical significance and any modern-day parallels.

Safety Considerations:

- Ensure that costumes are comfortable and do not pose tripping hazards. Avoid using sharp or heavy accessories that could cause injury.
- Use soft, non-toxic materials for props, especially if they mimic weapons or tools. Avoid any sharp edges or hard surfaces that could cause harm.
- When preparing historical meals, be mindful of any food allergies and dietary restrictions within the family.
- If the reenactment takes place outside, be aware of the weather conditions. Use sunscreen, wear hats, and ensure there is adequate shade to prevent sunburn and heat exhaustion.
- Keep an eye on younger children throughout the day, especially during activities involving props or food preparation.

Troubleshooting Tips:

- **Historical Accuracy:** Focus on the learning experience rather than perfect accuracy to keep the activity fun and engaging.
- **Costume Malfunctions**: If a costume piece breaks or doesn't fit properly, have safety pins, sewing supplies, or adhesive tape on hand for quick fixes. Improvising with scarves, belts, or other household items can also save the day.
- **Prop Issues**: If a prop breaks or isn't working as intended, substitute with another household item. Encourage creativity and flexibility to keep the reenactment fun and engaging.
- **Food Prep Challenges**: If a historical recipe isn't turning out as expected, have some modern ingredients and recipes on hand as a backup. Focus on the experience and learning rather than perfect authenticity.
- **Time Management**: If activities are taking longer than expected, prioritize the most engaging and essential parts of the reenactment. It's okay to skip or shorten less critical elements.
- **Script Problems**: If scripted scenes feel too rigid or aren't working, encourage improvisation and let family members add their own twist to the reenactment. This can make the experience more dynamic and enjoyable.

Cleanup Tips:

- If the reenactment took place outside, make sure to collect all decorations, props, and any trash. Leave the area as clean as you found it.
- Organize as you go by keeping a designated area for props, costumes, and other materials when not in use. This will make it easier to put everything back in its place afterward. Store costumes and props for future use or donation.
- Assign specific cleanup tasks to each family member to make the process efficient. For example, one person can act as the "costumer" to collect and organize costumes, another can be the "props master" to manage and store props, and someone else can be the "kitchen steward" to clean up the food area.

Variations and Adaptations:

- **Historic Cultural Celebration**: Instead of focusing on a specific event, recreate a cultural celebration from the past, like a medieval banquet, an ancient Roman feast, or a Native American harvest festival. Include traditional dances, songs, and food to immerse everyone in the experience.
- **Myths and Legends Day**: Instead of historical events, focus on legendary figures and folklore from different cultures. Reenact the stories of King

Arthur, Greek gods, or Viking sagas, and bring mythical tales to life through role-play and storytelling.

- **Skills Workshop**: Focus on learning and practicing skills from the chosen era, such as weaving, Calligraphy, or wood working. This hands-on approach can make the historical experience more immersive and educational.
- **Living History Museum**: Set up different "exhibits" or stations around your home or yard, each representing a different aspect of the chosen time period (e.g., a blacksmith shop, a marketplace, a home). Family members can take turns acting as guides or historical figures at each station.
- **Historical Cooking Show**: Turn the meal preparation into a cooking show, where family members explain the historical significance of the dishes they are preparing and demonstrate the cooking techniques used during that time period.
- **Historical Challenges**: Create a series of challenges or tasks that were common in the chosen era (e.g., building a simple structure, solving a puzzle, or even mummifying Dad). Compete or collaborate to complete these tasks.
- **Historic Newsroom**: Turn the reenactment into a newsroom where each family member is a reporter covering a major historical event. Write "news articles" or film news segments about significant moments, from ancient battles to space exploration, giving history a modern twist through the lens of a journalist.
- **Alternate History Reenactment**: What if a famous event had gone differently? Explore alternate history by reenacting key moments and imagining different outcomes. For example, what if the Wright brothers' plane hadn't flown, or what if ancient Rome never fell? This variation opens up endless creative possibilities.
- **History-Themed Game Show**: Create a quiz or trivia game about the historical period you're exploring. Family members can compete in teams, answering questions or completing challenges based on historical knowledge. Add buzzer rounds or physical tasks like reenacting a famous speech or solving a period puzzle.

Benefits:

- **Enhances Historical Understanding**: Immersing in a historical period through reenactment provides a deeper and more memorable understanding of history than traditional learning methods.
- **Develops Research Skills**: Preparing for the reenactment by learning about the chosen time period or event enhances research abilities, teaching valuable skills in gathering, analyzing, and applying historical information.

- **Stimulates Creativity and Imagination**: Designing costumes, planning scenes, and role-playing historical figures fosters creativity, allowing each participant to express their interpretation of history in imaginative and artistic ways.
- **Promotes Empathy**: Stepping into the shoes of historical figures helps cultivate empathy and a greater appreciation for the challenges and achievements of people from different times.
- **Strengthens Bonds**: Collaborating on recreating historical scenes encourages active communication, joint problem-solving, and mutual support. Whether it's working together to design costumes, plan scenes, or act out key moments, the shared effort and teamwork foster a sense of accomplishment and strengthen connections through meaningful, creative interaction.
- **Improves Communication Skills**: Reenacting historical speeches, debates, or dialogue improves public speaking and communication skills, encouraging clear expression of ideas and perspectives.

OUTDOOR FUN

Get outside as a family for memorable adventures that strengthen bonds and create lasting memories! Go on a Geocaching Treasure Trek, using GPS to find hidden treasures together while exploring nature. Organize a Family Olympic Games day, complete with fun challenges like balloon pop relays and hula hoop contests—guaranteed to bring out the friendly competition and laughter. For a more relaxed yet magical experience, host a Backyard Film Fest, complete with cozy blankets, fairy lights, and favorite family movies under the stars. These outdoor activities offer a mix of adventure, physical play, and togetherness, creating moments that everyone will cherish.

70

GEOCACHING TREASURE TREK

Gear up for a modern-day treasure hunt that combines outdoor adventure with the excitement of discovery. Geocaching is an activity where you use GPS coordinates to find hidden containers, known as caches, placed by other adventurers. These caches can be hidden anywhere—from urban parks to remote forests. Each cache typically contains a logbook to sign and sometimes small trinkets to trade. It's a thrilling way to explore your surroundings, enjoy the fresh air, and bond over the shared challenge of finding hidden treasures.

As you navigate to each cache together, the sense of adventure intensifies. With every successful find, there's a burst of excitement and shared triumph, reinforcing the connection between family members. The journey involves teamwork, problem-solving, and a lot of encouragement, transforming the simple act of walking into an exhilarating quest. Along the way, conversations flow naturally, creating an opportunity for bonding and learning more about each other in an engaging, fun-filled environment.

Materials Needed:

- ☐ Smartphone
- ☐ Geocaching app (e.g., Geocaching® by Groundspeak Inc. [free])
- ☐ Pen for signing logbooks
- ☐ Small trinkets for trading (optional)
- ☐ Sturdy shoes and weather-appropriate clothing
- ☐ Water, snacks or packed lunches
- ☐ Sun protection
- ☐ Insect repellent (optional)

Step-by-Step Instructions:

1. **Download an App:**
   - Begin by downloading and installing a geocaching app on your smartphone.
   - Set up an account and familiarize yourself with how to search for caches in your area.
   - Let family members help by exploring cache options or reading about the locations together to build excitement.
2. **Choose Your Geocaches:**
   - Select several caches based on their difficulty level and proximity to your current location. For younger kids, choose easy-to-find caches. If your family is up for a challenge, you can include a mix of easy and moderate caches.
3. **Prepare for the Trek:**
   - Pack a small backpack with essentials such as water, snacks, sunscreen, and a pen for signing logbooks.
   - If you're planning on trading items, pack a few small trinkets (e.g., toy cars, coins, keychains) to exchange at caches that offer this feature.
   - Ensure your smartphone is fully charged before heading out. Consider bringing a portable charger to ensure you have a backup power source.
   - Check the weather forecast beforehand and pack accordingly—bring extra layers, rain gear, or a hat and sunglasses depending on the conditions.
4. **Navigate to the First Cache:**
   - Using the geocaching app or GPS device, follow the directions to your first cache.
   - Involve your children by letting them track the distance and help read the coordinates aloud as you navigate.
   - As you walk, talk about the surrounding area—point out landmarks, discuss what the cache might look like, or encourage guesses about where it could be hidden.
5. **Search for the Cache:**
   - Once you're close, the real treasure hunt begins! Search together, checking hiding spots like under rocks, in tree trunks, or behind park benches.
   - Look high, low, and in unexpected places—caches can be cleverly hidden.
   - Encourage everyone to take turns guessing the best hiding spots. This

promotes teamwork and makes each discovery more satisfying.

6. **Find and Sign the Cache:**
    - Once you've found the cache, celebrate the success! Open it together, sign the logbook with your geocaching username or your family's name, and note the date.
    - If the cache includes trinkets, take one and leave one in its place (if you've brought items to trade). This keeps the adventure going for future geocachers.
7. **Move On to the Next Cache:**
    - After securing the cache, head to the next one using the GPS or app to navigate. Each new location offers a fresh challenge and an opportunity for more exploration.
    - Use the journey to bond, chatting about the first cache's hiding spot, what other treasures you might find, or simply enjoying the natural surroundings together.
8. **End the Day:**
    - Once you've completed your geocaching trek, reflect on your finds, the challenges faced, and the fun moments shared along the way. You can even log your finds on the app or website as a way to track your geocaching adventures.

Safety Considerations:

- Research the area where you will be geocaching. Check for any potential hazards, such as rough terrain, wildlife, or restricted areas, and plan your route accordingly.
- Be cautious of wildlife, especially in remote areas. Know what to do if you encounter animals such as snakes, bears, or other potentially dangerous creatures.
- Carry a basic first aid kit to handle minor injuries like cuts, scrapes, or insect bites.
- Ensure all family members know basic safety rules such as staying close to the group, not touching unknown plants or animals, and what to do if they get separated.
- Have a plan for emergencies and ensure your phone is charged. Know the nearest location to seek help if needed and inform someone of your location and expected return time in case of any unforeseen situations.
- If you're exploring areas with tall grass or wooded regions, regularly check for ticks during and after the activity. Promptly and properly remove any that are found. Wear long sleeves and tuck pants into socks to minimize exposure.

Troubleshooting Tips:

- **Difficulty Finding Caches:** Use the app's hints and previous logs for additional clues. Look for hiding spots that might not be obvious, such as under rocks or within hollow tree stumps.
- **GPS Signal Issues:** If you're having trouble getting a GPS signal, try moving to an open area away from tall buildings or dense trees. Sometimes, simply restarting your device can help reestablish a stronger connection.
- **Cache Missing or Damaged**: If you suspect a cache is missing or damaged, log your findings in the app to inform other geocachers and the cache owner. Consider bringing a small replacement container to help maintain the game if needed.
- **Battery Life**: Make sure to start with a fully charged device and bring a portable charger to ensure you don't run out of battery while out in the field. Conserve battery by dimming the screen and closing unnecessary apps.

Cleanup Tips:

- After signing the logbook and exchanging trinkets, ensure the cache is securely closed and placed back exactly where you found it.
- Take a moment to document your findings and any maintenance issues with the cache in the app. Reporting issues helps maintain the quality and enjoyment of the geocaching community.
- Practice "Leave No Trace" principles by ensuring you leave the area as you found it. Pick up any trash you see, even if it's not yours, to help keep the environment clean and beautiful for others.

Variations and Adaptations:

- **Themed Caches:** Choose a specific theme, such as nature, history, or architecture, and search for caches that are placed near related sites. For example, in a historical theme, the caches might be near monuments, old buildings, or historic landmarks.
- **Photography Geocaching**: Incorporate photography into your geocaching adventure. Take pictures of interesting locations, wildlife, and landmarks you encounter. Create a photo journal of your journey.
- **Geocaching Challenges**: Take on specific geocaching challenges, such as finding caches in every park in your city, completing a cache series, or finding caches with different difficulty ratings.
- **Educational Geocaching**: Integrate educational elements into your geocaching adventure. Place caches that include interesting facts about local history, geography, or wildlife. This turns the activity into a fun

learning experience for both you and the future adventurers who discover the caches.

- **Charity Geocaching Event**: Organize a geocaching event to raise awareness and funds for a charitable cause. Participants can donate or get sponsors for each cache they find, turning the adventure into a meaningful contribution to a good cause.
- **DIY Geocaching**: After a successful hunt, create your own cache to hide for others to find. Work together to choose a clever location, add a logbook, and leave small items for future geocachers to trade. You can track the cache online and see who discovers it over time.

Benefits:

- **Promotes Physical Activity**: Searching for caches involves walking, hiking, or climbing, promoting physical movement and an active lifestyle in a fun, adventurous way.
- **Enhances Problem-Solving Skills**: Locating hidden caches using GPS coordinates and deciphering clues sharpens problem-solving skills, teaching participants how to think critically and adapt to new challenges.
- **Encourages Teamwork**: Solving clues and navigating to each cache requires effective communication and collaboration, allowing participants to work together, share ideas, and contribute unique strengths to achieve a common goal.
- **Boosts Mental Health**: Spending time outdoors and engaging in a fun, rewarding activity like geocaching can reduce stress and improve overall mental well-being.
- **Builds Perseverance**: Searching for caches, especially when they're cleverly hidden, requires persistence. Participants learn the value of patience and the reward that comes from sticking with a challenge until the end.
- **Strengthens Bonds:** The shared excitement of successfully finding a cache fosters closer relationships, as participants work together, celebrate achievements, and encourage each other throughout the hunt.
- **Promotes Exploration and Adventure**: Geocaching is an exciting way to explore new locations, whether they're urban parks or remote forests, inspiring a lasting appreciation for adventure and sparking curiosity about the world.

71

FAMILY OLYMPIC GAMES

Transform your local park into an exhilarating arena with a Family Olympic Games day, filled with fun and friendly competition. Set the stage with a variety of events, from hula hoop contests and balloon pop relays to tug-of-war and three-legged races. The excitement builds as each event unfolds, with everyone cheering and celebrating each victory. The diverse activities ensure that there's something for everyone, making the day welcoming and entertaining.

The highlight of the day is the camaraderie and the spirited competition that brings out the best in everyone. As awards are handed out and photos are taken, the sense of achievement and togetherness shines through. This vibrant, energetic day not only provides a great workout but also strengthens family bonds, creating a treasure trove of joyful memories and a tradition to look forward to year after year.

Materials Needed:

- ☐ Materials for your chosen games (e.g., hula hoops, balloons, rope, bandanas)
- ☐ Cones or markers for setting up courses
- ☐ Stopwatch or phone with a timer
- ☐ Prizes, medals or ribbons for awards (homemade or found online; optional)
- ☐ Camera or smartphone for capturing moments
- ☐ Water, snacks or packed lunches
- ☐ Comfortable outdoor clothing and footwear
- ☐ Sun protection
- ☐ First aid kit (optional)

Step-by-Step Instructions:

1. **Choose the Events:**
   - Gather the family together and brainstorm a variety of games everyone would enjoy. Ensure there are activities suitable for the different ages and abilities in your family.
   - Plan around four to seven events, depending on the size of your family and the time available.
   - Make sure to include a mix of physical challenges, balancing skills, and both individual and team events
2. **Set Up the Games:**
   - Choose a local park or open space that has enough room for running, relays, and other activities. Check the weather in advance to ensure it's suitable for outdoor games, and pack accordingly (e.g., extra layers or rain gear if needed).
   - Set up cones or markers to create lanes for races and to designate specific event areas.
   - Mark start and finish lines, and make sure there's enough space between each event for comfort and safety, especially for races or tug-of-war.
3. **Kickoff the Games:**
   - Gather the family for a fun opening ceremony. You could play some music, create a family chant or cheer, and explain the games and rules.
   - Let everyone know that the goal is to have fun, and encourage cheering for all participants, regardless of who wins.
   - Consider pairing parents and children together for partner activities to promote bonding and teamwork, encouraging intergenerational cooperation and fun.
4. **Compete and Have Fun:**
   - Begin with a warm-up session and stretching exercises to prevent injuries and prepare everyone's muscles for physical activity.
   - Start the games and cheer each other on. Encourage a fun and supportive atmosphere.
   - For a full experience, play multiple rounds of each game. This keeps the excitement going and allows everyone multiple chances to compete.
   - Take lots of photos and videos throughout the games to capture the fun and excitement of the day. To make sure no great moments slip by, consider designating someone as the official photographer so

everyone can stay in the moment.

5. **Award Ceremony:**
    - Conclude the event with a fun award ceremony! Hand out homemade medals, ribbons, or certificates to all participants to celebrate their efforts. You can create categories like "Fastest Racer," "Best Teamwork," or "Most Creative Hula Hoop Moves."
    - Take family photos with everyone holding their awards or posing together in funny victory stances. This is a great way to capture the spirit of the day and create lasting memories.

Safety Considerations:

- Ensure all activities are age-appropriate and safe for participants.
- Ensure the playing area is free from hazards like rocks, sticks, and uneven ground that could cause trips or falls. Mark any potential danger zones clearly.
- Ensure everyone stays hydrated by drinking plenty of water before, during, and after the games. Have water bottles readily available.
- Be aware of any health conditions or allergies that participants may have. Ensure that those with medical needs have their medications and are comfortable participating.
- Encourage participants to pace themselves and take breaks as needed to avoid overexertion or heat exhaustion, especially on hot days.

Troubleshooting Tips:

- **Overcrowding**: If the park or chosen location gets too crowded, adjust the layout of the games or consider setting up in a more secluded part of the park to minimize interruptions.
- **Participation Issues**: If some family members are hesitant to join certain activities, offer them roles like timekeeper, scorekeeper, or referee to keep them engaged.
- **Disputes or Competitiveness**: If friendly competition turns into disputes, remind everyone that the goal is to have fun and bond. Emphasize good sportsmanship and consider implementing a "cool down" period for any heated moments.
- **Participant Fatigue:** Plan a mix of active and less strenuous events to keep energy levels balanced.
- **Time Management**: If the event is running longer than expected, prioritize the most popular or important games and shorten others. Keep an eye on the schedule to ensure a timely conclusion.

Cleanup Tips:

- Assign specific cleanup tasks to each participant to make the process quick and efficient. For example, one person collects and stores all the game equipment, while another tidies up the snack area.
- Carry extra trash bags to collect any litter or discarded items during the event. Make sure to dispose of them properly in nearby bins.
- Before leaving, do a final sweep of the area to ensure no personal items, trash, or game materials are left behind.

Variations and Adaptations:

- **DIY Medals and Awards**: Before the activity, involve your family in creating personalized medals and awards using craft materials. This can include making medals out of clay, cardboard and aluminum foil, or creating certificates for different achievements, like "Best Team Spirit" or "Most Creative Competitor."
- **Surprise Challenges**: Include unexpected challenges throughout the day, such as sudden dance-offs or trivia quizzes. These surprises keep the event lively and unpredictable.
- **Themed Olympic Day**: Choose a specific theme for your Family Olympic Games, such as "Ancient Greece," "Superheroes," or "Wild West." Decorate the area and dress up according to the theme to make the event more immersive and fun.
- **Scenic Location Olympics**: Host the games in a scenic location like a beach, a forest clearing, or a mountaintop. The beautiful surroundings enhance the experience and provide great photo opportunities.
- **Universal Family Olympics**: Plan a variety of activities that elderly family members and those with disabilities can comfortably enjoy. Include a mix of games such as a trivia challenge, a storytelling contest, an arts and crafts competition, ring toss, cornhole, and lawn bowling to ensure everyone can join in the fun.

Benefits:

- **Promotes Physical Fitness**: Engaging in various athletic activities helps improve cardiovascular health, strength, flexibility, and overall fitness for all family members.
- **Encourages Outdoor Play**: Organizing the games in a park or backyard encourages outdoor activity, which provides numerous health benefits, including enhanced mood, better sleep, and increased vitamin D levels from sun exposure.
- **Encourages Healthy Competition**: Friendly competition during the games teaches important life skills such as sportsmanship, resilience, and

the ability to handle both wins and losses gracefully.

- **Teaches Conflict Resolution**: Disagreements during competition offer real-time opportunities to learn and practice conflict resolution, teaching the importance of compromise, communication, and fairness.
- **Strengthens Bonds**: Shared experiences and friendly competitions create opportunities for laughter, encouragement, and positive interaction, fostering a deeper connection among family members.
- **Builds Confidence and Self-Esteem**: Successfully participating in and completing various games boosts self-confidence and self-esteem, especially when efforts are recognized and celebrated.

Kick-Start Your First Family Olympic Games

Ready to pole vault into your first Family Olympic Games? Here's a handy list of games with all the materials and instructions you need to get started. These activities are designed to be easy to set up and loads of fun for everyone involved.

Balloon Pop Relay

- **Materials Needed:**
    - ☐ Bag of balloons
    - ☐ Foldable chairs (one per par team)
- **Instructions:** Participants race to a chair, sit on a balloon to pop it, then run back to tag the next team member. The first team to have all members pop their balloons and return wins.

Tug-of-War

- **Materials Needed:**
    - ☐ Sturdy rope to tug and to indicate the winning line
    - ☐ Bright tape to mark the center of the rope
- **Instructions**: Teams pull on opposite ends of the rope, trying to pull the other team past a designated point. The team that pulls the other past the winning line wins.

Three-Legged Race

- **Materials Needed:**
    - ☐ Bandanas or fabric strips to tie legs together
    - ☐ Cones for marking the race path
- **Instructions**: Pairs of participants tie their inside legs together and race to the finish line. The first pair to cross the finish line wins.

Hula Hoop Contest:

- **Materials Needed:**
    - ☐ Hula hoops (one per participant)
- **Instructions:** Each participant takes a hula hoop and starts hooping. The goal is to keep the hoop spinning around the waist for as long as possible. The last person with their hoop spinning wins.

Olympic Theme Generator

Looking to keep your Family Olympic Games exciting and new each time? Here's a list of creative themes to inspire your next event, ensuring every game day is filled with fresh fun and endless laughter.

Ancient Olympics

- **Description:** Bring the classic Olympic spirit to life with a series of time-honored sports, focusing on running, jumping, and throwing for a true athletic challenge.
- **Activities:** Sprint races, relay races, broad jump, "shot put" with bean bags, "discus" throws with Frisbees, and "javelin" throws with pool noodles.

Wacky Olympics

- **Description:** Incorporate silly and unconventional events that are sure to bring laughter.
- **Activities:** Wheelbarrow races, costume relay races, dizzy bat spin race, balloon pop challenges, and funny face contests.

Water Olympics

- **Description:** Perfect for a hot day, these water-based games will keep everyone cool and entertained.
- **Activities:** Water relay races, sponge toss, slip-and-slide races, and water balloon volleyball.

DIY Olympics

- **Description:** Get creative with homemade equipment and activities that encourage family members to invent and participate in unique events.
- **Activities:** Homemade obstacle courses, DIY bowling with soda bottles, homemade target shooting with nerf guns, and creative arts and crafts challenges.

Indoor Olympics

- **Description:** Great for rainy days or if you prefer staying indoors, these activities can be done in the living room or any open space inside the house.
- **Activities:** Paper plane flying contest, sock basketball, balloon volleyball, scavenger hunt, and musical chairs.

Cultural Olympics

- **Description:** Celebrate different cultures with themed games and activities from around the world.

- **Activities:** Chinese jump rope, bocce ball, piñata, Scottish caber toss (using pool noodles), and traditional dance contests.

These themes offer a creative framework to tailor your Family Olympic Games to your family's preferences, ensuring each event is unique and engaging. They help keep the games fresh and exciting, sparking new ideas and fun every time. Embrace the variety and make each event a memorable experience!

72

BACKYARD FILM FEST

Set the stage for an unforgettable movie night by creating a cozy outdoor cinema in your backyard. Begin by setting up a simple projector and screen, or even use a light-colored wall or sheet as your screen. Decorate your space with blankets, cushions, and twinkling fairy lights to give it that special touch of magic. As the sun sets and the stars emerge, settle in for a night filled with laughter, thrills, and storytelling magic that rivals any theater experience.

From picking the perfect film to preparing everyone's favorite snacks, the whole family can get involved in creating the evening's atmosphere. Whether it's an action-packed adventure, a classic comedy, or a heartwarming family tale, each film becomes an experience that sparks conversation and connection. As you share popcorn, cuddle under blankets, and watch the movie play out against the backdrop of the night sky, you'll create memories that last far beyond the rolling credits.

Materials Needed:

- ☐ Projector (Affordable options are widely available online)
- ☐ Thick white sheet or portable screen
- ☐ Laptop or media player
- ☐ Speakers (Using your existing home speakers outside works great)
- ☐ Extension cords
- ☐ Appropriate audio cables/adapters (if not wireless)
- ☐ Blankets, cushions, or outdoor chairs
- ☐ Fairy lights or lanterns (optional for ambiance)
- ☐ Snacks and drinks (popcorn, candy, soda, etc.)
- ☐ Insect repellent (optional)

Step-by-Step Instructions:

1. **Choose the Movie:**
    - Have each family member suggest a movie they would like to watch. Once everyone has made their suggestion, take a vote to decide which movie will be featured for the evening.
    - In case of a tie, use a fun tiebreaker to decide the winning movie. This could be a quick game of rock-paper-scissors, a coin toss, or a short family trivia question. The winner gets to choose the movie from the tied options.
2. **Set Up the Screen:**
    - Check the weather forecast before setting up. Avoid setting up the equipment if rain or strong winds are expected. If unexpected weather occurs, have a backup plan to quickly move the equipment indoors.
    - Plan to start the setup about 30-60 minutes before sunset to ensure you have enough time to get everything ready. This allows you to test the projector and sound system in the natural light before it gets dark.
    - Hang a thick white sheet or set up a portable screen in your backyard.
        - If using a sheet, secure it with clothespins or clips to a fence or rope stretched between two supports. Secure the bottom of the sheet to the ground with weights or stakes to keep it taut and wrinkle-free.
    - Ensure the screen is positioned so that everyone has a good view.
3. **Prepare the Projector:**
    - Connect the projector to your laptop or media player.
    - Position the projector at an appropriate distance from the screen and adjust the focus for a clear image.
    - Test the setup to ensure the movie is displayed correctly.
4. **Set Up Sound:**
    - Connect your speakers to your laptop or media player.
    - Place the speakers in positions that evenly distribute sound throughout the viewing area.
    - Do a quick sound check to ensure everything is working properly.
5. **Arrange Seating:**
    - Create a cozy, inviting atmosphere by spreading out blankets, cushions, or chairs for comfortable seating. Add pillows, throws, or bean bags for extra comfort.
    - Ensure everyone has a clear view of the screen.

6. **Create Ambiance:**
   - Hang fairy lights or lanterns around the backyard for a magical atmosphere (optional).
   - Prepare snacks and drinks, and set them up in an easily accessible area.
7. **Enjoy the Movie:**
   - Wait until it is fully dark before starting the movie for the best viewing experience.
   - Gather the family, settle into your cozy setup, and start the movie.
   - Relax and enjoy the film together under the stars, sharing laughs and moments with your loved ones.
8. **Critics' Corner:**
   - After the movie, gather everyone for a review session where each family member shares their ratings and thoughts on the film. Discuss favorite characters, memorable scenes, and any interesting themes.
   - For added fun, write down your reviews or record a video to document your family's unique perspectives. You can even come up with fun categories like "Best Performance," "Most Exciting Scene," or "Funniest Moment," and vote for your favorites as a family. It's a playful way to see how everyone's opinions compare!

Safety Considerations:

- To prevent the projector from overheating, ensure it has proper ventilation by placing it on a hard, flat surface that doesn't block its vents. Take breaks if necessary to allow the projector to cool down.
- Ensure all extension cords and cables are kept away from walkways to prevent tripping. Use outdoor-rated extension cords and protect connections from moisture.
- Check local noise ordinances and be mindful of the volume to avoid disturbing neighbors, especially if watching the movie late at night.

Troubleshooting Tips:

- **Uncooperative Weather:** Have a backup plan to quickly move the equipment indoors if unexpected weather occurs.
- **Blurry Image**: If the projector image is blurry, adjust the focus and ensure the projector is at the correct distance from the screen. Check the projector's manual for optimal distance guidelines.
- **Sound Issues**: If the sound isn't clear or loud enough, check all connections between the speakers and the media player. Make sure the volume is turned up on both the media player and the speakers. Ensure your speakers are powerful enough for this activity.

- **Inadequate Brightness**: If the projector image appears dim, check the projector's brightness settings and ensure it is set to the highest level. Move the projector closer to the screen if needed.
- **Weak Wi-Fi Signal**: If you're streaming the movie and experience buffering or connection issues, try downloading the movie in advance or move the Wi-Fi router closer to the viewing area.

Cleanup Tips:

- Make cleanup part of the movie theme. For example, if you watched a superhero movie, pretend you're superheroes saving the backyard from a mess.
- Gather and properly store all equipment, including the projector, screen, speakers, and extension cords. Keep cables neatly coiled and secure to prevent damage.
- Clean up any food or drink residues that might attract insects. Wipe down tables and seating areas to ensure they are free from sticky residues.

Variations and Adaptations:

- **Drive-In Style**: Create a drive-in movie experience by setting up cardboard "cars" for younger kids to sit in while they watch the movie. Decorate the cars together before the show.
- **Themed Movie Nights**: Choose a theme for the evening such as "Disney Classics," "Superhero Movies," or "80s Throwback." Encourage family members to dress up according to the theme, decorate accordingly, and prepare themed snacks.
- **DIY Concessions Stand**: Set up a concessions stand where family members can "buy" snacks with play money. Assign someone to be the concessions operator for a fun twist.
- **Popcorn Tasting Bar**: Set up a popcorn bar with various flavors and toppings. Have each family member create their own popcorn mix before the movie starts.
- **Movie-Themed Games**: Play a game related to the movie you're about to watch. For example, if the movie is about space, you could play a "space trivia" game or "alien charades," where players act out different space-themed words or phrases without speaking, and others guess what they are.
- **Interactive Movie Crafting**: Before the movie starts, have a craft session where everyone makes their own movie tickets, popcorn bags, or crafts related to the movie's theme.
- **Cook-Along Movie**: Pick a movie related to food or cooking, like "Ratatouille" or "Julie & Julia," and create a special movie night feast

together before the screening.

Benefits:

- **Encourages Teamwork and Collaboration**: Involving everyone in setting up the outdoor cinema, from choosing the movie to preparing snacks, promotes teamwork and collaborative effort.
- **Promotes Outdoor Enjoyment**: Transforming the backyard into a cozy cinema allows the family to enjoy the fresh air and the natural environment, combining entertainment with the benefits of being outdoors.
- **Cultivates Open Communication**: Discussing movie choices and sharing thoughts about the film afterward encourages open communication, helping improve listening and decision-making as everyone shares their preferences and ideas.
- **Strengthens Bonds:** Sharing a movie night under the stars in a relaxed setting encourages conversations, shared laughter, and emotional connections, creating lasting memories and enhancing family relationships.
- **Inspires Creativity**: Setting up a backyard cinema offers opportunities for creativity, from designing the layout and decorations to preparing themed snacks, making it a fun and imaginative project for everyone involved.

ABOUT THE AUTHOR

Z.J. Ramsey is a passionate advocate for involved fatherhood and the author of *Bond Like a Boss!*, a treasure trove of enriching activities designed to strengthen the bond between fathers and their children. Drawing from personal experiences and a deep commitment to empowering dads, Z.J. understands the transformative power of active parental involvement. The absence of a father figure during childhood fueled a mission to equip dads with practical tools for creating cherished memories and building strong, meaningful connections with their children. Through *Bond Like a Boss!*, Z.J. aims to inspire fathers everywhere to embrace their pivotal role in their children's lives, fostering fulfilling childhoods and laying the foundation for happier, more resilient adults.

www.ingramcontent.com/pod-product-compliance
Lightning Source LLC
LaVergne TN
LVHW010049170826
845678LV00012B/2090

* 9 7 9 8 9 9 6 3 2 6 5 0 1 *